Methods in Development Research:

Combining Qualitative and Quantitative Approaches

Edited by
JEREMY HOLLAND
with
JOHN CAMPBELL

ITDG
PUBLISHING

Published by ITDG Publishing
The Schumacher Centre for Technology and Development, Bourton Hall,
Bourton-on-Dunsmore, Rugby, Warwickshire CV23 9QZ, UK
www.itdgpublishing.org.uk

ISBN 1 85339 572 2

ITDG Publishing is the publishing arm of the Intermediate Technology
Development Group. Our mission is to build the skills and capacity of people
in developing countries through the dissemination of information in all
forms, enabling them to improve the quality of their lives and that of
future generations.

Designed and typeset by Christian Humphries
Printed in United Kingdom

Acknowledgements

This book stems from a conference on Combined Methods in Development Research held at the University of Wales Swansea in July 2002. We are extremely grateful to the Department for International Development for their financial support for the conference and to all the participants for making the conference such a success. We particularly thank contributors for accepting with good grace editorial condensing or restructuring of papers that appear in this book.

Many thanks to Eric Pawson and his colleagues at the Department of Geography, University of Canterbury in Christchurch for providing office space and support during a sabbatical spent editing this book, and to the Davie family for social support. Finally, a huge thank you to colleagues at ITDG Publishing and their anonymous reviewers for a winning combination of patience and rigour.

Contents

Figures

Tables

Boxes

Acronyms

ACP	African, Caribbean and Pacific
ADDs	Agricultural Development Divisions (Malawi)
AIDS	acquired immunodeficiency syndrome
AIMS	assessing the impact of microenterprise services
ANOVA	analysis of variance
CBA	cost–benefit analysis
CDS	Centre for Development Studies (Swansea, Wales)
CEPFOR	Commercialization of non-timber Forest Products in Mexico and Bolivia: Factors Influencing Success Project
CER	Centre for Economic and Social Studies (Uzbekistan)
CERES	*Centro de Estudios de la Realidad Economica y Social* (Centre for Studies on Economic and Social Reality – Bolivia)
CGIAR	Consultative Group on International Agricultural Research
CIDA	Canadian International Development Agency
CONANP	National Commission of Protected Areas (Mexico)
CSSSC	Centre for Studies in the Social Sciences (Kolkata, India)
CUBOS	Conservation Through Use of Tree Species Diversity in Fragmented Mesoamerican Dry Forest Project (Honduras)
DAC	Development Assistance Committee
Danida	Danish International Development Agency (Danish Agency for International Development)
DFID	Department for International Development (UK)
DG	democracy and governance
DGCD	Conservation and Development Directorate (Mexico)
DHS	demographic and health survey
DPIP	District Poverty Initiative Programme
EFI	extremely food insecure
EPAs	extension planning areas (Malawi)
FCP	free-choice profiling
FEWS	famine early warning system (Malawi)
FGD	focus group discussion
FI	food insecure
FPM	flavour profile method
FS	food secure
GDF	grassroots development framework
GIS	geographic information system
GTZ	*Deutsche Gesellschaft für Technische Zusammenarbeit* (German Agency for Technical Cooperation)
HDI	Human Development Index
HIV	human immunodeficiency virus
IA	impact assessment
ICBF	*Instituto Colombiano de Bienestar Familiar* (Colombian Institute of Family Welfare)

ICRAF	World Agroforestry Centre (formerly International Centre for Research in Agroforestry)
IDPs	internally displaced persons/people
Imp-Act	Improving the impact of microfinance on poverty: Action research programme
IRDC	International Research Development Centre (Canada)
ISED	Institute for Socio-Economic Development (India)
JASPEV	Jamaica Social Policy Evaluation
JVSV	*Jibika Vikas Samaj Gavesna* (India)
LFA	logical framework analysis
M&E	monitoring and evaluation
MDGs	Millennium Development Goals
MDP	Mediterranean Democracy Programme
MFO	microfinance organization
MFR	managing for results
NCCDS	Nabakrushna Choudhury Centre for Development Studies (India)
NGO	non-government organization
NR	natural resources
NSMP	Nepal Safe Motherhood Project
NTFPs	non-timber forest products
OECD	Organisation for Economic Co-operation and Development
PA	poverty assessment
PALS	Partnership for Adolescent Sexual and Reproductive Health Project (Zambia)
PCA	principal components analysis
PE	participatory evaluation
PF	performance framework
PLA	participatory learning and action
PM&E	participatory monitoring and evaluation
PMF	performance measurement framework
PPA	participatory poverty assessment
PRA	participatory reflection and action
PRA	participatory rural (or rapid) appraisal
PRODERS	Regional Sustainable Development Programmes (Mexico)
PRRO	Protracted Relief and Recovery Operation (Columbia)
PRS	poverty reduction strategy
PRSP	poverty reduction strategy paper
PSI/C	Population Services International Cambodia
QDA	quantitative descriptive analysis
QUIP	qualitative impact protocol
RBM	results-based management
REPOA	Research on Poverty Alleviation (Tanzania)
RRA	rapid rural appraisal
RSS	*Red de Solidaridad Social* (Social Solidarity Network – Colombia)

SDRC	Social Development Research Capacity Building Project
SEEP	Small Enterprise Education and Promotion (USA)
SEMARNAP	*Secretaria del Medio Ambiente, Recursos Naturales y Pesca* (National Secretariat for the Environment, Natural Resources and Fisheries) (Mexico)
Sida	Swedish International Development Cooperation Agency (Swedish International Development Authority)
SSC	Statistical Services Centre (UK)
STD	sexually transmitted disease
STI	sexually transmitted infection
TIP	Targeted Inputs Programme (Malawi)
TLM	temporal logic model
TOR	terms of reference
TPM	texture profile method
UNCSD	United Nations Commission on Sustainable Development
UNDP	United Nations Development Programme
UNEP	United Nations Environment Programme
UPPAP	Uganda Participatory Poverty Assessment Process
USAID	United States Agency for International Development
VDC	Village Development Committee (Nepal)
WDR	World Development Report
WFP	World Food Programme

General Introduction
Context and Challenges for Combining Methods in Development Research[1]

We are at an extraordinary moment in development research. Now, more than ever before, openness to methodological innovation and complementarity is creating exciting opportunities for an integrated approach to measurement, analysis, learning and change. Today, we are in a development context where international development practitioners are reaching greater consensus on what needs to be done, and how it should be achieved. This consensus allows more dynamic analysis and new partnerships, but also brings entrenched ideological positions to the fore. In this chapter, we explore the relationship between quantitative and qualitative research, examine the development context and map out a number of methodological and institutional opportunities and challenges that lie ahead, all of which are addressed by this book.

Combining methods: what do we know?

There is a widespread sense that the language of combined methods is used loosely and inconsistently. Concerns tend to focus on the use of the terms 'qualitative' and 'quantitative' to describe data collection methods and the types of data generated. Further, the term 'participatory' is sometimes used interchangeably with the term 'qualitative'.[2]

In clarifying the distinction between quantitative and qualitative research, we attempt to demonstrate the value to researchers of combining methods for development research. We do not hold the view that the epistemological differences between the research traditions make the task of combining methods impossible.[3] On the contrary, we believe that through careful and selective combination of methods and analysis of data the opportunity for adding value through innovative research is enhanced. We welcome this opportunity.

What is the difference between qualitative and quantitative research?

The use and abuse of the labels 'qualitative' and 'quantitative' research is unhelpful. While we do not want to be pedantic, it is helpful to provide a framework against which the reader can interpret the issues discussed in this book.

In 2001, a workshop held at Cornell University (Kanbur 2001b) brought together development practitioners and academics to reflect on qualitative and quantitative development research. The workshop identified five dimensions that collectively characterize the two research traditions (see Box a.1, page 2). Most contributors agreed that the points to the left of the spectrum were more qualitative in nature, while those to the right were more quantitative (Kanbur 2003b: 1–2).

Box a.1   *Qualitative and quantitative dimensions*
              of poverty appraisal

More qualitative research ←	→ More quantitative research
1. Non-numerical information	Numerical information
2. Specific (contextual)* population coverage	General (non-contextual)* population coverage
3. Active population involvement	Passive population involvement
4. Inductive inference methodology	Deductive inference methodology
5. Broad social sciences disciplinary framework	Neoclassical economics (and natural sciences)* disciplinary framework
* Words in parentheses added	*Source*: Kanbur (2003b: 1)

We recognize the importance of these five dimensions in underpinning the issues and themes of this volume, and explore them in greater depth below.

In order to provide a reasonably precise definition of the terms 'qualitative' and 'quantitative', we follow Hentschel's (1999) method–data framework, presented in Figure a.1 (see opposite page).[4] This framework focuses more narrowly on the first dimension in Box a.1, stating that the terms 'qualitative' and 'quantitative' should refer specifically to the type of data generated in the research process. Quantitative research produces data in the form of numbers, while qualitative research tends to produce data in prose or text form.

In order to produce different types of data, qualitative and quantitative research tend to employ different methods. This is the second spectrum in Hentschel's framework. Those methods that are applied across the population universe, often a country or region of a country, he labels **non-contextual**. Non-contextual methods are designed to achieve breadth in coverage and analysis. This requires that research is externalist or 'etic', dealing only with knowledge that can be transformed into abstract 'brute data':

> '*the sampling, the interview schedule, the training of enumerators and other aspects of best practice survey technique are designed precisely to collect information that is untainted by the particularities of the context in which it is collected.*' (Booth et al. 1998)

Non-contextual research typically uses the random sample survey as the main research method, applied across broad geographical areas and with large population samples.[5] The sample survey is driven by a **deductive** methodology (the fourth dimension in Box a.1) that is designed to produce quantitative data that can be statistically analysed. The aim is to measure, aggregate, model and predict behaviour and relations based on what can be observed and independently verified (what Shaffer calls an 'ideal of verification'). Deductive methods are associated with logical positivism, a school of thought that seeks to identify and capture a single external reality (Shaffer 1996).

In contrast, those methods that are applied to a specific locality, case or social setting might be described as **contextual**. Contextual methods sacrifice breadth of coverage and statistical generalizability in order to explore issues in depth:

'... [contextual methods] attempt to understand poverty (or other) dimensions within the social, cultural, economic and political environment of a (geographical or social) locality.' (Booth et al. 1998: 52)

Contextual research employs more **inductive** research methods, including ethnographic techniques such as participant observation, interviews, analysis of oral and documentary sources, and participatory tools, which are group-based and largely visual. These methods are designed to capture judgements and perceptions and to create space for researchers and participants to analyse complex and often non-quantifiable cause-and-effect processes, and the meanings that people impute to these processes.

In common with qualitative research, **participatory** research tends to employ more contextual methods and elicit more qualitative and interpretive information, but brings with it an important additional philosophical commitment to respect local (emic) knowledge and facilitate local ownership and control of data generation and analysis (Chambers 1994a,b, 1997). This aspect of ownership and control in participatory research is intended to provide space for local people to

Figure a.1   *Method–data framework (adapted from Hentschel 1999)*

	METHODS
	more contextual
* rapid assessments * participatory analysis * ethnographic investigations	* longitudinal village surveys
DATA	
more qualitative	*more quantitative*
* qualitative module of questionnaire study	* household and health surveys * epidemological surveys
	less contextual

establish their own analytical framework and to be in a position to challenge 'development from above' (Mukherjee 1995: 27). In contrast to the individualized observation and discussions of much qualitative investigation, participatory research focuses on public and collective reflection and action.

At its most extractive, participatory research simply uses a suite of participatory methods to improve outsiders' understanding of the local context (while adhering to certain ethical principles relating to behaviour, transparency and ownership). At its most political, participatory research is a process that shares elements of critical hermeneutics (Freire 1970; Habermas 1972, 1990) in which reflection is internalized and promotes raised political consciousness. This corresponds to the third dimension in Box a.1, in which population involvement shifts from passive to active. In this respect, there is a key difference in the position of the researcher in non-participatory and participatory qualitative research. In the former, the researcher becomes an interpreter of knowledge; in the latter, the researcher simply facilitates and channels the voices and analysis of others.

Participatory methods are by no means restricted to qualitative data output (see Part 2 of this volume). People map, count, estimate, compare and value using numbers during participatory research, often producing empirical insights that are very difficult to capture through conventional methods (Chambers 2003). Participatory methods are often quick and efficient, producing data in a timely fashion for evidence-based analysis and action. Most importantly, participatory research is effective because it can be empowering for different groups of stakeholders.

Finally, qualitative research and the interpretive, inductive tradition are firmly embedded in non-economic social science disciplines while quantitative research, with its logical positivist, deductive leanings, has a further-reaching disciplinary span (the fifth dimension in Box a.1). Social science has made more use of quantitative research because historically it has engaged in both positivist and post-positivist schools of thought (Uphoff 1992; Chambers 1997), with the US social-science tradition being more firmly embedded in the positivist school than the European tradition.[6] In contrast, economics and the natural sciences have largely failed to embrace qualitative research because of the positivist–empiricist embeddedness of those disciplines.[7]

Qualitative and quantitative research: strengths and weaknesses

Quantitative research has the comparative advantage of being able to enumerate and predict relationships for large populations, and for this reason data are assigned a high degree of confidence. It achieves this by simultaneously holding a range of variables constant in order to focus on the relationship between two or more specified variables. The observed relation between such variables allows analysts and policy makers to identify causal impact and covariant changes. By generating standardized numerical data, analysts identify longitudinal trends and, using statistical techniques, can aggregate data to compare findings across populations and geographical areas. Similarly, within population groups or areas numerical data allow estimation of the prevalence or distribution of a particular phenomenon or relationship.

While quantitative research prioritizes descriptive, analytical breadth of coverage, qualitative research is noted, above all, for its explanatory power and for the richness and depth of information it generates. Rather than standardizing to describe the norm, qualitative research seeks to explain difference. By seeking to understand social diversity and social interaction within population groups, including intra-household differences,[8] qualitative research attempts to explore the complexity and multiple realities of societies and communities. Qualitative research provides insights into the 'black box' of social and economic processes and relations which are poorly understood, ambiguous or sensitive in nature (see Chapter 11). Without these insights, deductive researchers and policy analysts tend to make interpretive leaps from bivariate description of the average situation to poorly considered social analysis that all too often supports, rather than challenges, existing ideologically normative positions.[9] The danger here is that what is not quantifiable becomes unimportant, while 'what is measurable and measured then becomes what is real and what matters' (Chambers 1995: 8).

In short, while quantitative methods produce data that can be aggregated and analysed to describe and predict relationships, qualitative research can help to probe and explain those relationships, and to explain contextual differences in their quality. Conversely, if qualitative research inductively throws up interesting, often surprising and sometimes counter-intuitive relationships and patterns, quantitative research is then able to ask 'how much?' and establish how confident we can be in these working hypotheses. This iterative relationship between describing and explaining provides the key to effective combination of methods and data (see Chapter 8), and is discussed further below.

Epistemology and social research

Contextual research can also be driven by an epistemological conviction that knowledge generated is subjective, and that a single reality is replaced by inter-subjective, competing worlds of knowledge (what Long and Long, 1992 describe as 'battlefields of knowledge') (Berger and Luckman 1971; Shaffer 1996; Chung 1997). These competing worlds are seen to be mediated by social identities, or fault lines, that characterize society and reflect different levels of social power.[10] Guba and Lincoln (1998) describe a 'post-positivist' or 'constructivist'[11] paradigm that encompasses a fundamentally different school of approaches to research than that of the positivist tradition. They argue that whereas conventional inquiry is linear and closed, constructivist methodology is 'iterative, interactive, hermeneutic, at times intuitive, and most certainly open' (Guba and Lincoln, 1998: 183).

According to this epistemological position, qualitative research stresses the interpretive or hermeneutic nature of knowledge construction, and recognizes that there are different interpretations of reality, so that data lose their independence and become a social product. If we throw in the researcher as active in this process of knowledge construction, no longer able to hide behind an 'independent' data set, then we are left with a double hermeneutic (Giddens 1974) – knowledge is interpreted by local people/respondents and is then reinterpreted by outsiders/researchers. Researchers are encouraged to recognize their agency and their social distance from those being researched. This prompts emphasis in anthropological training on reflexivity – a self-conscious awareness of the relationships on which the fieldwork experience is based (see Chapter 8).

This epistemological tension creates a challenge for those promoting methodological pluralism in the use of research methods. Our position in this debate is strongly influenced by Hammersley's (1998) notion of subtle realism. We accept that people construct their world, and recognize that a key task for researchers is to document and understand these different constructions. We also accept that the researcher's account of these constructions is itself discursively constructed. But we also take from realism the proposition that these discursive constructions (realities) exist independently of the researcher's subsequent construction, interpretation and representation of them.[12]

If so, the researcher's account can be more or less valid, depending on how closely it represents the discursive constructions (realities) of the object of research. The emphasis then shifts away from the rather sterile epistemological tension between constructivist and positivist positions[13] and towards empirical validity. Here our position is similar to that adopted by Sechrist and Sidani (1995: 78) who argue that qualitative and quantitative methods are equally 'empirical, [and] dependent on observation'. Indeed, both types of method depend on the same tasks and aims: describing their data, constructing explanatory arguments from their data, 'and speculating about why the outcomes they observed happened as they did' (Sechrist and Sidani 1995: 78). We are all part of a scientific community with shared norms (Box a.2).

Putting shared scientific norms into practice

This shared normative position hinges on recognition of certain key principles which underlie good research. The first challenge is theoretical (see Campbell and Holland, 2005) and the second challenge is methodological in nature, namely the need for our findings to be representative, reliable and objective.

As Chapter 2 makes clear, the issue of representativeness can be addressed through robust sampling protocol. Certainly there remains a

Box a.2   *Norms of the scientific community*

1. Universalism	Regardless of who or where research is conducted, it is judged on its scientific merits
2. Organized scepticism	Research should challenge and question all evidence and subject each study to intense scrutiny
3. Disinterestedness	Scientists must be neutral, impartial, receptive, and open to unexpected observations and new ideas. They should not be rigidly wedded to a particular idea or point of view
4. Communalism	Scientific knowledge must be shared with others; it belongs to everyone. The way in which research is conducted must be described in detail. New knowledge is not formally accepted until other researchers have reviewed it and it has been made publicly available in a special form and style
5. Honesty	Scientists demand honesty in all research
	Source: Neuman (2002)

tension between depth (allowing analysis, diagnosis and process) and coverage (increasing the precision of inference and extraction), but this can often be resolved through increasing resources and/or fitting the data to larger surveys. There also remains a tension in participatory research between purposive sampling and/or self-selection of samples, on the one hand, and probability-based sampling on the other. Here, Ian Wilson argues for greater use of segmented research in which random and standardized segments are applied separately from contextual and flexible research methods and procedures. Wilson also suggests that we should make more use of participatory methods to identify sampling frames and stratify populations. Barahona and Levy (2002) argue that the need for standardized segments can be reduced by using key informants more effectively to gather observable data that otherwise are collected inefficiently from randomly sampled households.

Once representative sample population groups have been identified, we still face the considerable challenge of demonstrating that qualitative information is reliable and objective. The reliability of information in natural sciences and economics can be defined as the extent to which each repetition of the same instruments will yield similar measurements. Quantitative data generated by standard survey instruments are made reliable by employing closed questions that generate discrete, precise units of data. The objectivity of data refers to the extent to which multiple observers can agree on a phenomenon. This is ensured in the natural sciences and economics by removing the influence of the researcher on the research process.[14]

There is much scepticism about the reliability and objectivity of data generated by conventional household research. This scepticism is

Box a.3   *Achieving trustworthiness in qualitative research*

A set of alternative trustworthiness criteria has been established against which observers can judge findings from qualitative research. These are: credibility (for internal validity); transferability (for external validity); dependability (for reliability); and confirmability (for objectivity).

Credibility can be enhanced by:

1. **prolonged engagement** – investing sufficient time to provide scope for the study by learning context and culture, testing for misinformation and building trust

2. **persistent observation** – providing depth to the study by identifying the elements in the situation that are most relevant

3. **triangulation** – cross-checking information by use of multiple and different sources, methods, investigators and theories*

4. **peer debriefing** – exposing researchers to disinterested peers in order to probe biases and explore meanings

5. **negative case analysis** – continuously revising a hypothesis until it accounts for all known cases

6. **referential adequacy** – archiving data for future reference

7. **member checks** – testing interpretations and conclusions with members of those stakeholder groups from whom data were originally collected.

Transferability is not the objective of qualitative research, which instead aims to provide a database, with working hypotheses, that allows users of information to make informed judgements. The **dependability** of qualitative information can be enhanced through overlap methods (equivalent to triangulation) and stepwise replication (parallel investigations by research teams). Finally, **confirmability** can be enhanced through research journals, triangulation, and a confirmability audit (which records the process of inquiry and the end product).

---

* Chambers (1997: 159-60) makes the point that group-based participatory research has the added advantage of improving trustworthiness through what he calls 'group visual synergy' or 'observable mutual checking'.

Source: Lincoln and Guba (1985)

---

summarized by Herring (2003) as stemming from errors introduced by the 'social relations of production of data,' which he argues can easily become systematic. In the first instance, these non-sampling errors can be introduced at the point of data collection by the behaviour of questioners.[15] Herring's point echoes the latter part of Chambers's (1983: 53-4) withering reflections on non-sampling error in empiricist research, in which the respondent is portrayed as a 'tiresome complication' in the generation of data.

At a higher level of social production, survey data can quickly become politicized in policy analysis because of strong incentives to massage the figures. Even when surveys have been properly conducted and their data carefully analysed, the data can nevertheless become the subject of controversy if they do not fit with prevailing perceptions of patterns and trends.[16]

But this scepticism regarding questionnaire surveys applies most often to the sociopolitical processes in which the method is embedded. Certainly, the political nature of data production applies equally to qualitative data. Herring (2003) observes that:

'Failing to understand the relations of power and interests that condition the production of either qualitative or quantitative data reduces the confidence that can be placed in the results.'

In this regard, White (2002a) makes a useful distinction between data analysts, who look for the interpretation most consistent with the data, and data miners, who know what they are looking for and keep digging until they find it: 'Then she stops and that is the story she tells.' Because data miners are equally comfortable using either quantitative or qualitative data,[17] the key to rigour in all research is the proper application of techniques.

Here, standard statistical deductive techniques need not claim a monopoly. Lincoln and Guba (1985), for instance, present a set of 'alternative trustworthiness criteria' for qualitative research to strengthen credibility, transferability, dependability and confirmability.[18] They map out concrete ways of enhancing the trustworthiness of qualitative research according to each of these criteria (see Box a.3, opposite).

By carefully designing research it is possible to enhance the validity and reliability of our findings. Analysis can be strengthened further through the flexible adoption of research questions (see Chapter 1) backed by powerful theoretical frameworks (Campbell 2002).

Applying combined research to international development: the context

The above discussion maps out a perspective on combined methods designed to guide readers as they delve into the more detailed case study material presented in this book. Here we examine the changing context for the very distinct application of combined methods to development research by briefly reviewing recent debates about policy and practice in international development.

Converging discourses

During the past decade, the international development community has united behind a renewed focus on poverty reduction – a cohesion powerfully reflected in the common objectives presented by the Millennium Development Goals[19] (see Box a.4, overleaf).

During this period of convergence on development objectives, there has also been some dramatic movement in how development agencies think about poverty. During the early part of the 1990s, a narrow focus on the poverty line drove poverty reduction. The World Bank notably

Box a.4   *The Millennium Development Goals*

1. Eradicate extreme poverty and hunger

2. Achieve universal primary education

3. Promote gender equality and empower women

4. Reduce child mortality

5. Improve maternal health

6. Combat HIV/AIDs, malaria and other diseases

7. Ensure environmental sustainability

8. Develop a global partnership for development.

Source: www.undp.org/mdg/goalsandindicators.html

introduced the poverty assessment in the wake of its 1990 *World Development Report* as part of a process of strengthening the poverty focus of its Country Assistance Strategies; most poverty assessments identified two poverty lines, leading to an identification of the poor and a subset of these who are very poor. An important consequence of this construction of a 'universal' poverty line was that there tended to be a lack of motivation for the eventual choice of where the poverty line was drawn; in other words, there was no attempt to identify the underlying dimensions of poverty in any particular society or context. This lack of motivation undermined the ability of the poverty assessment to provoke useful poverty and policy analysis.[20]

A decade later, discussion and thinking about poverty has moved on apace.[21] New, dynamic and powerful analytical frameworks emerging among the international donor community are a testament to this shift of thinking. These frameworks have evolved from work by Sen (1981, 1985, 1997) on entitlements and capabilities, and from the food security literature of the 1980s (Devereux and Maxwell 2001) and later work on vulnerability (Swift 1989; Moser 1998). The implementation of the frameworks for research has been fuelled by a dawning recognition that the poor themselves have a sophisticated understanding of what it means to be poor. The frameworks share a conceptualization of poverty as multi-dimensional and complex, and introduce a more dynamic and entitlements-focused analytical approach to poverty assessment.[22]

Throughout the 1990s, debates about human rights and development increasingly converged (Häusermann 1998). During the same period in which development agencies have embraced multi-dimensional analytical frameworks, human rights concerns have developed from a first-generation, 'negative' concern with protecting individual civil and political rights to a broader and more developmental concern with ensuring economic, social and cultural rights linked to progress towards the Millennium Development Goals (DFID 2000).[23]

Converging strategies

This convergence of discourse – the developmental approach to rights and the dynamic approach to poverty[24] – has enabled development agencies, with varying degrees of forcefulness, to engage with what Moore and Putzel (1999) call the 'politics of poverty'. The rights-based discourse, in particular, politicizes poverty analysis and refocuses attention on the institutions and processes that determine development outcomes.

For the United Nations Development Programme, the World Bank and bilateral agencies such as the UK Department for International Development, empowerment represents a liberal concern with and operational focus on enabling people actively to claim their rights as citizens (Gaventa and Valderrama 1999).

Convergence of thinking on empowerment is reflected in a new consensus on how to reduce poverty, recently described as a 'new "New Poverty Agenda"' (Maxwell 2003), and captured broadly by the World Bank's *World Development Report 2000/01: Attacking Poverty,* with its three-legged approach of opportunity (through growth); security (through measures to manage risk more effectively); and empowerment (through participation and increased responsiveness among state institutions).

This poverty-reduction consensus, influenced as we have noted by more dynamic and process-based understandings of the causes of poverty, has moved the international position considerably away from that laid out by the World Bank in 1990, which focused more narrowly on economic growth as the engine of poverty reduction, supported by investment in human capital. Criticisms of the World Bank's lack of attention to resource distribution as a constraint on growth and poverty reduction (Tjonneland et al. 1998) have been replaced by acknowledgement of a greater emphasis on distributional equity (Maxwell 2003) and on material and political notions of empowerment (Moore 2001).

Indications of change in the way that development is managed and delivered have accompanied this more 'political' approach to poverty reduction strategies. Management thinking in development has been influenced by new approaches that challenge the reductionist and technical ways managers in professional development tackle complex problems of political process. Forms of engagement by development agencies are changing, with a move away from positivist linear management to more flexible and adaptive learning. This is particularly evident in the monitoring and evaluation of development interventions (Estrella and Gaventa 1998). New management thinking promotes a shift from hard to soft systems methodologies in which bureaucracies using information systems become learning organizations that behave flexibly and improve outcomes by empowering people (Peters 1989; Senge 1990; Pasteur 2003).

The adoption of a process approach in projects coincides with a major shift in development agencies' thinking about appropriate entry points for development assistance. Bilateral and multilateral agencies are now beginning to work more closely together in engaging with the upstream sector and policy analysis and design. The fact that this type of engagement is messier, more complex, less linear and less controllable merely serves to accelerate the perceived need for a process approach to management.

Although these shifts have created a context that is more open to political participation and institutional change, there are warning signs that the process part of the 'new New Poverty Agenda' is nevertheless ideologically driven and methodologically formulaic. This is particularly the case with the current methodology for implementing the agenda, the Poverty Reduction Strategy Paper. This has led to concerns about the supply-driven and conditionality-burdened cultivation of political processes (Craig and Porter 2002; Maxwell 2003), as well as the tendency for functional forms of participation to mask conflicts of interest: Maxwell (2003) uses the illustration of urban consumers favouring lower prices versus rural producers favouring higher prices.

Opportunities and challenges

The development context reviewed briefly above provides a number of extraordinary opportunities for combined methods in development research. In analytical and methodological terms, the scene is set for new standards of combined qualitative and quantitative research. Multidimensional and dynamic thinking about poverty is encouraging iteration and sequencing of the descriptive and the diagnostic which moves beyond the standardizing, depoliticizing and consensus-based tendencies of positivist research. Process approaches to development and to the management of development are creating more opportunities for institutional engagement and change through research, with more and more people participating in new forms of empowering research. At the same time we are faced with a coalescing ideological policy position among development agencies that has dangerous implications for the social production of data – this is perhaps the greatest challenge for combined research. Below we discuss these methodological and institutional opportunities and challenges in more detail.

Methodological opportunities and challenges

Improving reliability and representativeness
After Carvalho and White (1997), we explore some of the opportunities that exist for combined methods. Integration of research methods can be achieved relatively easily by adopting more robust technical procedures that will improve the reliability and representativeness of qualitative and quantitative data (Chapters 3–5). Sampling theory and its application is a crucial area of integration, with a particular concern among social statisticians with an ecumenical bent that decisions on sampling may presently be underconceptualized in qualitative literature,

including the definition of units and levels, comparison of sample segments, achieving representativeness, deciding on sample size, and the combination and phasing of studies. This is discussed in greater depth in Chapter 2.

The many opportunities for shrewd sequencing of methods are increasingly recognized and promoted within many areas of development research. We have discussed the increasingly flexible application of methods in poverty assessment. Another particularly strong area of innovation with sequencing is in impact assessment and project evaluation (Chapters 4 and 12). Approaches to merging findings for better action have also been pioneered by social statisticians and economists, who argue that appropriate statistical approaches can greatly facilitate the handling and analysis of qualitative information and provide a helpful structure for further qualitative interpretation. They make the point that many qualitative researchers are unclear why statistical approaches are needed, and what their benefits are. Those with a qualitative background are unsure when their data are appropriate for the application of quantitative approaches, and how their data could best be handled to provide generalizable conclusions. Savitri Abeyasekera (Chapter 6) considers the wide potential for quantification and statistical analysis, and van Oirschot and Tomlins (Chapter 7) discuss an example of objective quantification of perception data.

Resolving trade-offs

Some writers have raised concerns that overstretching the integrationist route will erode the comparative advantages of different methods, and Appleton and Booth (Chapter 8) explore the implicit trade-offs between contextual depth and universal coverage when combining development research methods and data. Their viewpoint is that if we blur the methodological boundary to the point where contextual methods are used (often inappropriately) to convert qualitative interpretation among a wide range of social actors and groups into standardized aggregated data, researchers risk producing at best 'unmotivated' data, and at worst bad data.

There is an attendant danger that the standardizing tendency brings with it an opportunity cost of diverting finite energies and resources in qualitative research away from explanatory analysis. Here there are warning signs from poverty assessment, with the tendency for qualitative research to be used as a supplement to enrich descriptive analysis, rather than as a tool for analysing complex and highly contextual social relations. Anthropologists Booth et al. (1999) comment:

> *'While anthropological work can help to enrich statistical poverty profiles, a more important contribution may be in documenting the variable, fluid, complex and contested categorizations and relationships that constitute the reality that poverty-reduction efforts must contend with on the ground.'*

Analytical integration

The emergence of new, dynamic frameworks for poverty analysis demonstrates the potential for analytical integration of different types of data in development research. Yet the experience of recent research processes[25] shows that this type of integration is far from straightforward. More than anything, the problems encountered point to a theoretical gulf between traditions that is not mentioned in the typology of Box a.1, but which has enormous implications for analysis. Qualitative research tends to be guided by a theoretical model of power-infused social relations. This type of conflictual analysis does not sit comfortably with the consensus-based theoretical lens of quantitative descriptive analysis.

Nowhere has this been more sharply highlighted than in the recent functionalist and depoliticized love affair with social capital among Washington-based neoliberal economists keen to explore market performance in relation to the 'missing link' of collective action (e.g. Grootaert 1998). The reaction from non-economist social scientists, career observers of social relations yet convinced of their conflictual nature, has been robust (e.g. Harriss and de Renzio 1997; Fine 1999).

Institutional opportunities and challenges: beyond institutionalized methods, knowledge and power

Bridging disciplines, meeting minds

We believe that challenges to combining methods are not a function of intractable epistemological differences. More important, we argue, is the huge gulf of understanding that separates different disciplines and which needs to be bridged if we are to make the most of a new climate of dynamic analysis in development and of process engagement with local researchers.

The prevailing tendency of social scientists from different disciplines is to conduct research among their own disciplinary peer group, but within the overall disciplinary hegemonic hold of economics.[26] One major influence on continuing unequal separation (McGee 2001) arises from a lack of respect for and suspicion of the rigour of qualitative research on the one hand, and of the trustworthiness of large-scale surveys on the other (White 2002a). Apropos this issue, White concludes that:

> *'the real question here is one of professional respect, trust and integrity. Just as economists quite readily take as "right" the regression results they find in published papers, they should accord the same professional respect to presentations of qualitative material. Members of all disciplines should be on the look out for shady practices which distort patterns in the data.'*

A related hurdle is the language of disciplines. In recent times, there has been some convergence within the social sciences, particularly through the use of the 'asset–vulnerability' discourse. Yet there remains a powerful language barrier between disciplines – erected, some would argue, to protect and privilege their members (Chambers 1997) – that creates foreign and esoteric worlds that intimidate and exclude.

Democratizing research

This language barrier masks a far more significant vertical structure of institutional exclusion of 'them' – the researched, the beneficiaries, the primary stakeholders – from development research and its outcomes. A major institutional challenge lies in democratizing a research process that maintains these hegemonic positions among the development élite:

> 'As important as how you gather info and what type of info you elicit, is the issue of "who controls information, how the information is used and by whom and what information can do to inform policies".' (de Haan 2000)

The academic community is a powerful arbiter of good quality research, and yet seems further away than ever from being a truly democratic platform for knowledge generation and discourse in which non-academics are seen as legitimate participants. Development research has much to learn here from the principle of ownership underpinning the participatory research tradition. Ensuring local ownership might suggest a different set of trade-offs around the methodological pluralism promoted in this book. We consider these issues further in Chapters 15 and 16.

Within a broadly democratic research environment, different groups of actors will emerge with different information needs and research priorities (de Haan 2000). For civil society actors, access to information and dialogue are crucial for citizenship participation for the progressive fulfillment of rights (Gaventa, J. and Valderrama, C., unpublished background note, 'Participation, citizenship and local governance', June 1999). At the national level, evidence-based policy is fuelled by timely and relevant flows of information. For donors, the growing number of sector-wide programmes and the promotion of new policy and partnership frameworks make new demands on donor agency staff to negotiate with a wider range of institutions and to implement joint evaluations (de Haan 2000) and to continue capacity-building in development research (Chapter 17).

Development management: process and learning

Earlier we linked knowledge acquisition to a perspective on institutional learning that originated in management theory and has diffused across to the highly technocratic world of development management. Integrated and democratized development research provides an opportunity to fuel process approaches to development management that emphasize knowledge-sharing over hoarding, and user democracy over authoritarianism (Chambers 1997). These themes are explored further in Chapters 13 and 14.

As development agencies become increasingly comfortable with these new ways of working, they will realize that the real challenge lies beyond stripping away bureaucratic fixations with counting the things that go into and defining and counting the things that come out of development interventions. They will recognize that, far from being neutral bystanders, they are political agents in one part of a development process that transforms many institutions.

Embedding research in policy process

Combined development research is not just about a neatly designed pluralist package of methods;[27] if it is to have an impact it must be embedded in policy process. Practitioners and researchers must commit themselves to identifying the (usually chaotic and non-linear) institutional and policy context, and to stretching policy spaces (McGee 2002) for development interventions in order to embed the research process. Here, knowledge brokers or actors can play an important role in connecting research and policy communities, through advocacy, policy networks, and filtering and championing information for greater impact (Stone et al. 2001; Chapter 20). A policy community listens when it has interest, capacity and openness (Clark 1999). Practitioners must also recognize the disjuncture between policy-making and policy implementation (Sutton 1999). In the context of decentralizing administrations, where poor people's main point of contact is local government, this is where the research-to-policy connection is most likely to be forged.

Policy embeddedness also demands that development research is salient (perceived as relevant); credible (perceived as valid and believable); and legitimate (perceived as fair and open) (Clark 1999). Practitioners must use the full range of methods to increase support and legitimacy, to broaden stakeholder involvement, and to create new alliances. Working within institutional contexts should not give way to easy solutions based on externally engineered institution-building, which can often simply provide actors with a convenient institutional 'escape hatch' which actually exerts friction on institutional change (Biggs and Smith 1998: 243). Nor should institutional engagement be depoliticized and 'deprocessed' to a one-off technical approach driven by neat stakeholder analysis and project management tools. There is no blueprint for institutional change – coalitions of interest groups are a complex mix of consensus and conflict, and are constantly changing (Biggs and Smith 1998).

Unsettling the social production of development ideologies

There is a final, broader challenge that is addressed at times in this book, sometimes directly but often obliquely. This is the relationship between the research process as evidence-driven and empirical, and the policy process as ideologically driven and political. Above we discussed briefly how research-generated information is transferred to and absorbed by policy audiences, and referred to the social production of knowledge in a politicized context. The final challenge for combined development research is the Himalayan one of unsettling the social learning process (the internalization of values and ideals underpinning a particular idea or concept; Stone 2000) that feeds and reinforces prevailing ideological orthodoxies about development.

Kanbur (2001a) describes a moment in the late 1990s when the finance (or free market) 'policy constellation' distanced itself from what he calls the civil society (or process and participation) constellation.[28] They backed this up by a process of 'policy messaging' regarding their non-negotiable economic policy fundamentals. This ideological tension played itself out in the production of the *World Development Report 2000/01* (World Bank 2001) from which Kanbur, the Report's director, resigned shortly before its publication (Wade 2001). The process by which the content of the report was finally resolved reflected 'the [political] field of power in which the Bank operates' (Wade 2001: 1435) and indicates that a process seen by the *World Development Report* team as serious, independent, evidence-driven social science could not seal itself off from ideologically driven reaction. This reaction from within the financial constellation (especially the US Treasury) focused particularly on the draft report's qualification of the Bank's creed that liberalizing and opening up economies automatically helps the poor; its qualification of growth-centred policy in the conclusion that (apparent) widening income inequality was bad for growth;[29] its new focus on empowerment through scaled-up participation and more accountable state institutions; and its insistence that safety nets must be in place prior to market reform. The final document retained some of these elements, but with a stronger policy message on the fundamentals of the financial constellation ideology:

> '[The World Development Report] is a political document in the sense that as the Bank's flagship, its message must reflect the ideological preferences of key constituencies and not offend them too much; but the message must also be backed by empirical evidence and made to look "technical".' (Wade 2001: 1435)

Ultimately we must ask, 'Can combined research approaches challenge the social production of knowledge that feeds the normal ideological discourse on development?' Kanbur argues that the key to bridging the growing divide on key areas of economic policy is greater dialogue: 'trying to understand legitimate alternative views on economic policy' (Wade 2001). Certainly, as we argue here, greater pluralism across disciplines, methodologies and analytical frameworks will help challenge the social construction of ideological norms, realities or 'regimes of truth' that characterize dominant development discourses:[30]

> *'The challenge is not therefore changing people's consciousness – or what's in their heads – but the political, economic and institutional regimes of production of truths.'* (Foucault 1980: 132)

Part I
Combining forces with qualitative and quantitative research

Introduction
Bridges and fences for
combined methods

The General Introduction has laid the groundwork for further discussion in a number of important areas. We have identified and acknowledged the epistemological and methodological differences that exist between the two broad research paradigms, but confirmed that this should not create a barrier to shrewd pluralism in the use of methods and data that lie in the qualitative and quantitative camps. Here we note the 'sentiment of complementarity' (Kanbur 2003b) evident in recent forums, including the Cornell workshop (Kanbur 2001b), and Swansea conference. This convergence of thinking in development research draws on earlier discussions (Carvalho and White 1997; Chung 1997; Hanmer et al. 1997; Booth et al. 1998), and mirrors much earlier statements on methodological pluralism (Miles and Huberman 1984).

How can qualitative and quantitative research be combined?

From these ecumenical beginnings we have established that different methods and sources have their own advantages but cannot replace each other, and have indicated that qualitative and quantitative methods and data are often more powerful when combined, at different levels and in different sequences. Carvalho and White (1997: 18) usefully describe three ways of combining the best of qualitative and quantitative approaches: **integrating** methodologies for better measurement; **sequencing** information for better analysis; and **merging** findings for better action. We elaborate briefly on these three areas below.

During the design and fieldwork phases of research, thoughtful sequencing allows for a number of ways of mixing or integrating methods and data for better measurement. Sequencing is rarely a two-step process, the reality being a larger number of steps or iterations between qualitative and quantitative research. Single steps within this longer process might include:

1. Survey used to select qualitative investigation sample.
2. Survey highlights priority issues to be covered.
3. Qualitative analysis identifies knowledge gaps to be filled by survey.
4. Qualitative analysis enables surveys to predict more accurately which issues (sectoral, cross-sectoral or other) and which options are important to local people and what explanations they might give, thus improving the definition of survey modules and questions and the categories of choice of answer available.[1]
5. Qualitative analysis identifies what is highly contextual information and therefore what should **not** be subject to standardizing quantitative methods.

6. Qualitative research suggests the importance and means of construction of indicators[2] that usefully complement or replace existing indicators.

7. Insights from qualitative and quantitative studies help define population subgroup sampling frames.

8. Qualitative analysis (including that of key informants) helps determine appropriate stratification of the quantitative survey and subsequent disaggregation of survey cross-tabulation analysis (e.g. along gender, age, socioeconomic, political, sociocultural or ethnic lines).

Sequencing methods and data can allow for **examining**, **explaining**, **confirming**, **refuting** and/or **enriching** information from one approach with that from another, for better analysis. Means of sequencing might include:

A qualitative study generates working hypotheses that can be further examined through quantitative research with specific predefined questions.

A contextual study is conducted as a subsample of larger, non-contextual surveys. This allows for comparisons to be made between the results of contextual investigation and those of larger surveys for the same community.[3]

Qualitative investigation assesses how important the average is at the local level, i.e. how important the heterogeneity of local conditions is for challenging the worth of abstracted/standardized findings or conclusions.

Qualitative research explains relationships, trends and patterns emerging from a survey.[4]

Qualitative investigation triangulates (verifies or refutes) survey results.[5]

Qualitative research enriches analysis of relationships, trends and patterns emerging from surveys through new learning.

During the analysis phase of research, the emphasis shifts to ensuring data are merged sufficiently for improved analysis and policy influence. Analytical frameworks powerfully shape the use and interpretation of data.[6] Dissemination and learning require crucially that normative ideological positions are open to change. Booth et al. (1998: 14) comment on the potential power of participatory poverty assessments to 'bring to the fore and articulate as policy relevant, the dynamic processes behind vulnerability and persistent poverty', but warn that 'this involves ... addressing issues that may not easily be recognized as relevant to policy, and do not sit very easily within current policy frameworks, but which nonetheless cry out for consideration at this level.' The dissemination and learning phase also brings into focus the importance of process, democratization and empowerment through research, themes that are picked up in the final section of this book.

A number of important principles emerge from this brief discussion. The first is the principle of **methodological triangulation** of data, investigator, theory and method (Denzin 1970). We wrote in the General Introduction about triangulation as a means of improving the trustworthiness of qualitative research, and triangulation is widely recognized as a working principle of the participatory reflection and action tradition because of the increased likelihood of non-sampling errors in this type of research (Chambers 1994a,b). Here we suggest that triangulation should cut across schools of thought, disciplines, theoretical frameworks, researchers,[7] populations, stakeholders, key informants, methods and data. Single-strand methods are weak and vulnerable; triangulation, representing 'robust eclecticism' (Booth et al. 1998: 6), strengthens understanding and increases confidence.

A second principle is that of moving iteratively between description and explanation through flexible use of methods and data. Researchers who adopt and adhere to a blueprint research process often become victims of their own rigidity. Indeed there are certain elements of research that need to be predesigned (particularly the sampling protocol and the standardization of methods and data for research segments that will be aggregated), but even here there is ample opportunity for sequencing through piloting and pretesting in order to produce the right kind of standardization.[8]

A third important principle is that of equity, or what McGee (2003: 135) calls 'equality of difference'. By promoting various forms of mixing, we are moving methodological discussion away from a norm in development research in which qualitative research plays second fiddle to conventional empiricist investigation. This means, for example, that contextual studies should not be used simply to confirm and window-dress the findings of non-contextual surveys. Instead they should play a more rigorous role of identifying errors or puzzles, reshaping working hypotheses, and continually testing normative views (Booth et al. 1998: 12), or even of replacing (when appropriate) large-scale, clumsy and lengthy surveys that tend to overgenerate information in an untimely fashion for policy audiences.

Achieving representativeness with qualitative and quantitative data

Development researchers usually set out to generate data and insights that, to some extent, can be generalized in order to produce lessons and guidance for future policy and practice. Data can be defined as representative or externally valid if a presumed causal relationship can be generalized across different types of persons, settings and times.

The problem of representativeness is usually one associated with qualitative data, and this is because the research that produces qualitative information is usually contextual. Contextual methods are used, for example, in anthropological enquiry to explore depth and produce qualitative insights. Participatory research uses contextual research methods in providing 'depth, richness and realism of information and analysis' (Chambers 1994a). With non-contextual research methods the emphasis is on breadth of coverage, and with breadth comes representativeness.

In many cases we can increase the representativeness, and therefore the usefulness, of context-specific data – both qualitative and quantitative – by applying sampling procedures that allow us to state how representative of larger populations these findings are. Uphoff (2003) rejects the 'tyranny' of 'statistical hawks' and their obsession with significance (a word he describes as 'one of the greatest misfortunes to befall us'), but points out that contextual studies need not ignore or reject sampling techniques. Instead:

> 'These (techniques) can give readers some idea of how common or frequent are the characteristics or experiences being reported. For an individual to report that he or she has been victimized by the police, for example, being defenseless because of his or her poverty, does not tell us whether this is a universal experience, a frequent occurrence, an uncommon thing, or a freak and completely idiosyncratic event. This is not to say that no information is valid unless it is accompanied by a detailed sampling procedure and a large enough sample to be able to establish statistical "significance". It is a plea for putting qualitative data into enough of a quantitative framework that they can be meaningfully interpreted.'

Certainly, sampling protocol demands that, as a first step, we should try to work in a relatively large number of sites in order to make reasonably precise generalized inferences that are representative of the (larger) population of interest, although the level of variability within a population is more important than population size in determining sample size (Barahona and Levy 2002). It may not be possible, due to constraints on time, money or human resources, to conduct in-depth research in sufficient sites in order to allow for variability. In cases where variability is low, this is less of a problem. If the population of a region, for example, has a demonstrably uniform economic, social, cultural and political make-up, then we do not need a large sample size. Stratification in sampling helps achieve greater uniformity of sampling frame. But in most instances the social universe is highly variable and complex, and we would need to sample enough sites to take account of that heterogeneity even after stratifying populations to reduce likely variability.

In these instances of research in a small number of sites, the best we might be able to do is to fit the data from the sites to a larger target population (Booth et al. 1998) while acknowledging that the small site coverage has implications for the representativeness of the data. An existing statistically robust household survey sample frame (from a living standards survey or census) can be very useful for fitting the profile of a small-scale qualitative study population to a broader population. This at least allows for some reasoned discussion and assessment of the representativeness of findings from qualitative research.[9] The very least we can do is make indicative statements or working hypotheses that can be followed up through less contextual, less open-ended research. This is discussed further in the section below on combining methods and data.

Next, when choosing research sites (geographical communities) and research units (population groups) within sites, probability-based selection (or random sampling) is a method of selection that gives an equal chance of selection to all sites and all people. The advantage here is that researchers or enumerators are able to claim that their judgement has not been used for the selection (as happens when researchers look for the most interesting or extreme case studies). In cases when the number of selected sites is sufficiently large, we then have a good chance of including a representative set of sites and research units, and in addition will have a good idea of the diversity of circumstances present in the area of interest (Barahona and Levy 2002).

In most cases of development research, however, we are seeking to identify a particular target group that is of interest to us or to our clients. We might want to target, for example, an economically poor, rural, tribal community in a specific agroecological zone, or women of reproductive age in a particular community. By applying random stratified sampling[10] we can stratify the population universe before we apply probability-based selection. Careful sequencing of stratification and randomization through hierarchical (or multistage) sampling procedures then enables us to pursue contextual, in-depth research that produces both qualitative and quantitative information in sites and with groups that are representative of larger populations (Chapter 2).

One remaining problem is that in many instances, particularly in participatory research, it may not be desirable to select sites and groups randomly. Communities are often identified not because they are representative of a particular population profile, but because they are engaged in a particular project, programme or policy process. In these instances of purposive selection (selection on purpose), sampling is not random and is therefore potentially biased and unrepresentative. In these situations, if researchers see a benefit in generating information that is unbiased according to the conventions of statistical sampling, then they might consider either conducting additional participatory research in random stratified sites (without compromising the time and resource implications for participatory process in those sites), or fitting the purposive data retrospectively, as discussed above, while acknowledging that the lack of randomization has implications for the validity of the data.

Contributions

Part I expands on some of the technical challenges to combined methods raised in this introduction through a number of case studies that demonstrate the effective application of sequencing of methods in different policy and research contexts. Mike Jennings (Chapter 1) examines the process of focusing and mapping research through identification of research questions, set against a qualifying discussion of the iteration of inductive and deductive moments in development research. Ian Wilson (Chapter 2) provides a focused discussion of sampling protocol, and considers how it can be adapted and applied to research that is essentially qualitative and in-depth. Through a case study of innovation in impact assessment in the microfinance sector, James Copestake, Susan Johnson and Katie Wright (Chapter 3) explore the trade-offs inherent in standardizing methods and data for generalizability and the potential for thoughtful sequencing of methods. In the next two chapters, Gil Yaron, Jutta Blauert and Alejandro Sanguines (Chapter 4) and Tapani Tyynela (Chapter 5) reflect on the challenges in integrating qualitative and quantitative (income-based) data sets in impact assessment. Finally, Jennifer Briedenhann and Eugenia Wickens (Chapter 6) demonstrate the benefits of methodological sequencing in project evaluation.

Chapter One
Little white pebbles: getting the questions right and getting the right data

MIKE JENNINGS

Summary

A research project can seem a daunting proposition at the outset, when it might consist of nothing more than a tiny seed of an idea. The researcher must take this idea and develop it into a coherent set of research questions that provide direction and focus to the emerging project. Once the project has been identified and fleshed out, the task shifts to gathering evidence and data, to analysing the material collected, and to drawing conclusions. The need for clarity and coherence becomes apparent when the detail in the data starts to obscure the overall perspective and objectives of the research. Yet, while the research questions frame and guide the research process that follows, this is rarely a linear process, and the onus is on the researcher to allow for iteration in the dynamic relationship between research questions and emerging data. This chapter considers this process of establishing and revising the research questions to be pursued, concluding that only by asking the right questions will the right data emerge.

Introduction

In the fairytale *Hansel and Gretel*, the two children, abandoned in the forest at the whim of their mother, manage to find their way home having marked out their path with little white pebbles. There are times in the life of researchers, especially in the early days, when they feel like these two lost children, cast adrift in the forest of fieldwork, unable to see clearly through the tangled branches of data and methodology, overwhelmed by the quantity of information and the immense task of analysis and interpretation before the research can be written up and submitted. But through careful design of the research project, and in particular through basing the work upon a set of research questions that define parameters, focus and methodology, a trail of little white pebbles can be laid down to guide the researcher through this forest.

At the heart of the research process lies the research question (or rather questions) which forms the foundation of what is being discussed, analysed and reported on (Robson 2002). By describing the issue to be researched, the research questions provide the route map for the research project which is then pursued and resolved through careful design of research methods, through effective data collection and analysis, and in the final interpretation of that evidence.

The function of research questions

Research questions are required to complete three main tasks. First, the questions should provide a summary of the research project, explaining in short what exactly is being enquired into. The second task is to establish the parameters of the enquiry. A research project focusing on broad issues such as 'poverty', 'HIV/AIDS' or 'malnutrition' would need to qualified by a greater degree of precision in order to be accomplishable and useful (Marshall and Rossman 1999: 17–19). Third, the research questions should provide a clue as to what particular methodology or methodologies are going to be used in the course of data/evidence collection. As Mason (2002: 19) notes, the research questions form the backbone of research design, supporting the project that develops around it.

The task of constructing a research question can be seen as a process in which an edifice is constructed through the layering of questions. The research question consists of three layers of separate, but linked, questions: the basic summary of what the research is actually about; questions designed to establish what kind of research is being undertaken; and questions designed to draw out a methodology:

Foundation question:
what, where and when?

↓

Questions based on type of research:
is this project descriptive or explanatory?

↓

Questions to assist in selection of methodologies:
how?

With these points in mind the researcher needs to consider what types of knowledge the project is expected to generate, and therefore what types of questions need to be asked to meet the requirements of the project.

Knowledge generation: inductive versus deductive approaches

There are two main types of approach to generating knowledge, both of which lead to the formulation of differing types of research questions, the use of differing sets of methodologies for data collection, and differing outcomes. Using Kanbur's (2003: 1) typology discussed in the General Introduction, the deductive approach can be seen to fall more within a quantitative research type.

The deductive approach is theory-led, applying a theory or set of theories to social realities and testing how well they fit. For example,

Table 1.1 *Deductive versus inductive research*

Deductive research	Inductive research
Quantitative	Qualitative
Closed	Open-ended
Linear	Circular
One-off: testing hypotheses	Iterative: generating and continually testing working hypotheses
Theory-based	Rooted in lived experience
Fixed, static design	Flexible, changing design
Fact-oriented	'Knowledge'-generating
Top-down	Participatory

one might begin with a theory that particular types of HIV/AIDS intervention strategies are more likely to achieve positive outcomes. The research might then test this theory through a range of case studies (Preece 1994: 54–5). The conclusion of the research is already set through the deductive approach, and the research is designed to confirm, or reject, the validity of these theoretical conclusions.

The inductive approach reverses the process, beginning with various social realities and seeking to draw conclusions from the data that are collected through the research. In other words, the data are used to create a theoretical position, rather than (in the deductive approach) using the data to test that position. Again to take the case of interventions to contain and prevent HIV/AIDS, an inductive approach would begin with an examination of various types of intervention across a variety of settings, then use the data collected to draw conclusions as to which elements were critical to a successful strategy. Returning to Kanbur's typology, inductive inference relies more on qualitative data in reaching its conclusions.

Following Table 1.1, deductive research is fixed within theoretical premises, reliant more on quantitative data in its assessment of those hypotheses, and follows a fixed path from initial point of inquiry to final conclusions. In contrast, the inductive method is more reliant on a qualitative set of data and asks open-ended questions, research into which follows a more iterative approach. While deductive research remains largely within the theoretical world (albeit using research findings from the real world in order to support those theories), inductive research is more firmly rooted in lived experience, reliant on the context being studied for its conclusions and theories that emerge.

The foundation of the research – the research question – inevitably differs depending on the approach adopted by the researcher. If one approaches the issue of HIV/AIDS intervention strategies from a deductive approach, one might begin with the premise that successful strategies require a combination of multiple-agency action, strong leadership at all levels and among opinion-forming institutions (the church or mosque, for example), successful integration with local cultural and social mores, and a broad focus on socio-economic factors as well as the purely medical. The research that would flow from such a position would focus on gathering data and information from case studies that would test the hypothesis. The conclusion of this research is fixed (successful strategies require elements X, Y and Z), and once sufficient data have been collected adequately to test the validity of the theoretical position, the research can be said to be complete.

The inductive approach would begin with the question: 'What elements are necessary to a successful anti-HIV/AIDS strategy?', and would examine a range of interventions in order to identify both successful and unsuccessful policies. The conclusions are not known before the process of data collection and analysis, but are driven by the findings. As a result the conclusions are not fixed, but are reinforced over time with additional evidence. As Preece (1994: 54–5) points out, in the deductive approach a valid premise leads to a conclusion, but additional evidence does not add to the strength of the conclusion. Inductive approaches, by contrast, are strengthened by additional evidence. The conclusion may not be certain, as it is with deduction, but is probable based on the evidence available.

In reality the line between deductive and inductive approaches is blurred, and most research projects will combine the strengths of both. The applied nature of development studies, in particular, requires primacy to be given to the social realities within which the research is based. One might assume that, in the case of work designed within a policy framework, and particularly with participatory approaches that are underpinned by a shift in ownership of the research process, the inductive approach is the most appropriate. However, the deductive approach should not be discounted or abandoned: it has an important role to play in framing the parameters of the research, in giving shape to what might otherwise be an undefined (and hence unmanageable) project. It is perfectly possible, and perhaps advisable, to frame research questions in such a way that they borrow from the two approaches. To return to the example of anti-HIV/AIDS interventions, this third approach might begin with the premise that there are certain elements critical to the success or failure of such interventions (deduction). The actual research question 'what elements are essential?' is fundamentally inductive, relying on evidence to test the effectiveness of various elements from a variety of settings.

Finding the right questions

There are two broad types of research: descriptive and explanatory. Let us take as an example the issue of world hunger. 'World hunger' as a research topic is far too broad to be encompassed within a single project. At this stage, two questions are essential:

1. what aspect of world hunger is the project going to analyse?
2. what is the time frame of the proposed research project?

In this hypothetical example, the researcher narrows down the topic to focus on shifts in the numbers affected by world hunger. During the course of the twentieth century, the absolute number of people suffering from chronic hunger has shifted considerably in terms of both scale and geographical distribution of where hunger strikes hardest. Although the topic has been narrowly focused by the answer to the first research question ('what aspect of world hunger is this project considering?'), the topic needs to be further refined. During the first half of the 1990s, the number of chronically hungry people in the world decreased by 37 million; however, since 1995–7 the overall number has increased by more than 18 million people. Thus the researcher arrives at the research question that provides the foundation stone of the project: what happened to global shifts in absolute hunger during the 1990s?

The scope of the project has thus been set through a questioning process that sought to ask what aspect of a broader problem the researcher is most interested in investigating. The types of questions that follow this initial process will vary, however, according to the type of research to be undertaken. In order to answer the foundation research question, the descriptive and explanatory approaches require further questions to draw out a particular focus.

In descriptive research, the project is intended to show the shifts and cycles in hunger (rather than explain why they have occurred). Some of the questions that would inform such an approach might therefore include the following.

- What geographical area is going to be considered for study? Is the research looking at global trends, or picking a particular region or country (or perhaps countries for comparative purposes)?
- What is the time frame of the project? Although the research is most concerned with the post-1990 period, how far back is the researcher going to look for the roots of the post-1990 pattern?

The researcher might ask why descriptive research is important. Given that other research, in this example, has examined overall global trends in this period, what would such a project add to overall knowledge in this field? An inductive approach suggests that such a project would add to the weight of evidence, thus confirming (or even denying) the existence of the reported shifts. Moreover, a descriptive research project would be adding more detail, based on a particular region or country, or through comparative studies, to the overall picture. Thus although no new conclusions might be drawn out by the project (unless the study reveals flaws in the previously accepted evidence), the project is adding to an overall body of knowledge which serves to reinforce the acceptance of patterns in global hunger.

An explanatory approach to research is concerned less with showing that a particular trend has occurred (assuming, on the basis of other research, that it has), but rather asks why such a shift has occurred. The questions that this project might ask are therefore different from those asked in pure descriptive research. In looking at the same shift in hunger, in the same period, the questions that might be asked are:

- what factors have caused the increase in hunger since 1995–7?
- what elements changed from the early to late 1990s that might have had an impact on hunger?
- what is the importance of a particular factor (e.g. HIV/AIDS) in contributing to the upward shift?
- what elements in a particularly successful/unsuccessful intervention led to the increase/decrease in hunger in a particular area?
- what is the impact of hunger on issues of security and stability?

In reality, as with the differences between inductive and deductive approaches, the distinction between explanatory and descriptive research is often blurred, and it is rare that a researcher will rely purely on one or the other. It is unlikely that a research project will lead to fundamentally new conclusions. Rather, most will fit into a particular body of research on a specific issue or theme, and will add to the body of knowledge. Good research will tend to adopt elements from both descriptive and explanatory models, and the research questions will reflect this mix. Thus our research project on global shifts in hunger might be driven by the following set of research questions:

- what shifts in world hunger occurred during the 1990s?
- what happened in East Africa in this period?
- what factors contributed to a worsening position in food security in East Africa?
- what has been the impact of this at the household level?

A third model is also important in research in the social sciences, especially in development studies, operating as it does within a policy framework. Mikkelsen (1995: 214) refers to 'action-oriented' research questions which ask how people respond to the knowledge generated through the research process. In this model a final research question might be added: 'what interventions are most likely to achieve a positive outcome in restoring food security at the household level?' Adopting this approach leads to a more participatory model of research in which the qualitative data gathered speak directly to the immediate context from which they are gathered, and the community from which the data are collected acquires greater ownership of its generation and analysis (Chambers 1997).

Research in development studies is likely to involve a blend of all three approaches, although the balance will be dictated by the ultimate objective of the research, the interest of the researcher, and the requirement for a broadly participatory approach to data collection for methodological, philosophical and ethical reasons.

Linking questions to methodology

The final level of questions reflects the need to adopt a methodology for the research project. The specific questions outlined above fix the parameters of the study and focus the topic on a particular aspect. However, the research questions must also consider what is to be analysed – the unit of analysis. In both descriptive and explanatory models this might be decided by focusing on the particular level at which the research is going to be carried out. Is the project looking at national or regional statistics and reports, or considering the impact at household and community levels? If a project is using the household as the dominant unit of analysis – 'what has happened to hunger at the household level in rural Tanzania?' (descriptive) or 'why have certain households become more vulnerable?' (explanatory) – a methodology must be adopted that will elicit the required evidence. A project focusing on what has happened across several countries is likely to adopt a quantitative statistical approach in seeking to reach its conclusions, while assessments of vulnerability and insecurity might find qualitative data more appropriate. The types of questions asked in interviews, group discussions and questionnaires will be dictated by the particular terms of reference of the research questions. The research question, in suggesting the type of data required to reach an answer, thus leads the researcher to a set of methodologies that will draw out those data.

The importance of flexibility

There is an apocryphal story of a doctoral student in the mid-1960s who sought to ask why, in an age of nationalist struggles and the accession to power of indigenous governments, the Sultanate in Zanzibar had successfully managed to hold on to power. Within a few months of arriving to undertake fieldwork research, the revolution occurred and the Sultanate fell. Pondering the dilemma, the student simply rephrased the research question to 'why did the Sultanate prove unable to maintain its hold on to power?'

Research questions can be rendered unanswerable or unusable for a range of less dramatic or violent reasons. When the researcher begins to engage in fieldwork, sources of data assumed to exist might turn out to be missing; hypotheses that seemed to be central back in the home institution can, in the light of experience, become regarded as peripheral or unimportant. The research question, in other words, requires constant modification in the light of the experience of actual research. Without inbuilt flexibility the question becomes little more than a straitjacket.

In describing the process of formulating research questions and their importance in shaping the research project as it unfolds, it is

Figure 1.1   *The research process as a linear progression*

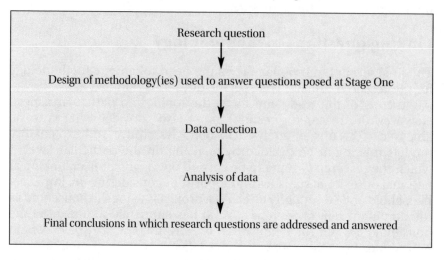

tempting to regard the research process as a linear progression from research question to final outcome. Figure 1.1 suggests how such a process might logically process.

However, given the unpredictable elements associated with research in the social sciences (especially when mixed methods are applied to research), the lack of flexibility inherent in a schema such as Figure 1.1 might serve to damage the research process fatally. The framing of research questions at the start of the process is an indispensable part of the research process, without which the rest cannot follow, yet the research questions are not intended solely to be a guide at the beginning stages, from which the rest logically and inevitably follows. In order to contribute and shape the research project, the questions must be framed and reframed constantly. Research rarely follows a linear progress; it is an iterative process, and at every stage in the cycle the research questions need to be modified and reframed. Such a process might look more like that in Figure 1.2.

The final conclusions might not, according to this cycle, be focused on the original set of questions outlined in the initial stages of the research project – questions that might, in the light of data collection and analysis, have been shown to be relatively unimportant or fundamentally flawed. Rather, the interpretation could be based on a set of questions outlined at any stage of research. The research questions, in other words, must combine a sharp focus with flexibility if they are to assist researchers effectively in their task.

Figure 1.2 *The research process as an iterative cycle*

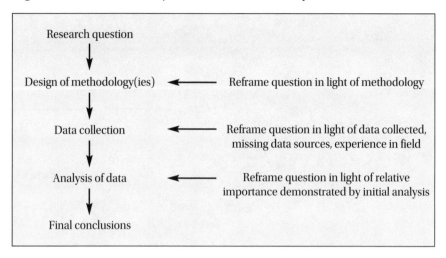

Conclusions

The research question is the road map of the research project. But, crucially, research questions are meant to enable research, to give it a focus, while allowing it to retain flexibility to deal with unexpected occurrences and the continual flow of new information that are the hallmark of most researchers' experiences. And, perhaps even more importantly, the research question should allow the researcher to provide a succinct, clear and unambiguous response to the inevitable question: 'so what is it exactly that you are doing?'

Chapter Two
Some practical sampling procedures for development research

IAN WILSON[1]

Summary

The concepts and principles of sampling theory can be expressed simply and applied sensibly to the complex realities of development projects. These complement the ontological and epistemological concerns and 'theoretical sampling' of qualitative researchers. They relate largely to studies where sampling should be representative so that conclusions can be generalized – usually studies preceded by relatively informal qualitative hypothesis-generating and scoping exercises.

This chapter summarizes the experience of advising, reviewing or participating in various projects of the UK's Department for International Development (DFID). It concentrates on hierarchical sampling situations with several levels of unit (e.g. region, district, community, household). These are common but problematic, involving practical decisions that may be underconceptualized in the qualitative literature. Applications are illustrated for some of the themes that may be explored in deciding the characteristics of a research design, including:

- defining units and levels, dealing with unequal units, defining unit size, determining which units qualify for inclusion, and how to cope with changes through time
- comparison of sample segments as an objective, factorial stratification structure
- representativeness and population coverage as an objective, objectivity–randomness and alternatives
- sample size compromises – multiple objectives, and the L-shaped data file
- distribution of effort over hierarchical levels, varying meaning of objectivity at different levels
- place of unequal distribution within primary units
- combining or phasing studies, table-top sampling, sampling read-through and livelihoods, problems of stratification, problems of targeting.

The argument of this chapter focuses on research funded because of a claim or implication (maybe not an explicitly stated promise) that it can be generalized to a domain that a development agency client regards as important. No distinction is made here between work done within sites that is quantitative, and that which is qualitative or participatory. This chapter is largely about evidence, rather than the qualitative or quantitative tools used to gather it.

Introduction

This chapter is about how, despite appearances to the contrary, elements of the quantitative approach to sampling can be applied to certain sorts of mixed-mode and qualitative research, and aid their generalizability. It is written from the point of view of statisticians familiar with teaching, and providing help to, non-statisticians. Our advisory input is often at stages of the research process when informal qualitative studies have already been carried out. Whether or not we were directly involved, we have, as long as we can remember, regarded mixing of methods – especially sequential mixing – as natural and inevitable. Early phase work involving scoping studies, consultation processes, prioritization and hypothesis-generating activities should be informal – what we now have to refer to as qualitative and, in the right circumstances, as participatory. Our perception is that in these more exploratory studies, so-called qualitative sampling is quite reasonably seen as staking out the limits of little-known territory, contrasting with the later-phase, detailed work to achieve proper coverage (often associated with descriptive statistical work, e.g. hypothesis-testing). It is when qualitative work is the main approach to this later-phase work that we see some potential for strengthening the sampling practice.

Limitations of traditional statistical theory

Sampling theory

Statistical sampling theory is a peculiarly – and regrettably – esoteric black art: most serious books are packed with formulae that are surpassingly boring and of very limited direct usefulness, except sometimes to the initiate. The starting points assumed are usually impossible hurdles for the development practitioner – in terms of both readers' mathematical hardiness (or foolhardiness), and the assumptions underlying the theory. A huge part of this theory is concerned with estimation of a single numerical quantity – not the most enticing objective to the qualitative researcher. Unsurprisingly, then, many researchers ignore the gobbledygook and jump straight in, with quite variable consequences. This chapter suggests a few slabs to pave a middle way.

Random sampling

For those who are exposed to sampling theory, the first big idea is that of random sampling. What people usually seem to recall later is that you must give every member of the population an equal chance of being picked – and this immediately loses many would-be researchers when they cannot enumerate the entire population, or when the units are not all equal (e.g. larger and smaller households).

You must, indeed, give every member of the population an equal chance of being picked if you want to work out the optimal properties of some mathematical estimators, but the important practical idea is both more basic and more interesting. This is that, in order to produce conclusions that can reasonably be defended as generalizing to a larger population, you must set up an objective (in principle a repeatable) procedure for sampling which prevents the implementers from choosing their informants in undisclosed and subjective ways – ways that invisibly bias the results by unknowable amounts. A clearly stated procedure, with careful arguments in its support, is referred to below as a protocol; a good one allows a fair assessment of what the sample does represent.

Another kind of claim frequently made for random sampling, but all too often overinterpreted and misunderstood, is that the results can reflect very precisely the population mean. This is the claim best supported by statistical theory, but not the most important way in which qualitative conclusions need to be backed up.

Furthermore, the claim to precision is true only if you meaningfully can, and successfully do: (a) elicit meaningful and accurate values, (b) sample at random, and (c) have a very large sample. A large sample allows us to select units disregarding the many complicated ways in which they may be characterized (e.g. human respondents' levels of education, social connectedness, access to loans, etc.). These will – as the sample becomes huge – be averaged out in the overall picture. There is no such claim at all if the sample size is very small, or if we do not want to ignore the characterizations.

Small samples are all too common because of lack of resources, but small sample sizes often do more harm than they need – and achieve less than they might – because of poor disposition of the resources available. This theme is developed below as we look at some of the realities of sampling as perceived in our professional practice, especially in advising or reviewing development agency projects.

Hierarchies of units

Information in hierarchies

Very frequently, social research reflects a broad social setting where we might be concerned, for example, with interviewing children as individuals; the primary care-giver or the head as representing the child's household; and/or the head of the village development committee to convey formal information about the community. Here there is a hierarchy of units – child, household, community, and maybe more levels.[2]

The largest sampling entities are referred to in the quantitative literature as 'primary sampling units', the next level down as 'secondary' and so on until we reach the 'ultimate' sampling units. An attempt to trace the impact of social and economic policies on the welfare of children, for instance, needs to link levels and trace pathways from the

> ### Box 2.1   *Hierarchical sampling: the DFID/Social Science Research Unit 'Young Lives' project*
>
> In this project, as well as policy monitoring we talk about four levels where both qualitative and quantitative information is collected: the site (sometimes called the 'sentinel site'); the community; the household; and the individual. The site is an administrative entity (a *mandal* in Andhra Pradesh; a commune or two in Vietnam) from within which we recruit 100 index children aged between 6 and 18 months at enrolment.

policy-making arena down to its effects on individual children, the ultimate units (see Box 2.1).

Resource allocation in hierarchies

Qualitative research design literature often fails to acknowledge how hierarchies should be considered in study design.[3] There is very often a resource trade-off that has to be thought about rather carefully – more sites means less information per site, and sometimes (as with the policy-tracking objective) the selections at one level bear critically on those at another. One of the main messages is that sampling strategies are incomplete and incoherent unless they define reasoning and procedures at all necessary levels. In the following we assume there is some hierarchical structure, and that this implies collecting information and addressing objectives at two levels, at least.

In reviewing DFID research projects, for example, the Statistical Services Centre has strongly criticized the design of studies where a couple of sites (each comprising a handful of villages) have been selected, and very intensive studies conducted within them – to the tune of a third of a million pounds in some cases – to give very large (indeed unmanageable and excessive) amounts of site-specific information.[4] The conclusion here is that too much effort has been expended within, and too little between, the primary sampling units. What did the sampling units represent?[5] We would have advised, or gone along with, (i) a not-very-different first phase with a few sites and quite a lot of households, then (ii) an additional light-touch second phase where some key results and predictions from the first phase were shown to apply to a range of other sites.

Protocols for hierarchies

The usual situation when sampling in a hierarchical setting is this. At the top level, the primary units are large entities about which a great deal is public knowledge, for example a geographical region is characterized – with varying degrees of relevance and accuracy – as to its climate, transport, ethnic mix, employment types, social problems, local government personalities and so on. In contrast, the bottom level of the hierarchy, the household or individual, is probably unknown to outsiders until after recruitment. Sampling at the top level involves selecting a very little of the vast amount of possible information and using this to provide a rationale for particular choices.

So-called random sampling has little or nothing to say at this level, and attempting to use it usually entails discarding or ignoring readily available information which might quite logically guide one's choices. In the author's view, doing so in order to make a claim to 'statistical' generalizability is usually bogus.[6] Any claim to objectivity, generalizability or broad usefulness will usually depend on a well argued case for the selection made. Hence a good protocol, at the top level of a hierarchy, will discuss the information that could be used as the basis for selection; will explain which of it is relevant, recent and reliable; and will illustrate clearly how the most appropriate information is used. It will admit that practicalities constrained the choices, and will assess the impact of restrictions so imposed.

At the bottom level, say the household, the external reader of a research report will never meet child Reddy, age eight, and is weakly positioned to interpret a researcher's unexplained procedure for selecting him. The contents of the protocol at this level are a quite separate issue: the protocol needs to assure the reader about different things, for example that researcher Mrs Rao recruited child Reddy following a purposeful, well-defined procedure, with adequate assurances of objectivity as one part of the requirement, alongside issues of ethics, qualifying characteristics and so on. The report of the implementation of this ultimate sampling unit protocol should again acknowledge, and assess the effects of, practicalities such as the 'hit rate' in judging what the achieved sample represents.[7]

Study objectives: estimation or comparison?

Crusading zeal for sampling rigour is often misplaced. Its importance depends on the topic, as well as the prevailing culture of the audience. If the objective of a study is to provide an accurate overall picture, sampling rigour is, of course, important.

Many studies are concerned not primarily with prevalences or population sizes, but with comparisons, for example between before and after, or between project areas and 'untreated control' areas. This usually imposes sample size requirements that sharply disagree with those for estimation objectives, whether the information collection process is quantitative or more qualitative. In a simple instance, a population split roughly 80:20 between two important strata should usually be sampled proportionately to produce an overall estimate; but to compare the two groups one with the other would usually suggest 50:50 sampling, so both groups are characterized equally well and the differences are as clear as possible.

There are many different contextual characteristics that might be taken into account in a process of comparison, and there is a great deal of theory in the statistical literature on experimental design, little

Table 2.1 *Comparing population groups and establishing hierarchies*

	High % scheduled castes		Low % scheduled castes	
Transport*	DPIP+	DPIP–	DPIP+	DPIP–
Good	–	Include	Include	–
Poor	Include	–	–	Include
*DPIP = District Poverty Initiative Programme				

mentioned in sampling theory but relevant here. At the simplest, each of these might again distinguish population members into two groups. For example, at the top level in a hierarchy we might have districts with high or low proportions of scheduled caste populations, with good or bad transport infrastructure, with early or late implementation of the District Poverty Initiative Programme, and so on. Similar multiple characterizations can appear at each of several levels in a hierarchy. For this example, we might propose a study in four sites at the level of choice of districts (a half-replicate of a factorial design) to obtain some information on the above three forms of groupings, as illustrated in Table 2.1.

Note that this element of design does not sit alone. It does not imply that the study at the next level of the hierarchy, within each chosen district, is qualitative or quantitative, cross-sectional or longitudinal, nor does it say how the study is structured within districts. We do not explore this theme further here, but note that the above is the merest mention of what can become quite a complicated balancing act when the levels are combined. It may be evident, even here, that some of the body cells of the table will be more common than others in the population, and we want to include relatively significant ones.

Combining and contextualizing studies

Multiple studies

Individual studies will often form part of a larger whole, where different themes are to be developed and explored over a period, as in many development projects. Research processes needing more involvement and time commitment from local people (and from researchers) will be restricted to smaller numbers than the briefer, shallower sections of the work such as responding to a short survey.

A simple version of this, which we refer to as the table-top, typically involves a relatively large number of people across a good number of places as respondents in a short questionnaire-based study at a relatively early phase, followed up with more intensive, deeper (probably qualitative) work in a few communities selected partly on the basis of the first study (Figure 2.1).

Figure 2.1   *Table-top sampling*

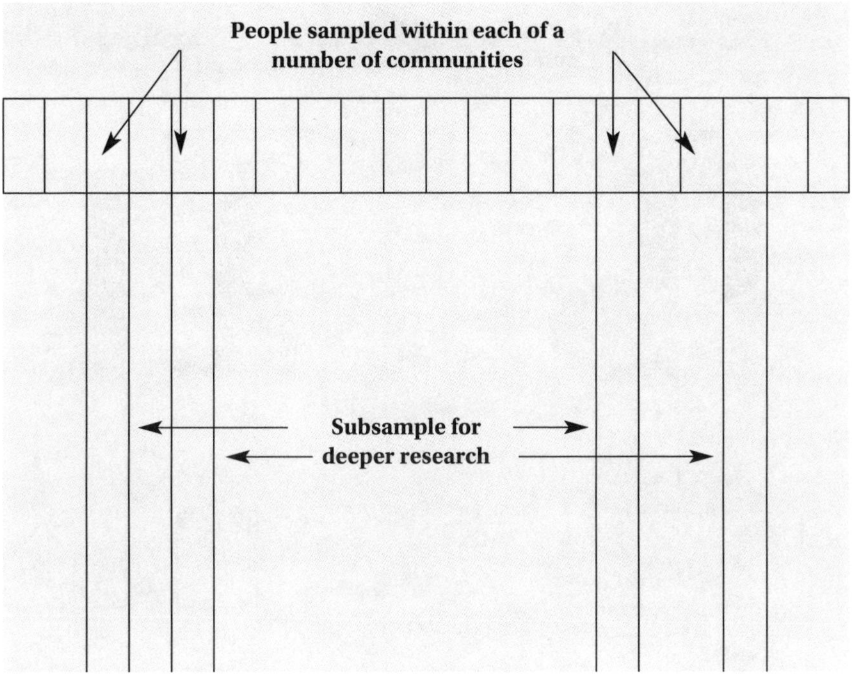

This provides some breadth which can justify the selection of in-depth study sites as being somewhat representative with respect to survey findings, rather than being 'just case studies'. There is also an element of read-through of data from the first-phase quick, shallow study to the deeper second phase, which may give some time-related information.

If a development project does carry out a succession of studies, the 'table legs' in Figure 2.1 may cease to be unitary and become more like piles of stones, each layer of stones representing a component study, participatory discussion, on-farm trial, etc. (Figure 2.2).

The greatest interest of the entomologist may be in the horizontal view of the shaded layer in Figure 2.2, representing data from, for example, pest management strategies. If there is the read-through suggested by the 3rd, 5th, 15th and 18th columns, then it is worth noting that the combination data from these compliant (and maybe much-burdened) communities also provides a vertical view which, with very careful thought about the studies, might be the 'livelihoods' view of the population.

Segmenting a study or articulating several?

Very often a single survey, whether formal and quantitative, or less formal and more open, is effectively a combination of several segments, each exploring a particular theme. There is a tendency to treat the survey

Figure 2.2 *Multi-study table-top sampling*

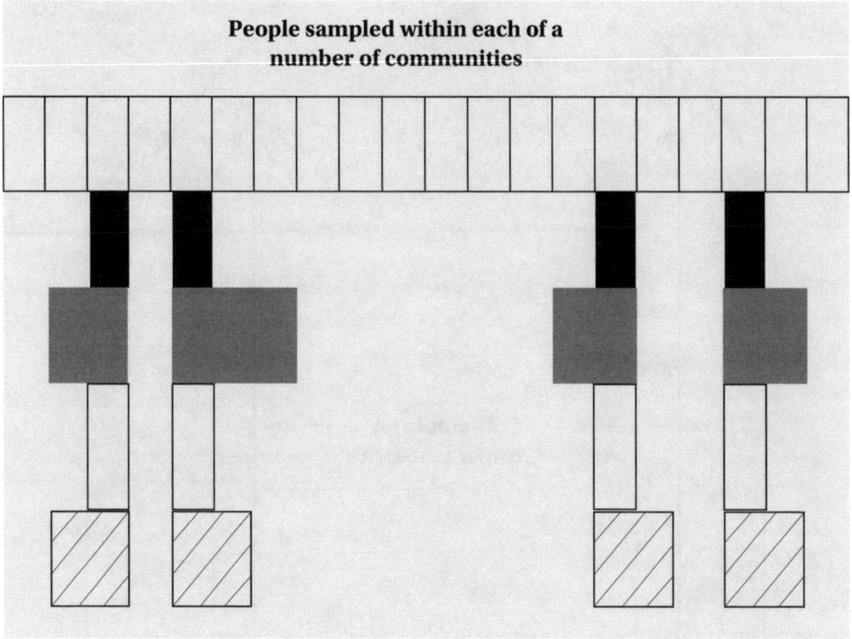

instrument as a unitary entity and to assume that every respondent must answer every question. Especially where a multi-disciplinary team has been involved in the design, we have seen survey instruments that have become far too cumbersome and burdensome. It appears there is often scope to prioritize within such surveys, saying that a core of questions must be answered by all whereas some other themes can be adequately covered by asking those questions of only a subset of the respondents (Figure 2.3). This assumes an effective study design so that analysis themes in module 1 do not require joint analysis with those in module 2.

Another way of thinking about this is to say that each of modules 1–3 in Figure 2.3 is a separate study which may be done by different researchers or at different times, but that the three studies have, by design, agreed on a set of common core questions that all will agree to use, with adequate commonality of training, interpretation and approach, so that the set of responses to this core can be amalgamated to strengthen its evidential power.

The above corresponds to a simple generalization of the common-place method in censuses where a percentage of the households receive a long form and the rest a short form. This creates an L-shaped data set. Figure 2.3 has multiple Ls.

Ranked set sampling

All the above notions are concerned with having both a relatively large group as the grounding for a study, and smaller groups which are more

Figure 2.3   *Main and subtheme coverage of segmented study*

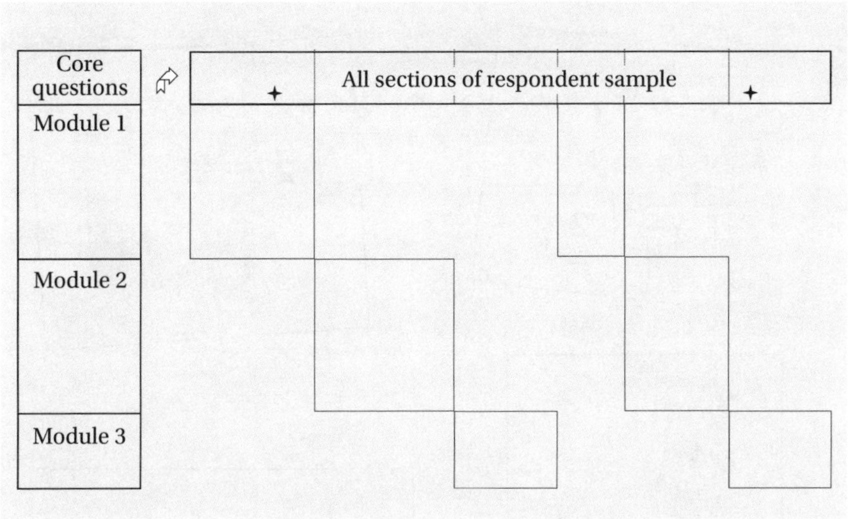

intensively studied when selected from that context. A different concept from sampling theory also operates at a conceptual level, where it is equally applicable to qualitative (including participatory) work, and brings with it some claims to objectivity of selection, lack of systematic bias, and generalizability. The ranked set sampling approach is illustrated in a simple case where there is a single key measure or characterization used to determine that the sample chosen is reasonable.

One frequent problem where ranked set sampling can help is the following. If there is no baseline study or existing sample frame available, we are denied the option that all the site selections could be made from a reasonable, if not comprehensive, list of communities. If there is no such list, how might we proceed, using more localized knowledge to help choose a few communities? Figure 2.4 (overleaf) illustrates how key informants can help to rank communities or villages according to a key variable such as food insecurity. Villages from each set of ranks can then be chosen randomly to be part of the research study (see Box 2.2 overleaf).

Sample stratification

Set in the context of communities, households and individuals, the above discusses the sampling issues that arise even if the units of study are all treated as interchangeable, for example, one community is the same as any other when sampling at primary unit level; within villages, households are treated as being undifferentiated, and so on. Of course this is usually not the case, and as well as worrying about hierarchies we need to think about male- versus female-headed households; occupation or livelihood characterizations; caste; religion, and the like.

The statistical concept of stratification is widely cited but not always relevant. Its essential meaning is not technical, and can be expressed

Figure 2.4   *Ranked-set sampling*

clearly by considering a wildly extreme case: suppose a population comprises subsets of individuals where every member is identical within each subset – in terms of the response we observe – even though the subsets differ from each other. We then need only a very small sample (of one) from each subset to typify it. In combination with information about how big the subsets are, we can typify the whole.

In reality, stratification can be very effective if the members who form a subgroup are a relatively homogeneous subset of the population, that is, they have a greater degree of similarity to one another in response terms than would a completely random subset. The education level of the head of household, the land tenure status, or other such factors used for stratification, bring together subsets of people who have something in common. Relatively small numbers of people can be supposed to typify each group, so the method is to some extent economical in fieldwork terms, although we probably need to search out all strata. Also, it is common that a report of a study will produce some results at stratum level, so it is sensible to control how many representatives of each stratum are sampled, so that the information base is fit for this purpose as well as to represent the whole population.

But stratification can also be highly ineffective. Populations are often divided into subgroups for administrative reasons, and results may be needed for separate subdivisions such as provinces. Unless the admin-

---

Box 2.2   *Ranked-set sampling: food insecurity in Malawi*

A participatory problem diagnosis study is to be carried out in four food-insecure village communities in one of the eight Agricultural Development Divisions of Malawi. How do we find these four communities? Four[8] Extension Planning Areas (EPAs, subunits of Agricultural Development Divisions) are selected at random from those that have featured in the Famine Early Warning System as having food-insecure communities. Within these, a set of qualifying criteria are set up which exclude unusual or atypical communities, e.g. trading centres adjacent to metalled roads. Four village communities per EPA are selected and it is verified that they qualify. Knowledgeable extension staff from each EPA (key informants) are asked to think about the past five years and to rank the set of four villages, say in terms of the proportion of their population who suffered three or more months of hunger in the year out of the last five with the worst rains.

The rankings (1–4) from the four EPAs are brought together. Taking the sets of ranks in an arbitrary order, the community ranked 1 in the first EPA is selected; that ranked 2 in the next EPA is selected; that ranked 3 is taken from the EPA that happens to be third in the review; and that ranked 4 from the fourth.

This set of four selected villages now has one per EPA, but also some claim to span the range of levels of food insecurity in the target area, and not to represent unconscious selection biases of the researchers, insofar as it has some elements of objectivity in its selection. The four villages selected are a set chosen in a 'random' way to be representative of a larger sample of 16. This sampling process has in no way affected the research methodology decisions which can now be made by the qualitative researchers working in each of the four villages.

The status in the entire population of the four villages ranked 1, say, will not be identical and, *a fortiori*, the differences between those ranked 1 and those ranked 4 will not be the same. This does not matter to the argument that we have an objective subset of a first sample of 16, and an enhanced claim to representative-ness. If the four constituent rankings are done at random, the resulting sample is neither better nor worse than a random sample of size four, while if it is better than random the resulting ranked set is better than that. Once again, the argument described here can be applied at more than one of the levels in a hierarchical sample. There is no bar to choosing four communities in this way, then having *n* households within each one selected on a similar basis.

---

istrative grouping happens to coincide with categories of participants who are homogeneous in response, it is not an effective stratification in the above sense. As an oversimplified example: if every village contains farmers, traders and artisans in vaguely similar proportions, villages will be of little relevance as a stratification factor if the main differences in livelihood situation are between farmers, traders and artisans.

The above suggests that the subsets by occupation correspond to clearly distinguished, identifiable groups, internally similar to each other but very different from group to group. In this clear situation, stratification – by occupation – is an obvious sampling tactic. In many cases, however, the groups are by no means so distinct, and the sub-divisions may be as arbitrary as the colonial borders of some African states. Usually this makes for ineffectual and delusory stratification.

Box 2.3   *Methods of stratification*

Pre- and post-stratification
Where stratification is meaningful, it is sensible to pre-stratify where the groupings can be detected before study work commences. In some cases the information for stratifying only becomes apparent during the study, and the cases are sorted into strata after the event (post-stratification). That does not allow the same control over the number of representatives included from each stratum, so it is usually a bit weaker, except where the fieldwork is necessary to decide on the stratifier to be used.

Participatory stratification
It is sometimes suggested that useful subdivisions of community members within communities can be achieved by getting them to divide into their own groups using their own criteria. This provides useful functional subdivisions for participatory work at local level. If results are to be integrated across communities, it is important that the subgroups correspond across those communities.

Thus a more formal stratification may require (i) a preliminary phase where stratification criteria are evolved by local participants; (ii) a reconciliation process between communities; and then (iii) the use of compromise 'one-size-fits-all' stratification procedures in the stratified study. If so, the set of strata should probably be the set of all subsets needed anywhere, including strata that may be null in many cases (e.g. fisher folk, who may be found only in coastal villages).

Quantile subdivision
Stratification is not natural where there is a continuous range rather than an effective classificatory factor. If there is just one clear-cut, observable piece of information which is selected as the best basis to be used, a pseudo-stratification can be imposed. For example, a wealth ranking exercise may put households into a clear order, and this can be divided into quantiles, for example the bottom, middle and top thirds; or four quartiles; or five quintiles. This permits comparisons between groups derived from the same ranking, such as the top and bottom thirds of the same village. As the rankings are relative, they may be difficult to use across a set of widely differing communities some of which are, overall, more prosperous than others.

This process hints at one way of choosing subsamples for later-phase, more detailed work, the table legs of Figure 2.1. One result of the broad, shallow table-top study – maybe a baseline study – could be a ranking or ordering of primary study units such as communities, and it would then be plausible to select a purposive sample to represent quantiles along the range of variation found.

Stratification for comparing groups
If, as above, we were intent on comparison, villages might be classified as near/remote from a metalled road; their land as mostly flat/steeply sloping; their access to irrigation water as good/poor – three stratification factors each at two crudely defined levels (and arguably more). The eight possible combination characterizations such as [near, flat, good] suggest that we might have eight subsamples, if possible. If each factor gave four levels, we would have 4 x 4 x 4 = 64. This illustrates a common difficulty, that possible strata are often all too numerous. Care is needed to select stratifiers of critical importance – if too many are used, the number of substudies to be conducted and reported can get out of hand.

Box 2.4   *Methods of targeted sampling*

General population screening
If the target population is a reasonably large fraction of the overall population, and if it is not contentious or difficult to ascertain membership, it may be possible to run a relatively quick screening check that respondents qualify as target population members, for example: 'Are there any children under 16 living in the household now?' As well as finding a sample from the target population, the hit rate of this method will provide an estimate of the proportion of the general population that the target population comprises, so long as careful records are kept of the numbers screened. If the target population is a small proportion of the whole, this method is likely to be uneconomical, although it may be possible to use key informants to elicit this information quickly and efficiently (Barahona and Levy 2002).

Snowball sampling
The least formal method of those discussed here is snowball sampling. The basis is that certain hard-to-reach subgroups of the population, such as drug-users or political dissidents, will be aware of others who belong to their own subgroup. An initial contact may then introduce the researcher to a network of further informants. The procedure used is serendipitous, and it is seldom possible to organize replicate sampling sweeps. Thus the results are usually somewhat anecdotal, and convey little sense of how completely the subgroup was covered or how large it really is.

Adaptive sampling
This relatively new method allows sampling intensity to be increased when one happens upon a relatively high local concentration of the target group during a geographical sweep, such as a transect sample. It provides some estimation procedures which take account of the differing levels of sampling effort invested, and is efficient in targeting the effort. Until now this method has been developed primarily for estimating the abundance of sessile species, and it is not yet in a form suitable for general use with human populations. It does not carry any suggestion of networking through a succession of connected informants, and is not a straightforward route to formalizing snowball sampling.

Targeted sampling

The sampling processes described above are mainly concerned with ensuring that the sample selected can be justified on the basis of being representative. In some cases, the aim is to target, exclusively or mainly, special segments of the general population, for example members of a geographically dispersed socio-economic or livelihood subgroup. If there is no sampling frame for the target group (and we are never going to enumerate them all), methods must be used to find target population members. There are several approaches to doing this. Mostly, the theoretical basis is less than perfect.

Protocol-derived replicated sampling

Here we offer a possible solution to the targeted sampling problem. The combination of ideas, and the idea of using it in the development setting, make this solution novel in the sense of being untried. It clearly needs further development through practical application. The notion of replicated sampling is highly adaptable as a basis of valid statistical inference about a wider population.[9]

We need to combine that idea with two other notions introduced here before using that of replication. The first is the idea of developing a prescriptive sampling protocol to be used in the field as a means of systematic targeting, say of particular households. The protocol prescribes, in detailed terms, how to reach qualifying households in practice. For example, suppose our target comprises 'vulnerable, female-headed rural households' in a particular region. This involves sorting out all necessary procedural details. One element might concern interviewing key informants at primary unit level (e.g. NGO regional officers), maybe presenting them with a list of 12 areas within the region, and getting them to agree on two areas where they are sure there is a high number of target households. There are numerous procedural steps at several hierarchical levels. Here the use of key informants is just an example, it is not an intrinsic part of every such protocol.

Samples are often derived in some such manner: they get at qualifying respondents cost-effectively, but the method usually carries overtones of subjectivity, and of inexplicit individual preference on the part of the selector. The protocol is supposed to address these difficulties. Naturally its development is a substantial process involving consultation, some triangulation, and pilot-testing of its practicability. It is thus a specially developed field guide which fits regional circumstances and study objectives, incorporating anthropological findings, local knowledge, and safeguards against fraud and other dangers, for example. The protocol is a fully defined set of procedures such that any one of a class of competent, trained fieldworkers could deliver a targeted sample with essentially interchangeable characteristics.

The second added notion is that if the protocol development involves appropriate consultation, brainstorming and consensus-building, then the protocol can be used to define the *de facto* target population being reached. Developers of the protocol can effectively sign up to accepting a term such as 'vulnerable, female-headed rural households' as the title of the population who are likely to be sampled during repeated, conscientious application of the protocol; and to accepting that the population sampled is a valid object of study, and a valid target for the development innovation(s) under consideration in the locale for which the protocol is valid.

Repeated application of the procedure would produce equivalent 'replicate' samples. These carry some statistical properties, provided that the sampling is regulated as described above, and the information-collection exercise within any given replicate is standardized.

When the procedure is replicated, it is necessary that at least a common core of results should be collected in the same form, and recorded using the same conventions, in each replicate, and it is for these results that we can make statistical claims.

For example, suppose we record the proportion (x) of respondents within a replicate sample who felt their households were excluded from benefits generated by a farmers' research committee in their community. The set of x values from a set of replicate samples from different places now has the properties of a statistical sample from the protocol-defined population. Even though the protocol itself encompassed various possibly complicated selection processes, we can, for example, produce a simple confidence interval for the general proportion who felt excluded.

The important general principle that follows from this is that if we can summarize more complicated conclusions (qualitative or quantitative) instead of a single number x from each replicate, then we can treat the set as representing, or generalizing to, the protocol-defined population. There are interesting ways forward, but the practical development and uptake of such a notion poses adaptive research challenges if the concept is put to use in the more complex settings of qualitative work in developing countries.

Conclusions

Except for the last section on protocol-derived replicated sampling, the ideas discussed in this chapter are familiar to many sampling statisticians in their natural milieu. They usually deal with number data, and have a strong focus on producing numerical estimates; given rather stringent assumptions, they produce error bounds on estimates. In difficult development settings these assumptions are often unrealistic, and the set of objectives is much wider than estimation of a single quantity. Even though the mathematical superstructure of statistical sampling is inappropriate to mixed-mode and qualitative development research, its underlying commonsense ideas can contribute to research design wherever a claim to generalizability has to be argued.

Chapter Three
Impact assessment of microfinance: protocol for collection and analysis of qualitative data

JAMES COPESTAKE, SUSAN JOHNSON
and KATIE WRIGHT-REVOLLEDO

Summary

This chapter examines the practice and potential for innovation in microfinance impact assessment. The first section sets the context, discussing the nature of demand for and supply of information on the impact of microfinance. On the demand side, it makes a distinction between demand for organizational development from within microfinance organizations themselves, and from donors and regulators for public policy purposes. On the supply side, it argues that there is a case for more use of rigorous qualitative methods that occupy an intermediate position between 'positivist/quantitative' and 'participatory/interpretive' approaches. The Imp-Act programme is presented as an appropriate network within which a protocol to popularize the use of such an approach might be developed. The second section further clarifies the distinction between positivist/quantitative, participatory/interpretive and more rigorous qualitative methods. To illustrate the nature of the latter, we present brief case studies of how such tools have been used by the authors in Kenya, Zambia, Malawi and Peru. The following section takes a further step, suggesting what a standard protocol for a more rigorous qualitative impact protocol (QUIP) might look like. We conclude by emphasizing the key reasons why QUIP might meet unsatisfied demand and outlining the steps required for its future development.

The context: microfinance impact assessment

Demand for impact assessment information

Microfinance services contribute to development by adding value: benefits to society should exceed costs. Most of the costs and benefits are borne by the providers and users of the services, but there may also be important side effects, or what economists call externalities, on other people and society at large. These are referred to below as wider impact. The day-to-day business of microfinance is primarily concerned with direct impacts. Here the key equation is whether costs of provision are less than the benefits (net of transaction costs) to clients. If they are, then business is possible, with benefits shared between provider and user according to the price that is struck between them. The scope for business can be enhanced by lowering the cost of providing services, as well as by developing new products that better serve the needs of clients.

This takes us to the first rationale for seeking to understand the impact of services on users. The better the understanding of users – their livelihoods and relationships, values and norms, particularly in relation to managing money – the more likely it is that providers will be able to improve the quality of services they can offer.

But there is a second reason why impact assessment (IA) may be important. Where the indirect impact of microfinance is large and positive, there may be a case for public subsidy of microfinance services. Likewise, if there are significant negative effects then there may be a case for taxing them. Either way, policy-makers need information on the nature and magnitude of wider impact.

The literature on this topic tends to divide into two types, corresponding to the two rationales for IA outlined above, and the distinct information and decision-making systems corresponding to each. This distinction is illustrated in Table 3.1. The first places greater emphasis on how to convince more detached decision-makers in the public policy domain; the second is concerned with management of microfinance organizations. The two columns may also be viewed to some extent as a historical progression. For as the so-called new wave of microfinance has spread and deepened, so the emphasis on IA for public policy has given way to a preoccupation with IA for internal organizational learning.

Perhaps the most important rule of IA is to be clear about why it is necessary, and for whom; hence this distinction is useful. But an overemphasis on such a simplistic classification of IA may also be dangerous. More specifically, it is easy to associate each source of demand for IA with distinct methodologies for its supply.

Supply of impact assessment information

Impact assessment for public policy tends to be particularly associated with 'impact proving' using more positivist methods, or quantitative data collection, analysed statistically (Hulme and Mosley 1996). Impact assessment for product development or organizational learning, in contrast, tends to be associated with 'impact improving' using more participatory methods, or reliance on interpretation of mostly qualitative data (Woller 2002). The former is regarded as more expensive, but more scientifically rigorous; the latter is cheaper and aims to be credible. 'Rigour' here may be taken to mean that findings can be logically deduced from stated assumptions, and empirical evidence presented for peer review. 'Credibility', in contrast, consists of the use of acceptable processes for the generation of findings that are plausible when compared with knowledge from other sources, including the personal experience, as participant observers, of microfinance providers themselves.

Table 3.1 *Contrasting sources of demand for impact assessment*

	Impact assessment for public policy	Impact assessment for product development
Who for?	Donor	Service provider
When?	Donor-led agenda of promoting increased provision of microfinance (historical where supply of services is deficient (weak competition)	Organization-led agenda of seeking to cut costs and improve customer loyalty in order to survive (strong competition)
What for?	Is public money better used (at the margin) to subsidize microfinance services or for other purposes?	What can be learned from clients in order to improve prospects for organizational survival?
Outcomes	Green/red light for replication of 'best practice' models (e.g. village banking, solidarity groups) without much differentiation of users	Product differentiation in response to diverse local demands of different categories of user

A historical dimension can again be added to the distinction. Expensive, rigorous, positivist IA can be set up as a straw man to justify the shift to more cost-effective, credible, interpretive IA (Cohen 1999; Hulme 2000). The former can then be linked to top-down replication of microfinance services (demanding impact information for public policy), and the latter to the more participatory processes of product development (demand for IA for organizational learning and innovation). This can then be conflated with a more general paradigm shift or fashion change from a top-down, blueprint, technology transfer vision of development practice to a bottom-up, process-oriented and participatory vision (Chambers 1997).

The problem with this line of thinking is that it discourages the development of methodologies for IA that do not fit neatly into either category.[1] For example, participatory and interpretive methods of IA also play an important role in moulding public policy. Likewise, quantitative methods are also integral to much market research. The trade-off between rigour and cost-effectiveness may also be more complex. For example, combinations of quantitative and qualitative data collection may generate data relevant for both internal and public policy purposes (Copestake et al. 2001b). The distinction also suggests that only positivist methods can be rigorous, thereby neglecting many traditions within the social sciences of rigorous analysis and interpretation of qualitative data (Moris and Copestake 1993).

The purpose of this chapter can now be restated with greater clarity. It is to contribute towards development of microfinance IA methods that (i) are both impact-proving (rigorous) and improving (cost-effective and useful); and (ii) can meet both internal (organizational development) and external (public policy) demand. In particular, we argue the need for a clearer protocol for qualitative analysis based on the in-depth, semi-structured narrative or long interview. Before doing so, a brief digression is necessary about the process of methodological innovation.

The process of methodological innovation

Like all innovation, development of methodologies, tools, instruments and protocols cannot be viewed as an entirely rational process. Promising ideas have to be elaborated and thoroughly tested. It must be possible to explain them easily to potential users, and they must acquire currency and legitimacy within communities of users. Semantics, relationships, resources and power are important. A key issue is the extent to which flexibility, heterogeneity and sophistication of product design have to be traded against uniformity, scale of production and robustness.

In the field of development practice there is a wealth of experience with IA methods – good, bad and ugly. Many NGOs and aid organizations have their own in-house methods, including some adapted specifically for microfinance (Simanowitz 2001). There is also a vast and diverse academic literature on microfinance IA. It is also possible to identify a relatively small number of more influential institutional players in this field during the past decade. Perhaps the most widely known are the five SEEP/AIMS tools developed by USAID in collaboration with the Small Enterprise Education and Promotion (SEEP) Network, a US network of enterprise-oriented NGOs. The Consultative Group to Assist the Poor has invested in promoting first an intermediate impact survey tool, and more recently a standard tool for assessing the relative poverty of microfinance clients. MicroSave-Africa, with support from DFID and UNDP, is perhaps the market leader in establishing and branding industry standards for market research using participatory methodologies.[2]

It is beyond the scope of this present chapter to assess the relative usefulness of these different brands and their distinctive products. Nor is it appropriate to explore critically the tendency towards establishment of global standards.[3] However, it is important to locate any new proposal in the context of an already crowded and confused quasi-marketplace. First, the key question about a new proposal is not whether it constitutes a truly new and original methodological idea – if such a thing is indeed possible. Rather, is there scope for selecting and developing known but diffuse ideas into a 'product' that augments the range of such products that have industry recognition and acceptance? Second, achieving this requires substantial investment not only in product design, but also in product testing and marketing. Are such resources available and likely to be adequate? Third, and particularly in the context of development practice, there is the issue of legitimacy of any new product. Who has been involved in its development, and how?

The institutional context for this particular proposal is the authors' participation in Imp-Act (Improving the impact of microfinance:

Action research programme, *www.imp-act.org*), a three-year action research programme involving 29 microfinance organizations (MFOs) around the world, sponsored by the Ford Foundation. The programme's main aim is to improve the effectiveness of MFOs by strengthening the mechanisms by which they learn about the impact of their services, particularly on poverty. It emphasizes that progress in IA is partially determined by techniques and skills of data collection and analysis, but also by the relationships and feedback processes within which IA tools are used. Imp-Act sets out to move away from donor-oriented IA towards practitioner-focused processes of listening and learning. Each participating MFO has developed its own pilot IA plans, to fit specific organizational contexts, objectives and stakeholder needs. A mixture of quantitative, qualitative and PRA/PLA (participatory reflection and action/participatory learning and action) tools are being used. At the same time, the project seeks to facilitate interaction between participants in order to prompt the development of generic solutions to the problems and challenges each organization faces.

One of the most important issues emerging from the first year of the Imp-Act programme has been the need to develop a simple, cost-effective, replicable and credible method for collection and analysis of qualitative data. This chapter is part of the process of responding to this need. It is hoped that it will contribute towards developing a standard protocol that can be tested and developed during the remaining two years of the programme. This is just one of a number of themes that are in the process of discussion.

Towards more rigorous qualitative impact assessment

The previous section suggested that there is scope for development of a standard protocol for more rigorous qualitative IA. Table 3.2 (overleaf) distinguishes between approaches that are based on individual interviews and group-based activities. In the context of the microfinance industry, there are particular reasons for obtaining a better understanding of causal pathways linking provision of services to diverse effects. The industry still tends to assume a very direct chain of impact leading from access to loan capital, to improved micro-enterprise performance and thus to increased income and poverty reduction. But impact research to date has exposed a far more diverse range of pathways and outcomes (e.g. Sebstad and Cohen 2001; Marr 2002). This diversity poses major problems for the design of fully precoded questionnaires for quantitative surveys. Both individual interview and group-based data collection methods can help overcome this limitation. But in both cases there is a need for greater rigour, by which we mean mechanisms to enable peer reviewers to audit the process by which conclusions are derived from documented evidence and stated assumptions. The scope of this paper is mostly limited to how to enhance rigour in the use of individual semi-structured interviews. But

Table 3.2 *Methods for supply of impact assessment information*

	METHODS		
	Positivist	**Qualitative, based on individual interviews**	**Qualitative, based on group activities**
Data collection	Sample survey using closed questionnaire	Random sample of semi-structured narrative interviews	Focus group discussions and events
Data analysis	Interpretation of statistical tables and multiple regression analysis	Interpretive reports based on narrative notes and transcripts Can also be used for systematic scoring of types of impact.	Verbal and experiential learning among participants. Interpretive reports. Can also be used to generate numbers
Epistemology	Rigorous statistical inference and peer review	Rigorous qualitative analysis and peer review	Process transparency and expert judgement
Potential strengths	Rigour. Possibility of quantitative estimates of impact. More convincing to sceptical outsiders	Richness in detail and understanding of differential (including personally sensitive) impact	In-built triangulation. Potential for shorter feedback loops from suppliers to users of information. Ability to pick up unexpected and unmeasurable impact
Potential weaknesses	High cost and time lags. Restricted to measurable impact indicators. Reveals little about causation. Difficult to counter selection bias problems	Demonstrating that findings are representative of wider populations. Lack of clarity and consensus about how to achieve rigour	Participants may hide important facts from peers as well as facilitators. Risk of response bias makes it hard to convince outsiders of the reliability of findings

there is obviously similar scope with respect to group methods, as well as for comparisons of the two.

There is a vast literature on the use of qualitative methodologies in the social sciences (e.g. Hammersley 1992; Moris and Copestake 1993; Bernard 1994; Denzin and Lincoln 1994; Maynard and Purvis 1994; Silverman 1997; Flick 1998). There is also no shortage of literature on the use of open-ended individual interviews, particularly if this is broadly defined to include, for example, the long interview (McCracken 1998); the life story (Atkinson 1998); the in-depth interview (Chirban 1996); and oral testimonies (Onselen 1993). One dimension of variation within this literature is the extent to which interviews are structured. In general it can be argued that the more open the format, the more skilled and time-consuming are the tasks of interviewing, data analysis and interpretation. Given the emphasis of this chapter on the need for methods that are relatively cost-effective and useful, it follows that the emphasis in this chapter is on methods that are towards the more structured end of the spectrum. The remainder of the section elaborates by presenting brief case studies of the use of semi-structured interviews by the authors in Kenya, Zambia, Malawi and Peru.

Towards a standard protocol for the use of in-depth interviews

In this section we suggest what a standard protocol for such an approach might look like, with reference to case-study illustrations. For ease of reference, this prototype protocol is called the 'qualitative impact protocol' or QUIP (the word 'quip' defined as a 'pointed saying').

Objectives, sample selection and scope

A key consideration is that a QUIP should be able to provide information on impact quickly, cost-effectively and reliably enough to facilitate organizational learning. This can be done in two ways, although these are not mutually exclusive. First, specific one-off studies may be commissioned to examine particular aspects of impact in relation to specific concerns about performance that the organization wishes to address. Second, qualitative interview material may be accumulated in a database over time. One important advantage of the qualitative interview is that benefits (in terms of useful data) accrue continuously in relation to the number of interviews carried out, whereas meaningful positivist analysis requires a critical minimum sample size, as well as inclusion of a control group.[4] QUIP should be useful for managers who are interested in understanding problems with specific subgroups of clients for which they can commission a quota sample of interviews. At the same time, adoption of a standard protocol should permit findings from batches of interviews to be integrated cumulatively into a standard database for further, wider analysis.

As with any research, the first step is to identify the questions that the research seeks to answer (see Chapter 1). While the overall question of impact may be clear, specific questions about impact pathways or outcomes arising from specific aspects of programme design, or additional questions about wider impact, will vary between organizations and over time.

This raises the question of sample selection, and how representative findings can be from smaller but richer data sets (see Chapter 2). The important point is to emphasize that there are a range of choices between the purely anecdotal case study and the fully statistically representative sample. Qualitative data are most useful where they can be combined with a clear typology for stratification of the MFO's client portfolio.[5] Researchers can then use quota sampling to update the profile of the different client groups.[6] The aim is not to estimate average statistics for all clients, but to ensure that management and other stakeholders improve their understanding of the diversity of impact across the entire client portfolio.

Turning to consider the scope of data collected, a major potential strength of a QUIP is that it would offer managers a broad, holistic understanding of the impact of their services – at business, household, individual, community and market levels. Clients are likely to talk first about the direct impact of participation on their own business activities and income. But with appropriate probing they can then be encouraged to talk about direct non-material impact on their understanding (e.g. of business management), perception/attitudes (e.g. self confidence), and relationships (with MFO staff, other group members and kin; Chen 1997). More experienced clients can also be used as key informants for discussing wider or indirect impact on overall access to financial services, market opportunities, supply constraints and community activities.[7] The open-ended scope of the approach is important because reliability depends, in part, on the consistency of respondents' explanations for why certain kinds of impact are more marked than others.

This broad scope of interviews contrasts strongly with IA based on precoded questionnaire-based approaches, which have to be more precise and selective about research hypotheses. On the other hand, efficiency of data collection and analysis does require that interviews are clearly planned and structured around broad domains of impact. There is also scope for combining in-depth interviews with quantitative sample survey-based work. The case studies in this chapter illustrate the range of possibilities. In Kenya (Box 3.1), open and closed questions were combined sequentially in a single interview schedule. The main drawback of this was the resulting length of the interview. In Zambia (Box 3.2), the in-depth interview was a repeat interview building on baseline findings about the same clients from a closed questionnaire a year earlier, which also served as the sample frame. In Malawi (Box 3.3), repeat in-depth interviews were undertaken in parallel with an impact survey, but with separate clients, ruling out the possibility of being able to combine and then jointly analyse quantitative and qualitative data. Another option is to supplement in-depth interviews with data routinely collected by the MFO, for example at the loan appraisal stage.

Preparation for fieldwork and conduct of interviews

Given the more open-ended nature of the data-collection process, adequate training of field researchers is particularly important. One set of issues, highlighted by the Peru case study (Box 3.4), concerns how interviews are set up and initiated. Another is the ethical dimension. Many essential principles of good ethical practice have been outlined in the literature and applied by researchers in the field. However, proponents of participatory methods go further, suggesting that data collection and analysis should empower informants (Chambers 1997). Not all MFOs adhere to such a participatory ethos – some are designed for service delivery rather than empowerment. Nevertheless, guidelines

Box 3.1   *Impact assessment with MFO clients in Kenya*

Under the British Aid for Small Enterprise programme of DFID, impact assessment was required of a programme of grant support for six Kenyan MFOs. An independent marketing research firm was hired to conduct an initial round of single-visit qualitative interviews with a random sample of 15 clients per MFO (Research International 2000). The work was designed both to provide useful feedback to MFOs themselves about their own clients, as well as to build up a broader, sector-wide picture of direct impact for DFID.

The questionnaire schedule comprised three closed-question sections and three open-ended narrative sections, as follows. **Section A** (closed) collected basic information about the identity of the respondent. **Section B** (open) started with the generative question: 'To start off, tell me a little bit about yourself, and the people you live with.' The interviewer was also given four preset probing questions to use if necessary, to ensure that the respondent's narrative account covered all key aspects of the life and livelihood of the respondent and her family. **Section C** (closed) then supplemented this narrative with key quantitative data on household composition and income. **Section D** (open) explicitly raised the issue of access to and use of financial services, including those of the MFO. Again, the interviewer was also given optional probing questions to use to maintain the flow of the narrative if necessary. All questions were printed in Swahili as well as English. **Section E** (closed) again supplemented the narrative with key quantitative data on loan use, but the fact that these questions came after the narrative section ensured that they did not guide the narrative section. **Section F** (open) closed the interview by asking respondents to explain in their own words what plans they had for the future – for themselves personally, for other members of the family, and for their business activities.

Where respondents agreed, narrative sections were tape recorded. The interviewer also typed up a summary of the narrative sections to a tight word limit, drawing upon memory, field notes and the tape recording as needed. (The tape recordings were then filed, so that the research supervisor could carry out a random audit of whether typed narrative summaries were consistent with them.) The field supervisor and interviewer then met to review the narrative summary and agree, against agreed criteria, what level of impact it represented – the two most important were sustainable income generation and employment creation. These were scored on a scale of one to five, then entered in a single database along with precoded data from the three closed sections of the interview schedule. In other words, the attribution problem was addressed by making a judgement about the plausibility and consistency of respondents' own narratives. The impact scores could then be analysed through cross-tabulation against precoded variables.

Each MFO received a report comprising a six-page summary of the findings of each interview, together with a summary of what they collectively revealed about impact in relation to seven hypotheses. Findings were generally more negative than they were used to hearing, and evoked a defensive reaction, including criticisms of the research team. However, this was perhaps more a reflection of lack of ownership of sensitive findings on the part of the MFOs than weaknesses in the underlying methodology. DFID scored impact against each hypothesis so that it could be entered into the database for analysis along with the data obtained from the closed sections of the questionnaire.

Box 3.2   *Impact assessment with MFO clients in Zambia*

In Zambia semi-structured interviews were used as part of an ongoing three-year programme of impact monitoring and assessment for a DFID-sponsored MFO starting up on the Copperbelt (Copestake et al. 2001a). An initial impact survey was carried out on a matching sample of one-year-old and new or 'pipeline' clients using a closed questionnaire. In-depth interviews were then carried out a year later for a randomly selected subsample of this survey, in order to improve understanding of the causation of impact. They also elicited data on information less easily collected through a standard questionnaire, such as changes in intra-household relations. Data were mainly collected through semi-structured interviews with individual clients, supplemented where possible with discussions at the group level and with other members of selected clients' households.

Attribution of impact was again based primarily on the coherence of respondents' own accounts of causal chains linking their membership of credit groups to changes at the individual, business, household and community levels. Particular care was taken to encourage respondents to discuss changes arising specifically from their participation in the programme, rather than changes that might have occurred anyway. The plausibility of their account was also cross-checked against information from direct observation, the original sample survey interview, and discussions with loan officers and other group members.

The first section of the interview format recorded basic factual and coding information about the client. Separate sections then dealt, in turn, with changes in household circumstances, changes in business activities, experience as a group member, impact on individuals, and views of other household members. Each section was initiated by an open-ended, generative question designed to encourage respondents to describe their experience in their own words in as free and fluent a way as possible. A standard set of prompting questions was also prepared for each section to assist the interview as and when the respondent stopped talking. In many cases it was not necessary for the interviewer to ask all these questions; rather they served as a checklist of topics to be covered. Each section closed with one or two precoded attitudinal questions which asked respondents directly, taking into account the previous conversation, to sum up how participation in the programme had affected them.

As in Kenya (Box 3.1), notes on each narrative section of the interviews were typed up immediately after the interview, and used as a point of reference for attributing an impact score to the client against different criteria. These data were then entered into a database along with responses to the attitudinal questions and statistical data about the respondents from the survey a year earlier. An aggregated index of impact was also calculated. This enabled the sample to be divided into a group for whom overall impact was 'clearly positive' and a group for whom impact appeared either negligible or negative. Statistical data from the first survey round were then used to analyse possible determinants of this differential impact. Finally, the data were analysed and written up as a short report by cutting and pasting data from each narrative summary into sections covering different types of impact, including the four dimensions of individual impact (material, cognitive, attitudinal and relational) highlighted by Chen (1997).

Box 3.3   *Impact assessment with MFO clients in Malawi*

The third case study also comes from DFID-sponsored impact research, in this case of a microfinance programme in Malawi (Johnson et al. 2002).

Research in the Central Region of Malawi had two components. The first was a quantitative survey of approximately 400 interviews, comprising borrowers and a comparison group. This was based on two rounds of interviews carried out a year apart using a fully precoded questionnaire. To complement this, a panel of 20 borrowers were selected for qualitative interviews. The purpose of this component was to gain a better understanding of impact pathways and variables mediating outcomes on clients. These interviews were carried out quarterly over a year, involving participants in a total of five interviews.

Sample selection aimed to capture diversity in members' experience of the programme and of group dynamics. This was done through a two-stage process of selecting groups with varied performance, and selecting members within them of different wealth levels. These selection processes were carried out using participatory ranking methods with MFO staff and group members in turn, followed by random selection within the ranked categories.

All interviews were semi-structured. They covered respondents' basic household and livelihood information, participation in the village bank in terms of loan history and performance, views about the operation of the village bank, their experience, and views on any other effects the village bank had on their lives. Basic household data were updated on each occasion to ensure the current status of the household could be captured. Interviews were taped and later transcribed as narratives. Analysis involved overall assessment of the information given by the analyst as to whether the impact of the programme had been positive, negative or ambiguous for material welfare (in some cases opinions contradicted reported facts). Narratives were reviewed both against a pre-existing set of questions about material, cognitive, perceptual and relational impact. Explanation of the impact pathways and mediating variables was established by analysing the narratives for emerging themes and patterns that could explain the impact outcomes.

The revisits were of critical importance to the research. Through this approach, the interviewer developed a close rapport with the respondents, and was able to probe more deeply into the reasons why decisions were taken. They also enabled a much more consistent picture of household dynamics to be built up, and the development of a more detailed understanding of the environment in which the programme was operating. Moreover, it became possible to identify the differences between what people reported (what they wanted us to hear) and the reality of the actual events they experienced. Compared with the single-visit approach, revisits enabled a high degree of confidence in the data set to be developed. They also generated data that would not have been captured in a single round, about the ways in which businesses stopped and started in relation to women's own skills, experience, marital status, domestic situations, seasonality and loan programme design.

Box 3.4   *Impact assessment with MFO clients in Peru*

Doctoral research, conducted over a period of 18 months, critically reviewed the extent to which microcredit could be empowering for women in low-income rural and urban locations of Peru (Wright 2001). In this case the emphasis was less on how representative data were, and more on understanding the social processes affecting microcredit outcomes. It also 'gave voice' to a diverse group of women and their husbands or partners, and provided source material on how microcredit agencies interacted with other institutions at the community level. An important feminist theoretical standpoint was to articulate the perspectives of multiple participants (Henwood and Pidgeon 1995: 23).

The sample comprised over 150 women participating in a range of microcredit schemes operating in Lima and Cajamarca. Care was taken to ensure the sample included households at different stages of the life cycle, including single, separated and married women, heads of households and widows. Interviews were structured around a standard list of questions, with responses transcribed from a tape recording or noted down by the researcher. Data collected covered socio-economic profiles, micro-enterprise activities, political economic context, and perceptions and aspirations for the future, with life-history methods considered the most appropriate technique for gleaning this kind of information.[8] Detailed interviews in both rural and urban areas took the form of guided conversations, mostly in women's homes (which often doubled up as their workplaces) and in markets. The advantage of interviewing women in their homes was that it allowed the observation of relationships and interactions between family members. Where possible, second and third interviews were conducted with the same informants, for them to have the chance to think about the issues over a longer period of time.

This relatively slow and open-ended fieldwork strategy highlights important issues affecting the quality of data that any protocol for qualitative IA would also have to address. For example, during the interviewing stage much emphasis was placed on the construction of questions and techniques outlined by Foddy (1993), such as the importance of the ordering and wording of questions. The questions were then carefully piloted. At this point in the research process the need to rephrase the questions drawn up meant that the researcher's prejudices and preconceptions as a western woman were revealed, and her identity was questioned. For example, the question: 'What problems did you experience?' did not get a response. Women in rural areas were sensitive to the suggestion that they 'had problems', so the question was rephrased to 'What makes you angry?' This rewording unlocked the key to the real issues and proved to be the turning point in this research (Wright 2003).

---

for ethical practice must be incorporated into the protocol. In order to build trust and minimize response bias, respondents need to understand who researchers are, what the data are being collected for, and how they will be used. There is also the fraught issue of whether respondents should receive any material incentive or 'token of thanks' for agreeing to participate. The best approach will clearly be culture- and context-specific, limiting the scope for a standard, prescriptive protocol. However, there may still be scope for preparing some kind of decision tree to help guide researchers through a range of options.

A second set of issues concerns design of the interviewing schedule, including framing and phrasing of questions. A trade-off exists between questions that act as prompts and open-ended questions. In the former, the researcher introduces new elements or invites responses to a specific topic. Such questions risk not allowing informants to answer using their own categories, rather imposing categories based on the prejudices of the researcher and thus tainting the nature of the response. But without some structure, interviews may become unacceptably time-consuming or irrelevant.

There is no substitute for the skills of the researcher in sensitively addressing this dilemma. However, less experienced researchers can be assisted not only through training but also through development of a flexibly structured interview schedule. The first element of structure is to identify a broad agenda of topics to be covered, starting with the most general ones and moving on to those that relate directly to the service under review. Each topic can be introduced with a predetermined and tested, open-ended, 'generative' question, leaving informants free to talk in their own terms. Researchers may then also be given a set of optional supplementary questions, phrased to raise issues but not to suggest answers. Even if they are not used, these can serve as a useful checklist of what is covered by unstructured narrative. In the final analysis, some trade-off is necessary. Pragmatists have to learn to be more patient, while academic purists have to be realistic. The pay-off is that such an approach should improve understanding of issues, such as group dynamics and power relations in the wider community, which can negatively affect the operation of development projects, but which organizations currently neglect.

Data entry and analysis

Having discussed the need for attention to question design and data collection methods, we now return to the major task – to devise a simple, replicable, timely and cost-effective way of analysing the data collected. Feedback from the first year of the Imp-Act programme suggests that lack of clarity regarding how to go about systematically analysing qualitative data inhibits MFOs from using this approach more.

Broadly, we suggest that there are two ways of analysing the data, and that these can be used either in isolation or to complement each other. The first is to produce a written report summarizing the findings from a set of individual in-depth interviews. Starting with typed written summaries, this can be done by sorting excerpts from each using a list of topics. This work can be done using a qualitative data analysis package such as 'NUD*IST', by using cards, or more simply by cutting and pasting text in a word processing package. The analysis is illustrated in Table 3.3 (overleaf). Reading the table downwards by column, we have excerpts from the fictional narrative summaries (see also Tables 3.4 and 3.5). This can then be turned into a report that moves systematically through the topics in the left-hand column. Thus under 'wider market'

Table 3.3   *Illustration of qualitative analysis of narrative summaries*

Topic/level	Respondent 1	Respondent 2	Respondent 3
Business activity	Selling fish	Selling fish	Selling fish
Material impact on business	She was able to purchase stock in bulk (+)	She took on a second stall in the market (+)	Her capital was used up so she stopped trading (–)
Material impact on household	She bought more food for the family (+)	Her children had to help her in the market (–)	They had to skip meals in order to save money for repayments (–)
Material impact on individual	She was able to buy better clothes (+)	She felt tired all the time (–)	She went hungry more often (–)
Cognitive impact on individual	She learned how to borrow money again (0)	She was forced to learn how to manage her time better (+)	She decided never to manage money (+)
Perceptual impact on individual	She started to make more plans (+)	She became less lazy (+)	She lost confidence (–)
Positional impact on individual	She became less dependent on her brother for cash (+)	She made friends who helped her out on the stall (+)	She returned to ask for more from her husband (0)
Financial market impact	She opened a bank account too (+)	She shifted her savings from the cooperative (0)	She started saving small amounts of money (+)
Wider market impact	More women used loan money to enter the business (+)	More women used loan money to enter the business (0)	Customers insisted on buying on credit (0)
Wider social impact	She became more confident at public speaking (+)	She learned about the market by talking to other members (+)	She fell out with old friends who had to cover for her arrears (–)

impact there is reasonably strong evidence that increased access to credit resulted in the market for fish becoming more competitive. Note that the fuller and more explicit the links from narrative summaries to the general report, the more rigorous are the findings, in the sense that peer reviewers can trace the evidence on the basis of which generalizations are made. Reliability is increased further by randomly auditing the quality of narrative summaries against archived tape recordings of the original interviews.

The second way of analysing narrative summary data is by using simple scoring methods (Boxes 1 and 2; Chapter 7). In the above case, for example, impact has been classified by the interviewer on a three-

Table 3.4   *Responses to attitudinal questions**

	RESPONSE			
Question	Better	Worse	No change	Not sure
S8 Overall, how has your economic situation changed since the last interview?	8	6	1	1
S9 How does this compare with other people living in your area?	7	3	1	5
T7 Overall, how profitable are your business activities now compared to a year ago?	7	6	1	2
T8 How does this compare with other people (but not in your trust bank) doing this business?	6	5	0	5
V4 Overall, how has belonging to a trust bank affected you as a person	11	1	2	2
W5 How has the welfare of your household been affected by the respondent joining a trust bank?	7	5	1	3

* Data fully analysed and discussed by Copestake and Mlotshwa (2000)

point scale (+, 0, -). Adding these scores horizontally facilitates analysis of overall impact in relation to each level; adding the scores vertically produces a single impact score for each respondent (+8, +3, -4). These scores can then be analysed by cross-tabulation against statistics about the respondent, their business, location and so on.

Such scoring is an imperfect and subjective process.[9] Yet the pay-off is that complex findings from numerous interviews can be summarized, analysed and presented to others much more easily. The quality will depend on the reliability and level of detail of the narrative summary, and the skill of the researchers. It may also be affected by the choice of scale and weights ascribed to different categories of impact, and there is considerable scope for experimentation with different ways of scoring. In the Zambia case, for example (Box 3.2), scores were elicited not only by subjective scoring by the researcher on the basis of the narrative summary, but also by asking respondents themselves to make an assessment immediately after concluding the open narrative section of the interview which raised the related topic. Comparable findings based on respondents' own questions and on simple scoring for the same sample of 16 interviews are reproduced in Tables 3.4 and 3.5 (above and overleaf).

Table 3.5   *Summary of scores derived from narrative summaries**

Hypothesis	+2	+1	0	–1	–2
Trust banks provide better services to continuing members during their second year	4	3	2	5	2
Sustained trust bank membership strengthens clients' business activities	5	3	2	5	1
It leads to material benefits to clients and to other household members	3	6	1	2	4
It resulted in increased (+2) or more stable (+1) employment	2	6	5	2	1
It improves clients' personal capabilities, self-confidence and capacity to plan	1	7	5	3	0
It strengthens their role in decision-making within the household and beyond	4	2	5	4	1
Other household members view trust bank membership positively	4	3	4	4	1

* Data fully analysed and discussed by Copestake and Mlotshwa (2000)
Key: +2, strong support for the hypothesis; +1, support; –2, strong support for the counter-hypothesis; –1, some support for the counter-hypothesis; 0, no support either way. ($n = 16$)

Research management, staffing and funding

In the context of the Imp-Act programme, most MFOs are interested in impact findings that can be used to feed into the development of new products or refinement of existing ones. The thrust of Imp-Act is therefore to experiment with approaches to IA that are within the means of MFOs themselves, and meet the needs of their stakeholders. In most of the projects it is MFO staff themselves who are implementing the research, albeit after being trained by external specialists and with their ongoing supervision and guidance. This approach has been facilitated by the existence of pre-packaged tools, particularly those developed by SEEP/AIMS and MicroSave-Africa.

It is tempting to infer from the above that, with clearer guidelines in the form of QUIP, MFOs can similarly be helped to make more use of qualitative methods using their own staff or directly recruited social science graduates. However, some caution is needed. Not only do more open-ended methods of interviewing and analysis require more specialized researchers (Copestake 2000); their value also resides in opening up more sensitive issues such as relations with field staff and group leaders. But this potential is less likely to be realized by researchers who belong to the organization itself. Larger MFOs may be able to afford to keep such specialists in-house and allow them sufficient autonomy from operations to avoid bias. But for most MFOs, there is a strong case for contracting out such work to specialist research consultants. MFO networks and technical support agencies may, in some instances, also be able to carve out a useful role in the provision or facilitation of such work.

Conclusions

This chapter highlights the need for a practical qualitative impact assessment protocol (QUIP). It raises issues that need to be addressed in devising such a protocol, and tentatively suggests the form it might take. Production of such a protocol would hardly represent an earth-shattering methodological breakthrough. Rather, it would represent a negotiated compromise between the canons of social science and the requirements of MFOs for methods that are cost-effective and replicable, yet also more rigorous and reliable than most current practice in this area.

By developing guidelines on data collection and analysis, it is hoped that MFOs will be able to make use of qualitative methods with more confidence and to better effect. This chapter represents only a first step towards production of such guidelines. To build credibility and acceptance, it is recognized that further design and testing is required, and it is hoped that the Imp-Act programme will provide a framework for this. In particular, this work will require a continued balancing act between standardization and flexibility: the former for consistency and ease of use; the latter to allow adaptation to specific conditions and ends. Methodological guidelines by themselves will not go far towards guaranteeing quality. Rather, the protocol must also contain guidelines on how the process of using the methodology should be documented to facilitate peer review.

Chapter Four
What determines successful sustainable development projects? Some evidence from the PRODERS experience in Mexico

GIL YARON, JUTTA BLAUERT and ALEJANDRO GUEVARA[1]

Summary

This chapter draws on the experience of an extensive monitoring and evaluation (M&E) programme in Mexico that is attempting to move from traditional to participatory monitoring and evaluation (PM&E) at local, regional and national levels. Even at an early stage in this process, there is a great deal to be gained from incorporating perceived impact measures alongside traditional cost–benefit analysis. Moving beyond this, the challenges include securing the right institutional environment; time scales that are consistent with learning as well as statutory reporting; designing in triangulation from the start; and allowing for very different perspectives at local, regional and national levels. It is important to be realistic and pragmatic in moving this process forward, offering incremental steps that encourage the development of participatory skills and political commitment.

Introduction

Policy makers and researchers alike are looking for appropriate methods and systems of M&E that can lead to better knowledge and better policy. The challenge faced by large-scale (national) programmes of poverty reduction or sustainable resource management, conservation or regional development policies is to move beyond the bipolar vision of depth versus scale, of numbers versus 'perceptions', of the local versus the national.

Considerable material is now emerging from the area of combining quantitative and qualitative methods, particularly in survey work (NRI/SSC 2001; Chambers 2003; Kanbur 2003a), and from work on participatory impact assessment in the agricultural and natural resources arena (Cromwell et al. 2001). This chapter presents partial results from analysis of an innovative programme of environmental projects in marginalized communities in Mexico. We draw on economic, social and institutional information from the evaluations of these projects to address the question: 'What determines success in this kind of project?' In order to do this we consider the importance of alternative definitions of 'success' emerging from community perceptions and those of other stakeholders, and address how measures of financial and economic impact at community and national levels can be elicited.

Figure 4.1   *Priority regions for Mexico's Programme for Regional Sustainable Development (PRODERS)*

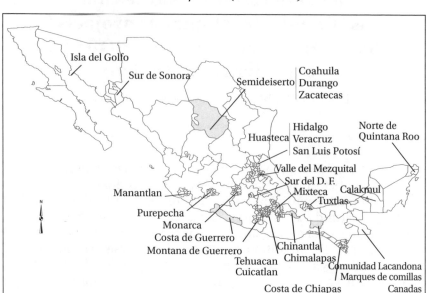

The detailed results of the evaluation are provided elsewhere (Yaron et al. 2002). In this chapter we briefly explain the PRODERS programme, and present a summary of the methodology used to analyse economic performance of projects within the programme and discuss alternative measures of success. The third section of the chapter presents a brief outline of the revised methodological approach that is presently being piloted with the aim of achieving a participatory quantitative and qualitative assessment process and reporting system. The chapter closes with broader conclusions and preliminary conceptual notes.

PRODERS: seeking means of evaluation

Like many other national-level development programmes, the large-scale evaluation of Mexico's Programme for Regional Sustainable Development (PRODERS) has presented complex methodological challenges. PRODERS, designed in recognition of the complexity of the policy and rural contexts, did not seek to provide simplistic programmatic answers, such as arguing only for larger transfers to rural producers, or for the establishment of stakeholder councils. It adopted an integrated approach designed to mirror complex reality on the ground and challenge sectoral and political interests at different levels of government.

PRODERS is an innovative programme of participatory regional sustainable development planning introduced by the Mexican environment ministry during the previous administration and continued under the new administration (Box 4.1). By the year 2000, PRODERS was operating in 24 of the 36 regions classified by the Government of

---

Box 4.1 *PRODERS: an overview*

The Programme for Regional Sustainable Development (PRODERS) provides an innovative[2] programme of participatory regional sustainable development planning, introduced by the Mexican environment ministry (SEMARNAP) during the previous administration and continued under the new administration as part of the Conservation and Development Directorate (DGCD) of the National Commission of Protected Areas (CONANP). The policy programme emphasized the need to address poverty reduction by going beyond simple transfer or targeting approaches, particularly if a change in natural resource management and conservation was to be achieved.

In each region, PRODERS aimed to:

- raise the quality of life of the population by means of environmentally and economically efficient productive systems
- apply regional planning instruments that incorporate the vision, and enhance the integrated participation, of both government and civil society
- build consensus among different social, economic and political actors in the definition of objectives, participants, strategies, commitments, modalities and timing which the transition towards sustainable development has to run
- design regional sustainable development models which would allow scenarios to be created, impact of policy actions to be evaluated, and projects and policies to be designed.

The three main principles of PRODERS were:

- it proposed an integrated, ecosystem perspective with a strategy designed to achieve ecological conservation and regeneration in balance with small-scale, sustainable rural production
- it supported a decentralized and participatory decision-making process for natural resource management that included the farmers and families affected and their authorities or organizations
- due to the complexity of the policy context, it recommended cross-sectoral management of the governmental and local budgets, as well as coordination of efforts for regional development between various ministries.

(Caravias et al. 1994: 25–30, 122–8)

The selected operational regions for PRODERS were within the Priority Areas defined by the Finance and Social Development ministries for action on poverty alleviation, and were regions of high ecological diversity or fragility, representative of the wide range of Mexico's different ecosystems.

The core strategy of PRODERS was that in each community and each region, socio-economic and environmental appraisals should be undertaken which would allow a baseline for fine-tuning local policy and planning and for identifying actors and conflicts in the region. It was crucial to bring together these different actors to allow a joint definition of objectives and strategies for the design of regional programmes, a process that initially involved stakeholder-specific or sectoral workshops.

Mexico as in need of immediate attention because of their extreme poverty or high ecological interest, covering some 173 million hectares and 7.7 million inhabitants (Figure 4.1). As the previous administration drew to a close, the Conservation and Development Directorate (DGCD) of the National Commission of Protected Areas (CONANP) had to summarize what it had achieved since 1996 and argue for its continuation and extension into other regions.

Needing to account for its use of funds to the Congress and Finance Ministry and other stakeholders, the DGCD had to undertake a large-scale evaluation. Where previous evaluations at national level (1997–8) had failed to produce information, data or processes with which either the ministry, consultants or participants (beneficiaries) were satisfied, the DGCD now aimed to produce in one year a combined report of impact on the socio-economic, environmental, participatory and man-agement aspects of its programmes. Arguing that national guidelines required this, PRODERS had to undertake the evaluation in all 18 states, but selecting 72 communities within the 24 regions for fieldwork.[3]

However, from the beginning it was clear that running such a large-scale evaluation with parallel strands of methodologies, with three to six months available for carrying out the work in all regions and training regional staff, and without a preliminary methodological design that allowed a complementary design of methodologies, was going to be not only exhausting and costly for all involved, but also would require the work to be done in an extractive form only, without a participatory approach to the impact assessment. The process also revealed two contrasting approaches: quantitative, questionnaire-based and econo-metric work, and more conventional questionnaires and structured interviews for social information or 'qualitative' data. From 2001 onwards, as well as dealing with the new administration and an ever-changing policy context, an attempt has been made to combine the qualitative and quantitative approaches to M&E by building on the lessons of the first phase, and to include a participatory aspect in the policy M&E, which had been one of the initial objectives of the programme. In this chapter, we report on the first phase of this work, and offer some pointers to the work currently in progress at the ministry where partic-ipatory M&E strategies and complementary use of qualitative and quantitative methods are being designed to set up a national M&E system, allowing for both quantitative and participatory approaches to be used **by**, and **with**, community and other stakeholders at the different operational and policy levels.

Methodology

Three different methodological approaches were used for the evaluation (see Table 4.1, overleaf). A team of national consultants trained regional consultants to undertake the questionnaire-based work in 72 commu-nities across the country and in national and regional offices of the environment ministry. By November 2000 results from three core areas of the impact studies were published (Guevara and Yúnez-Naude 2000), with environmental (monitoring) results in preparation for wider dissemination. Regional feedback workshops were then held in most regions to share some of the findings with regional actors.

Social participation and management (*gestión*)

One analytical and methodological strand focused on evaluation of social participation and management (*gestión*) at the regional level.[4] The following three aspects of PRODERS were analysed in this context:

- decentralization of decisions and strengthening of capacity at regional level
- intra- and inter-institutional coordination
- social collaboration (*concertación*) in planning, implementation and evaluation.

Within these broader programme fields, the following specific actions were appraised:

- integrated, strategic and participatory planning
- implementation of intra-institutional coordination (programmes within SEMARNAP)
- implementation of inter-institutional coordination (with institutions at different levels of government, and other ministries)
- concerted effort at programming investment
- feedback and relationship between local and regional policy and operational strategies
- articulation between sectoral strategic projects and integrated development of the region.

For this analysis, 22 case studies were produced from across the 24 states involved, and were then synthesized into a national report (Bartra 2000). The methodology used was structured interviews of key actors from public and civil society institutions at regional level.

Impact on community development (*transformación*)

The second qualitative strand of methodology focused on the programme's impact in terms of community transformation. The PRODERS model was designed to be based on participatory local planning of sustainable development plans, which were then to lead to specific productive and ecological projects coordinated by the ministry and a regional sustainable development council made up of stakeholders from government and civil society organizations. This strategy aimed to lead not only to poverty reduction, but also to a basis for sustainable livelihoods, community capacity for designing and managing sustainable production, and institutional coordination.

Table 4.1   Methodological approaches in the PRODERS monitoring and evaluation project*

	Phase 1 (concluded)	Phase 2 (concluded)	Phase 3 (starting)
Focus	Large-scale, rapid evaluation for reporting at end of year and of administration	Drawing on base line of Phase 1 and design of M&E system and process, with emphasis on participatory M&E – objective: base for a process of citizens' monitoring of policy and participatory M&E for institutional learning and reporting	Trial application and capacity-building of participatory M&E system and spread to pilot regions
Methodological approach	Essentially an extractive, externally driven evaluation based on primary documentary, interview and database (physical) material that produced both numbers and textual information on quantitative and qualitative aspects. Monitoring = physical, environmental data; Evaluation = social, economic data and aspects; **(rapid application, producing large sets of numbers)**	Design of indicators with institutional (national, regional) and non-governmental actors (regional and local); trial of field tools both for external M&E and for use by local and regional actors themselves, with a view to allowing idiosyncratic indicators alongside fixed, national ones, all fitting within a national framework of variables and categories that permits aggregation and comparative analysis. Monitoring = regular assessment of change (or reaching target); Evaluation = annual/biannual impact assessment for policy and programme adjustment – using grassroots development framework to define categories and variables for national analysis and location of indicators within these; **(design, trial phase)**	Pilot trials in two or three regions of M&E generating both quantitative and qualitative data for analysis, based on participatory methods and approach to who analyses and uses the information and analysis. Two-stage learning process to find correct praxis and for expanding the process for national and regional learning in a participatory way, while also generating the required numbers and analysis; regression analysis **(piloting and consolidation)**

	Phase 1 (concluded)	Phase 2 (concluded)	Phase 3 (starting)
Socio-economic aspects	Cost–benefit analysis (questionnaires administered by regional consultants, trained by national consultants)	Impact assessment of employment creation, income generation and efficiency, and incremental cost; rapid rural appraisal tools for quantitative random survey data needed for institutional indicators (to be aggregated to regional and national levels); rapid rural appraisal tools for indicator definition	As in previous phase, plus rapid rural appraisal tools to make cost–benefit analysis more accessible to local actors; wealth/well-being ranking
Environmental aspects	Deforestation rates, GIS; structured, closed questionnaires administered by national and regional consultants	Environmental indicators developed by national consultants and the institution (national, regional and local levels), institutional regional stakeholders (regional levels), and participatory methods used for indicator development at community and regional levels	Rapid rural appraisal / participatory rural appraisal and popular education methods to be used to achieve a combination of methods along with GIS and questionnaires on deforestation, soil conservation and biodiversity
Participation and management aspects	Structured interviews with regional actors from public and non-governmental sectors (15 interviews in each of 22 regions) (numbers generated for operation of Regional Councils on basis of 1–3 score). Structured and semi-structured interviews at community level regarding impact of small-scale community productive projects	Different teams trialling different methods, some more conventional, others more participatory rural appraisal-based methods and those of popular education to explore issues of participation/*gestión*; encouraging women and men to define their own indicators at village level	Participatory rural appraisal methods used for individual and group data collection and analysis; identification of 'institutional/ project well-being weighting'; linking to participatory land-use plans that the protected area regulation and PRODERS remit requires to link M&E more explicitly to participatory community and regional planning. Analysis of data to be undertaken by learning groups/accompanying committees; exchange to start with national and institutional actors
System (database)	Manual integration of various sources of data – subsequent analysis in SPSS	Theoretical design of relational database able to incorporate quantitative data from impact indicators and cost information with textual reports from communities and regions – aim is a policy tool	Implementation of relational database able to incorporate quantitative data from impact indicators and cost information with textual reports from communities and regions – aim is a policy tool

*Number-generating methodologies used or being developed are highlighted in bold type.

The impact assessment method was based on traditional social science methods of interviews with key informants (here limited to governmental actors); focus group interviews with community members using semi-structured interview guides; and some community-wide small questionnaires in the form of an opinion survey. The analysis from this work, as from the other two qualitative research strands of the first phase, was presented in narrative form using interview quotes and opinions expressed by regional consultants (Bartra 2000).

Quantitative methods

The third methodological component was a quantitative instrument: a household survey administered to a random sample of communities. This generated household expenditure data (to identify the poor) as well as project benefits (in financial terms) used for a cost–benefit analysis exercise. The broader economic cost–benefit analysis was undertaken at both community and national levels, and an attempt was made to include some environmental externalities (e.g. carbon sequestration) in the analysis. For a subsample, an extremely detailed questionnaire on all sources of income and agricultural production was used to generate data for a social accounting matrix.

One module of the household survey was designed to identify perceptions of the impact of PRODERS projects among beneficiaries and non-beneficiaries. A range of impact indicators was produced after consultation with key informants, covering income, employment, agricultural production, natural resource use and conservation, and community capacity to resolve problems and engage with outside institutions. These were subsequently piloted with communities (through group meetings and interviews) in various social and ecological environments, and a set of common impact indicators was used in the household questionnaire. One of the challenges faced by the national consultant in the training was to ensure that regional teams had a shared understanding of these indicators.

Moving towards participatory monitoring and evaluation

Several lessons from the first phase of the project, carried out on a large scale and in the context of the end of an administration, are being – cautiously – taken up by ministry and advisory teams for the second and final phases. In this section, the problematic aspects of Phase 1 are summarized, and the revised approach for the two subsequent phases of the project outlined.

The broad objective of the new approach is to move beyond M&E as merely a reporting and accounting tool that relies on extractive methodologies, both quantitative and qualitative. The objective is to avoid (as happened in many participatory poverty assessments during the 1990s) research simply providing a sounding board for the poor in policy debates and practice (McGee and Norton 2000: 45). While recognizing constraints of the bureaucratic context and financial norms and regulations, the proposed approach was to allow for a learning process by all concerned, one that would permit confidence in participatory M&E and an opening up of the institutional agenda to occur while setting in place a system of M&E at national level, but which could also be used by communities and regional institutions and actors. The potential for influencing policy, for seeing changes in policy in response to local and regional evaluation, is as much an objective as is the efficiency of the M&E system for institutional reporting to its minister, funders and the Presidency. For this to occur, a certain degree of institutionalization of M&E at local and regional levels is of central importance, as well as location and linkages within the central ministry.

The proposed first step in this new approach is to put into practice a modest version of the participatory monitoring and evaluation (PM&E) system. This allows for learning and confidence-building, with the full version to be implemented after this trial phase. Monitoring and core elements of the system are to be:

- a mixed set of stakeholder indicators – those relating to output maps addressing the four areas to be assessed (socio-economic, environmental, participation, administration) and those responding to four forms of information (quality, quantity, cost, time)
- local and regional learning groups (*comités de acompañamiento*) as multiple stakeholder groups designing indicators and involved in data analysis and dissemination
- a broader set of categories and variables applicable across the country which relate to the contextual regional sets of indicators
- data collection using collection sheets or record cards that allow both numerical input and the use of symbols
- community data to be collated at regional level and to be reported to state-level ministerial and national offices, allowing intercommunity and regional analysis, then aggregated at national level, with information returned to the regions
- methods to combine formal and participatory methods, depending on indicators and level of operation, with triangulation a constant feature
- targets to be set for future performance (PRODERS programme is currently under review).

Indicators for environmental, socio-economic and participation sectors of impact are designed by community and regional actors in the pilot regions. These will be combined with indicators decided on by institutional actors (such as those the programme and the ministry need to report on to the Congress and Finance Ministry). Prioritization will be undertaken and a fixed number of indicators from the regions will be included in the national set of indicators, while at regional level a fixed number of community indicators will be included for regional appraisal.

Methodological lessons and challenges

Our reflections in this chapter are general in nature, but relate to the wider questions posed by the challenge of combining methods in development research.

Cost–benefit analysis and project evaluation

We have found strong evidence that the Mexican Congress (and policy makers more generally) should not rely solely on cost–benefit analysis, even for periodic evaluation. Additional techniques are needed to identify what communities perceive to be benefits from government programmes. Introducing perceived impact measures or scales[5] across a range of areas – economic, environmental and social – strengthens the evaluation process. It is relatively easy to capture whether participants feel they now have a more effective voice, better access to resources, or an improved natural environment, but these are the kind of returns that cost–benefit analysis finds it difficult to incorporate, hence the projects that produced the best net returns were often not the ones that produced user satisfaction.

Household survey techniques that combine both cost–benefit analysis and perceived impact data allow these impacts to be quantified and related to other variables, such as spending on projects, poverty, and even information provided by key informants. This has helped to identify important factors associated with project success, but while suitable for occasional large-scale evaluation, this approach is too expensive for regular monitoring. It is possible, however, to use numbers generated from perceived impact scales as part of cheap participatory monitoring methods.

Institutional/policy environment

For effective participatory work at any scale, but particularly at national level, political and policy environments need to be in place or to be evolving alongside the design and trial phase of a complex methodology. In the Mexican case, the policy environment was conducive to a focus on poverty reduction, but stayed within the parameters of conventional indicators and data collection. Decentralization was non-existent to the municipal level, and the regional councils were not the institutions for anchoring this process that a participatory approach would have benefited from. Being located within a weak ministry (environment), but benefiting from the policy of interministerial collaboration on poverty reduction of which it formed part, PRODERS could not be eval- uated easily in terms of its impact on poverty reduction and sustainable livelihoods, and resource use more broadly, as the wider agenda it was part of was very complex. At the time of the Phase 1 work, the Director of PRODERS showed unswerving commitment to the M&E process for impact assessment. However, the extractive nature of the process that took place during Phase 1 was due as much to the political context during the evaluation (pre-election year) as to the differing methodological and political approaches of the teams involved.

Institutional timing versus local participation and learning

A long-recognized dilemma applies in this case: the time it takes for a participatory system or process to be set in place does not coincide with the timing of the reporting and financing cycles of government institutions and donors. Follow-up and working through potential changes in policy and local practice are often considered financially impossible (McGee and Norton 2000).

Communication

Two aspects of PM&E work are often misunderstood: the importance of communicating results and changes in policy or actions carried out in response to results; and the opportunity for contributing to communication and negotiation between different stakeholders. Negotiation over choice of indicators can help communication between actors, but increased understanding of the 'other' is always likely to be limited where indicators represent epistemologies that are diametrically opposite and where institutional timing for reporting is very tight, making listening and learning vertically and horizontally across actors too difficult.

Triangulation

The work with PRODERS was initially designed only marginally to include the principles of triangulation and complementarity of methods. The first cut at designing a national M&E system sought to address four core areas of programmatic work, to be evaluated separately. The stated intention had been to correlate sectoral learning (Toledo and Bartra 2000). However, separate teams of consultants were hired, and triangulation and intersectoral or disciplinary analysis were not designed into the process. This prevented complementary use and cross-checking of responses to questionnaires and semi-structured interviews. In the end, it became clear that the quantitative work was needed to report upwards to Congress and funders (Finance Ministry and international donors). The research design did not seek triangulation in order to cover different levels of programmatic intervention, and to draw conclusions relevant for policy change to occur.

Weighting indicators

We argue that however effective and participatory the process of indicator definition and analysis may have been at local and regional levels, the weighting that different stakeholders will give indicators defined by others will be crucial in terms of learning and change occurring during the monitoring phase and after the evaluation. Participatory and transparent prioritization and weighting of indicators will be key.

Epistemologies and scale

The perceptions, opinions and languages involved and expressed in M&E processes, particularly where these involve some level of participatory practice, will always be so varied as to make deeper understanding, as well as aggregation of data, immensely difficult. But listening to and recognizing perceptions and differing epistemologies is, we argue, a good starting point that can help bring about communication and effective triangulation. After all, the case of participatory budget monitoring, for example, is increasingly considered a case of solid participatory policy monitoring. This process does require training in budgeting and the reasons behind the budgeting and spending of the local, regional or national government. Learning about others through numbers may sound alienating, but it seems that the positivism represented by some methodologies is a problem only where the results are clearly used for a particular political end. Otherwise, villagers do not have a problem with creating numbers and analysing impacts on their lives in terms of quantitative and qualitative means of assessment. It is more difficult for those involved to do this analysis at regional and national levels, as it appears more abstract.

Potential for participation and numbers

The limitations of the first phase in the work with PRODERS, and the challenges we have faced so far in designing a participatory national M&E process and system, demonstrate that quantitative data is as important as qualitative. But what matters is who undertakes the data collection – who can use the indicators and turn them into an analysis that also serves other actors. First trials in the field have shown that community-based indicator definition that allows national aggregation is not difficult, but the categories within which results are discussed need to be agreed, otherwise numbers lose their meaning. Methodological frameworks such as the grassroots development framework are designed specifically to be a participatory tool for quantification and comparisons at scale (Ritchey-Vance 1998). Here numbers are no longer the only issue, but the analysis and agreement of categories and objectives of a policy also become important.

Conclusions

What emerges from this case study is that integrating participatory approaches into qualitative and quantitative work is possible, but where the political (institutional and community) context and capacity are not conducive, or the policy is not as participatory as has been claimed, then insistence on participatory practice high up the participation ladder is not of use from the beginning. We are trying to be realistic and pragmatic in how far participatory skills and political commitment can be taken. The two steps of the PM&E work – a 'mini' and a 'maxi' stage – are designed with this in mind.

In the end, the quantitative and qualitative mix will be conducive to policy analysis and national PM&E where stakeholders with the opportunity to evaluate see that they can control the process along with others, and that it leads to either (or both) a change in track of the policy under assessment, or/and an improvement in the targets or objectives, such as improved livelihoods, reduction in poverty, or a move to sustainable natural resource use.

Chapter Five
Combining qualitative and quantitative methods in evaluation-related rural tourism development research

JENNIFER BRIEDENHANN and EUGENIA WICKENS

Summary

There is an extensive ongoing debate about the relative merits of qualitative and quantitative research strategies. Researchers contend that both have advantages and drawbacks. This chapter applies that debate to a case study in the tourism development sector, arguing that the nature of the research topic promotes the adoption of a combination approach utilizing quantitative and qualitative techniques. Practitioners in the evaluation field who hold the view that both quantitative and qualitative methods contribute to all aspects of evaluative enquiries and can be used successfully together endorse this decision. The study, which is distinguished by an emphasis on the practical importance of research results, has been designed to ultilize a Delphi survey supplemented by open-ended interviews as chosen methods of data collection. The utilization of these complementary research methods facilitates the accommodation of disparate opinions, solicited from a diverse range of actors within the rural tourism domain.

Introduction

There is an extensive body of literature on research methodology, in which there is an ongoing debate about the relative merits of qualitative and quantitative research strategies and the possibilities for mixing methods. While the debate is ongoing between proponents of these two traditions, some theoretical contributions, particularly those by post-modernist thinkers, have strongly influenced the direction of recent methodological developments. This has led to the emergence of a hybrid approach, the defining characteristic of which is the flexibility it allows the researcher in combining both qualitative and quantitative research techniques (Wickens 1999). As Miles and Hubermann (1984: 4) acknowledge: 'in epistemological debates it is tempting to operate at the poles. But in the actual practice of empirical research, we believe that all of us ... are closer to the centre with multiple overlaps ... an increasing number of researchers now see the world with more pragmatic, ecumenical eyes.' Other researchers (Strauss and Corbin 1990; Wickens 1999) point out that the distinctions between the two 'traditional' approaches are not as precise as previously believed, and that it is no longer uncommon for researchers to use a plurality of methods.

Evaluation research

Patton (1997: xvii), quoting from Halcolm's *The Real Story of Paradise Lost*, humorously suggests that evaluation was born on the eighth day after the creation, when the archangel posed the following questions: 'God, how do you know that what you have created is very good? What are your criteria? On what data do you base your judgement? Just exactly what results were you expecting to attain? And aren't you a little close to the situation to make a fair and unbiased evaluation?'

The traditional, or banking, school of evaluation favours a scientific approach and the use of quantitative, measurable, objective methods of evaluation, based on prespecified criteria, in which standardized procedures are paramount (Rowlands 1991; Rubin 1995: 17–23). This approach elicits a high degree of managerial control and influence, with outsiders normally contracted as evaluators in order to increase objectivity. As little input is afforded to other stakeholders, the approach has the tendency of creating negative reactions among those affected by the evaluation outcome (Parlett and Hamilton 1972; Rowlands 1991).

The alternative, or dialogical, approach promotes the employment of qualitative, or subjective, methods in which dialogue, description and interpretation take precedence over measurement. Evaluation is seen as dynamic rather than static, and forms an integral part of the development process in which subjectivity is acknowledged and welcomed. The evaluation, which has an ethos of empowerment rather than control, recognizes that there may be different opinions. Negotiation and consensus form part of the process of evaluation that may be undertaken internally, by stakeholders, with the evaluator taking on the role of a facilitator (Parlett and Hamilton 1972; Rowlands 1991).

While Patton (1999: 9) describes evaluation as 'a rich feast of different approaches', others argue that consideration must be afforded to which methods are most likely to secure the type of information needed, taking into account the values, level of understanding and capabilities of those from whom information is requested (Taylor-Powell et al. 1996: 8). Echtner and Jamal (1997), however, affirm that researchers tend to approach the vagaries of tourism studies from the main discipline in which they themselves have been trained, rather than using holistic approaches to determine a universal spread of knowledge and attitude.

Both qualitative and quantitative data serve a purpose, with evaluators increasingly collecting data from multiple sources and perspectives, using a variety of data collection methods, thus allowing for a more complete representation of the problem under interrogation (Taylor-Powell et al. 1996; Curnan et al. 1998). Important issues for considera-tion when making methodological choices include the ease with which the data emanating from the evaluation can be understood, and its credibility in the eyes of the audience who will receive, and utilize, the results (Patton 1999: 9). The evaluation design additionally should be flexible and responsive enough to facilitate change or redirection, avoiding procedures which impose inhibiting controls (Curnan et al. 1998).

Other points that should be considered in deciding which methods to use include the financial resources available; the cultural perspectives of participants; and the credibility of the results emanating from the methods selected (Curnan et al. 1998). Evaluation professionals and authors repeatedly emphasize that the intrinsic worth of the evaluation process lies in its being focused on utilization and procuring commitment among participants through continuous strategizing, adaptation, prioritizing and relevance. 'No matter how rigorous the methods of data collection, design and reporting are in evaluation, if it does not get used it is a bad evaluation' (Patton 1999: 19).

A case study: rural tourism development in the UK and South Africa

Implementation of rural tourism development projects is often a long-term process in which a flexible approach, which calls for adaptation and change as emergent issues surface, is called for. One of the most fundamental 'knowledge gaps' (Patton 1999: 12), among both public and private tourism sectors, is an understanding of those elements that are essential to the success of rural tourism development projects, judged in economic, environmental, sociocultural, political and business terms. Implementation recurrently takes place in an *ad hoc*, haphazard manner (Butler 1993), and the subsequent failure of projects is commonplace. Most projects instigate change as a reactive measure aimed at overcoming a crisis, rather than proactively based on informed decision-making.

Evaluation in terms of tourism development projects is problematic and complex, and there is a need for a down-to-earth, clear, pragmatic evaluation framework, which is easily implementable, and cost-effective, as rural tourism projects are frequently small-scale and subject to financial constraints (Nelson 1993). Lack of tourism expertise, a need for capacity-building, and the creation of tourism awareness among rural communities have been identified as fundamental constraints of tourism development in rural areas. The public sector equally fails to understand the crucial role it is called on to play in creating an environment that is conducive to the development of tourism as an economic and employment-generating sector. Neither does it comprehend its role in managing the development of the industry in order to limit negative impacts resulting from overuse and damage to either sociocultural or environmental resources in developing areas (Pearce 1992; Hall and Jenkins 1995; Middleton and Hawkins 1998).

The case study in this chapter is based on the premise that rural tourism is eminently suited to small-scale, locally-owned tourism development. It suggests that identification of those elements essential to the success of rural tourism development projects represents one of the most critical issues facing the management of rural tourism today. The primary aim is to identify criteria that are clear, specific and prioritized. In addition, the study aims to establish who should be involved in the evaluation of rural tourism development projects.

Having deliberated the options, the study adopts a hybrid approach (Wickens 1999), combining both quantitative and qualitative methods of data collection with a view to minimizing the weakness of any single approach. The Delphi technique serves as the preliminary method of data collection. In addition, semi-structured interviews will be undertaken. Research will be conducted in both Britain and South Africa.

The Delphi technique

Linstone and Turoff (1975: 3) characterize the Delphi technique as 'a method for structuring a group communication process, so that the process is effective in allowing a group of individuals, as a whole, to deal with a complex problem.' As the method does not entail face-to-face interaction among respondents, it provides an enabling mechanism whereby conflicting opinion and hostile attitudes can be incorporated and dealt with, without the 'prima donna behaviours that may vitiate roundtable discussions' (Rosenthal 1976: 122).

Dunham (1998: 1) proclaims its purpose is to 'elicit information and judgments from participants to facilitate problem-solving, planning, and decision making' capitalizing on respondents' creativity while simultaneously maximizing the merits and minimizing the liabilities of group interaction. As the technique involves non-interactive groups, it is possible to employ experts based at considerable geographic distances.

The Delphi technique is widely recognized as a 'consensus-building tool' that has been applied as a means of cognition and inquiry in a variety of fields, including land-use planning, policy-making, organizational restructuring and tourism. The Delphi technique is said to be particularly appropriate in facilitating decision-making by a number of individuals in environments characterized by antagonistic or strongly opposed political or emotional factions, or when personality differences or intellectual style would be distracting in face-to-face settings (Rosenthal 1976: 121; Cline 2000). The technique is recommended in evaluation studies where conflicts between stakeholders are a disruptive influence and can become interpersonal and derail the focus of the study (Patton 1997: 151). Tourism evaluation, operating in a hostile environment with a plethora of stakeholders, each with their own overriding interests, agendas and areas of emphasis, is thus considered particularly apposite to use of the Delphi technique.

Strengths and weaknesses of the Delphi technique

Like all research methods, the Delphi technique has both its adherents and its critics. Critics claim that the method is based on a principle of achieving 'oneness of mind' through thesis, antithesis and synthesis, representing a continuous process through which consensus will supposedly occur (Stuter 1998). The method has been subject to extensive critique by Sackman, who views the Delphi as being unscientific, and by Armstrong, who questions the accuracy and reliability of a method

Figure 5.1 *Schematic representation of implementation of the Delphi technique**

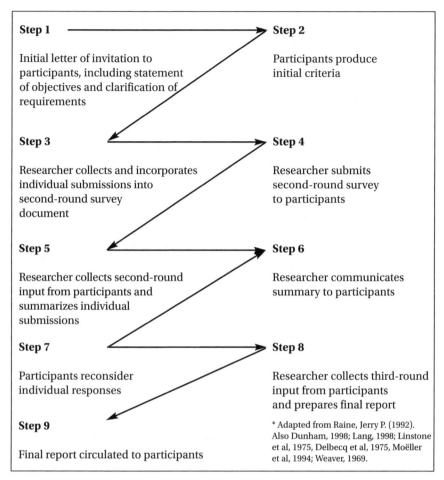

Step 1

Initial letter of invitation to participants, including statement of objectives and clarification of requirements

Step 2

Participants produce initial criteria

Step 3

Researcher collects and incorporates individual submissions into second-round survey document

Step 4

Researcher submits second-round survey to participants

Step 5

Researcher collects second-round input from participants and summarizes individual submissions

Step 6

Researcher communicates summary to participants

Step 7

Participants reconsider individual responses

Step 8

Researcher collects third-round input from participants and prepares final report

Step 9

Final report circulated to participants

* Adapted from Raine, Jerry P. (1992). Also Dunham, 1998; Lang, 1998; Linstone et al, 1975, Delbecq et al, 1975, Moëller et al, 1994; Weaver, 1969.

that has judgement and opinion as its basis (see *www.iit.edu/~it/delphi.html*). Weaver (1972) queries the methods of selection of the panel of experts, and the evaluation of their level of expertise.

The exclusivity of representation due to purposive sampling means that judgements are those of a selected group of people and may not be representative. This suggests that it is possible to obtain different results from different groups. Equally, the process of choosing participants is often not considered seriously enough, as it is their calibre that determines the quality of the outcomes of the survey, an issue of primary importance in group decision-making (Harrison 1995: 249). While direct control over the study by the researcher is seen by proponents as being among its benefits, others are critical of the level of influence and potential for bias in the design of questionnaires, the interpretation of responses,[1] and the processing of results, which may be significant (Salanick et al. 1971).

Proponents of the technique cite the fact that Delphic surveys provide a means whereby interaction between experts, who cannot come together physically but whose involvement may increase the validity of the information gathered, can be inexpensively facilitated. The opportunity to capitalize on the knowledge and experience of a group, representing a cross-section of expertise within the area researched, assists in providing researchers with a broad perspective of the issues under review as opposed to an isolated point of view. Equally, the anonymity of individual responses, removing the effects of prejudice, peer pressure and desire to conform, enhances the candour of respondents while simultaneously exposing agreements and disagreements.

The process of the Delphi study

The Delphi technique is a means of securing expert, convergent opinion solicited by the use of successive surveys and feedback (Figure 5.1). Each round of the survey is designed by means of focused questionnaires to elicit carefully considered group opinions, which can influence informed decision-making once the process is completed (Lang 1995). It enables participants with differing points of view and cognitive skills to contribute to those sections of the research topic on which they have particular knowledge and understanding.

The process, which is controlled by the researcher, permits participants to reconsider their own responses in view of group opinion, by means of iteration and feedback of the average responses of the group over a number of rounds. Respondents are informed of current consensus, but not harassed by arguments. Receipt of collective results from all participants allows them to refine and modify their opinions based on information generated in subsequent rounds of questioning. The ability of participants to establish the nature of the input sought from them, based on an understanding of the aims and objectives for which the study is being undertaken, is an important consideration. Equally significant is the degree to which participants are themselves interested in the problem under investigation. This is particularly significant in minimizing the dangers of frustration and loss of interest prior to completion of the process, which requires a significant commitment of time from participants (Delbecq et al. 1975; Andranovich 1995).

Phase Two of the study will comprise a series of open-ended, semi-structured interviews. The use of interviews as the second phase data collection method in this study is indicated by the need for face-to-face, in-depth exploration of issues, raised by respondents to the Delphi survey, which warrant more detailed investigation in the hope of gaining new insights into recurring problems. Topics that feature prominently in the South African response include the contentious issue of land tenure, cumbersome bureaucracy, role clarification, and the vulnerability of projects to political infighting and point-scoring. The complex problem of meaningful public participation is of consequence across responses from both countries, as is the delicate balance between environmental and social concerns weighed against the desperate need for development and income generation in many rural areas. The Delphi study has successfully gathered basic data, identified the major concerns in the tourism development community, and provided an understanding of the importance accorded to such issues by participants. It is, however, not possible to describe the intricacies of tourism development, its process, or the complexities of political interference in survey research. The Delphi technique is unable to generate the in-depth discussion, deeper understanding and useful response that should emanate from the interview process. Nor can it afford the opportunity for the interviewer either to experience the affective and cognitive aspects of informant's responses, or to seek the clarification necessary to gain full understanding if participants' responses appear unclear or ambiguous (Frechtling and Sharp 1997).

Conclusions

Gamon (1991) contends that, for any reputable evaluation, a solid base of evidence is essential and selection of an appropriate information collection strategy is thus imperative. In her opinion, the Delphi technique is particularly suited for evaluation focusing on the identification of problems and their possible solutions. Many researchers (Pill 1971: 57–71; Green et al. 1990: 51–62) affirm the cognitive value of the Delphi technique as a rapid, effective process of collecting and distilling expert opinion, and gaining consensus from a group of knowledgeable people. The study utilizes the process as a means of effectively structuring group communication and allowing the panel, comprising 60 individual experts, to deal with the research enquiry as a unit, thus facilitating the formation of a group judgement.

No single research method could elicit the comprehensive information sought by this study. While the Delphi technique is considered the most effective means of soliciting group input and consensual opinion-forming by a panel of experts utilizing a manageable method, it is unable to facilitate the in-depth discussion required to gain a fuller understanding of significant and contentious issues. Interviews alone could not have generated the means to elicit group input and opinion. The opportunity afforded by such interviews for face-to-face interaction and meaningful discussion in relation to important issues and critique of the draft evaluation framework is vital to the success of the study. The authors argue that utilization of these complementary research methods, which facilitate the accommodation of disparate opinions solicited from a diverse range of actors within the rural tourism domain, are essential to the successful outcomes of such studies, which are distinguished by an emphasis on the practical importance of research results.

The research outcomes are expected to generate knowledge for conceptual use, and to identify incipient problems and issues that will have an impact on the viability and success of rural tourism projects. The criteria against which projects will be evaluated are intended to influence decisions pertaining to whether or not a project should be implemented; to assist in formative decision-making relating to improvement of a project; or to facilitate decisions with regard to project funding. Evaluations undertaken during the life cycle of the project are expected to provide information relating to its impacts and resource utilization. It is hoped that findings from the study will be used to influence and lobby for the formulation, or modification, of rural tourism development policy. The policy environment may, in the long term, prove to be more important than either creativity or innovation to ultimate project success, and to the sustainability of the resources on which they are built and which they consume (Curnan et al. 1998).

The manner in which results of the study are presented, and the audience to whom they are presented, are of crucial significance if findings are to be utilized constructively. Where policy changes are indicated, the dissemination of information to both tourism stakeholders and the general public is worthwhile. Public attitudes and beliefs theoretically have an impact on bringing about policy change, while tourism stakeholders can speak both from experience and lessons learned from the evaluation process (Curnan et al. 1998).

Part II
Quantifying the qualitative in development research

Introduction
Reflections on quantifitication

Quantifying qualitative data

There is a long-established tradition in the social sciences of applying statistical techniques in the analysis of qualitative data (Mitchell 1980; Silverman 1985, 1993; Gilbert 1993), a trend that has expanded with the introduction of increasingly sophisticated techniques that allow ever-larger qualitative data sets to be analysed (Born 1997; White 2002a). Increasingly, policy analysis requires development research to explore a range of issues and problems that traditional forms of research, with their separation of qualitative and quantitative methods, prevent. Thus new concerns make it imperative that all research should be well theorized and designed (Campbell 2002) and that, where relevant, qualitative data should allow for a degree of standardization that comes with the use of statistical procedures. Quantification involves a degree of standardization that enables us to aggregate and compare qualitative issues across time and between populations. This is particularly useful for monitoring and evaluation, and involves the identification of a numerical indicator of a qualitative issue. A good example is the development of a $US/day income line as a global indicator of poverty.[1] This can be usefully combined with other, similarly constructed indicators to create indexes such as the UNDP's Human Development Index which combines indicators of economic wellbeing, health and knowledge.

Quantification can also involve respondents and participants giving a score to a qualitative issue, in much the same way that judges score ice skaters or divers against qualitative categories. Scoring produces cardinal data that can be aggregated and compared. This technique is popular in market research, but is also widely used in social and development research (Silverman 1966; Grandin 1988; Scoones 1995a). One interesting example of its use in development research was the scoring of the quality of social capital in Tanzania (see Box b.1, overleaf). The reliability of these figures, however, relies heavily on having some form of independent 'panel', with what Herring (2003) calls a 'shared cognitive field' and an 'ethnographic sensibility', that can confirm whether the scoring is being applied consistently.

Clearly there are dangers in relying on indicators, the principal one being that they have no explanatory power. They can also be particularly unhelpful if they do not capture the subjective reality in a reasonably accurate way.[2] But they can also be powerful in other ways, particularly as part of a process of change where they can galvanize actors into concerted action. By allowing for comparison of outcomes, trends and patterns, and for statistical probing of the influence of subjective variables on observable outcomes,[3] indicators can prompt further reflection and diagnosis, often between new alliances of actors. As long as quantification is not seen as a replacement for powerful qualitative analysis, then this can be a useful route.

Box b.1   *Quantifying qualitative data: social capital in Tanzania*

A social capital and poverty survey gathered qualitative data on association activity in 87 villages in Tanzania, comprising 1,376 households. The survey was conducted using the same population clusters targeted by an earlier household expenditure study. A social capital index was calculated from the survey relating to three aspects of social capital: (i) levels of membership in groups; (ii) the characteristics of those groups, including aspects of participation and inclusion; and (iii) the individual's values and attitudes, particularly with respect to their expressed level of trust in various groups and perceptions of social cohesion. Cardinal values were assigned to this index of social capital, which could then be analysed as an exogenous variable in income regressions (against household expenditure per adult equivalent). The magnitude of social capital's effect on incomes was impressively large, with one standard deviation increase in village social capital increasing household expenditure per person by at least 20–30 per cent. Econometric testing refuted the possibility of joint determination (by some other variable) and reverse causality. The policy implications of this analysis are significant: 'the investment of time and resources in building trust and self-organizational capacity of groups and municipalities is a pre-condition to sustainable change at the local level' (Narayan 1997).

Sources: Narayan 1997; Narayan and Pritchett 1997

Contributions

Part II of this book addresses the specific challenge of quantifying qualitative data in order to increase the comparability of findings. Appropriate statistical approaches can greatly facilitate the handling of qualitative information and provide a helpful structure for further qualitative interpretation. Arguing that this combination of methods has received insufficient attention from most qualitative researchers, Savitri Abeyasekera (Chapter 6) provides valuable guidance on the 'why, when and how' of quantification, with an emphasis on the collection and analysis of ranked data sets. Quirien van Oirschot (Chapter 7) illustrates how participatory visual techniques can, with the addition of a 'semi-expert trained expert panel' approach, be used to elicit quantified and comparable perception data, in this case on consumer preference. Finally, David Booth (Chapter 8) sounds a warning regarding attempts to overplay the quantification and integration card in combined methods research. Citing Bourguignon's (2003) analogy of seeing a mountain from two perspectives (by considering various perspectives one can obtain a fuller understanding of a multi-dimensional subject), he reminds us where the comparative advantage of participatory qualitative research lies with respect to standardized, survey-based data generation.

Chapter Six
Quantitative analysis approaches to qualitative data: why, when and how?

SAVITRI ABEYASEKERA

Summary

Although it is rarely stated in any explicit form, there is often a clear need in development research to provide generalizable results concerning a target population. Appropriate statistical analysis approaches can greatly facilitate the handling of qualitative information and provide a helpful structure for further qualitative interpretation. This combination of methods appears to have received little attention from most qualitative researchers, and there is some uncertainty about why such approaches are needed and when they are appropriate. Researchers are also often unaware of how their data could best be handled and fully utilized to provide generalizable conclusions. This chapter aims to address some of these issues. It provides an overview of some straightforward analysis approaches, and highlights the need to recognize data structure. The focus is on data in the form of ranks. Some discussion is included on how numerical values can be assigned to ranks. A brief overview is also given of analysis approaches suitable for other types of qualitative data.

Introduction

Much good development research produces qualitative data. Some of this contributes to addressing specific research questions, while other elements provide a more open-ended understanding of development dynamics and relationships. This chapter addresses the former element, concentrating on some quantitative analysis approaches that can be applied to qualitative data. Specific research questions can lead to a 'measure' of people's judgements, for example about what cooking oil they prefer; about what constraints they face putting their children through school; about what elements of government policy cause most problems for small traders; about the key reasons for the depletion of natural resources; or about the value of health information services. Such qualitative information gathered during development research can be analysed to provide conclusions that are applicable to a wider target population. Appropriate sampling is essential for this purpose, and it will be assumed in what follows that any sampling issues have been satisfactorily addressed to allow generalization of results from the data analysis to be meaningful (see Chapter 2).

Most emphasis in this chapter will be given to the analysis of data that can be put in the form of ranks, but some analysis approaches suitable for other types of qualitative data are also considered. Generally, ranks are better than scores for elicitation, as it is always easier to judge whether one item is better or worse, more or less important, than another item. However, the ease with which the information can be collected must be balanced against the fact that information from ranking cannot be analysed directly through quantitative means. Furthermore, ranks give no idea of the 'distance' between numerical values given. In the case of women's preference for cooking oils, for instance, we are not able to measure, from ranks, by how much they prefer one oil to another. Scores, on the other hand, have a numerical meaning, with 'best' or 'good' in some respect associated with larger scores. Scores also can have an absolute meaning, while ranks are always relative to the other items under consideration. So a rank of 1 is not necessarily a favoured item, it is just 'better than the rest'. Scores provide a ranking of the items but also something extra – a usable distance measure between preferences for different items.

The general questions of why and when to quantify are discussed first, but the main focus is on issues relating to the 'how' component of data analysis. It is not the intention to present implementation details of any statistical analysis procedures, nor to discuss how outputs resulting from the application of statistical software could be interpreted. The aim is to highlight a few types of research questions that can be answered on the basis of qualitative information; to discuss the types of data format that lend themselves readily to appropriate data analysis procedures; and to emphasize how data analysis can benefit from recognizing the data structure and paying attention to relevant sources of variation.

Why use quantitative approaches?

Quantitative methods of data analysis can be of great value to the researcher who is attempting to draw statistically meaningful results from a large body of qualitative data. The main beneficial aspect is that they provide the means to separate out the large number of confounding factors that often obscure qualitative insights. Once such quantifiable components of the data are separated, attention can focus on the exploratory and explanatory depths of understanding that qualitative research can elicit.

Quantitative analytical approaches also allow the reporting of summary results in numerical terms to be given with a specified degree of confidence. So, for example, a statement such as '45 per cent of households use an unprotected water source for drinking' may be enhanced by providing 95 per cent confidence limits for the true proportion using unprotected water as ranging from 42 to 48 per cent. Here it is possible to say with more than 95 per cent confidence that about half the households had no access to a protected water supply, as the confidence interval lies entirely below 50 per cent.

Likewise, other statements suggesting that some characteristic differed across two or more groups, for example that 'infant mortality differed significantly between households with and without access to a community-based healthcare clinic', can be accompanied by a statement giving the chance (probability) of error (say $P = 0.002$) in this statement – the chance that the conclusion is incorrect. Thus the use of quantitative procedures in analysing qualitative information can also lend greater credibility to research findings by providing the means of quantifying the degree of confidence in the research results.

When are quantitative analysis approaches useful?

Quantitative analysis approaches are meaningful only when there is a need for data summary across many repetitions of a research process, as in participatory focus group discussions that produce outputs such as seasonal calendars or Venn diagrams. Data summary, in turn, suggests that some common features do emerge across such repetitions. Thus the value of a quantitative analysis arises when it is possible to identify features that occur frequently across the many discussions with different research units aimed at studying a particular theme. If there are common strands that can be extracted and subsequently coded into a few major categories, then it becomes easier to study the more interesting qualitative aspects that remain.

For example, suppose it is of interest to learn about people's perceptions of what poverty means for them. It is likely that the narratives resulting from discussions across several communities will show some frequently occurring answers, such as experiencing periods of food shortage, being unable to provide children with a reasonable level of education, not owning a radio, etc. Such information can be extracted from the narratives and coded. Quantitative approaches provide the opportunity to study this coded information first, and then to turn to the remaining qualitative exploratory and explanatory components in the data. These can then be discussed more easily, unhindered by the quantitative components.

Data structure

The data structure plays a key role in helping to formulate the correct analysis of qualitative data through quantitative methods. Data structure refers to how the data can be visualized, categorized and described in different ways, largely as a result of the method of data collection. For example, focus groups in different agroecological zones may be categorized as male, female or mixed; and each group may be asked if they had one, two or three years' assistance with marketing their main cash crop. In the former case, the division by zone and gender must be recognized in the analysis, while in the latter case it may be relevant to consider possible trends across the periods for which assistance was received.

Thinking about the data structure forces researchers to focus on what constitutes replicates for data summarization. It also helps to identify the numerous factors that may have a bearing on those components of

Table 6.1 *Data set showing ranked preferences by a number of women regarding four types of oil**

Personal data		Oil			
Household size	Wage-earner?	Covo	Superstar	Market	Moringa
6	Yes	3	1	4	2
3	No	2	4	3	1
7	Yes	4	3	2	1
3	Yes	2	4	3	1
4	No	4	2	1	3

* The full data set extends over five villages, with 6, 8, 5, 11 and 14 women interviewed per village.

the qualitative information that cannot be coded. Often, the replicates may be several focus group discussions. If the data are to be summarized later over all groups, then some effort is needed to ensure the information is collected in the same systematic way each time. For example, a member of the research team may record the information that emerges from any participatory discussions in a semi-structured way. This systematization helps in regarding the sample, consisting of many focus groups, as a valid sample for later statistical analysis.

Considering the data structure also helps researchers to recognize the different hierarchical levels at which the data reside, for example community, focus group or household level. The data hierarchy needs attention during data analysis as well as when computerizing the information collected. If spreadsheets are to be used, then the data at each level of the hierarchy have to be organized in a separate sheet in a rectangular array.[1]

An example of a simple data structure is provided in Table 6.1, the study aim being to compare women's preference for four different oil types. Here there is structure between women: they come from five villages, they fall into one of four wealth groups, their household size is known, and they have been identified according to whether or not they earn wages by some means. The data should also be recognized as hierarchical, as the information resides both at the 'between-women' level (e.g. whether a wage-earner) and at the 'within-woman' level (e.g. their ranked preference for the four oils). Analysing the data correctly requires recognizing these components of the data structure.

In the above example, the ranking of oils merely represents an ordering of the items, and no numerical interpretation can be associated with the digits 1–4 representing the ranks. An alternative to ranking is to conduct a scoring exercise. For example, to determine the most preferred choice from a given set of items, respondents may be asked to allocate a number of counters (e.g. pebbles or seeds), say out of a maximum of five counters per item, to indicate their views on the

Table 6.2   *Data set showing scores given by farmers to the*
severity of pest attack on beans

Farmer	Ootheca*	Pod borers	Bean stem maggot	Aphids
1	4	2	1	2
2	5	4	1	3
3	4	1	2	1
4	4	5	1	4
5	1	2	1	1
6	1	4	1	2
7	5	1	1	5
8	2	5	5	3
Mean	**3.3**	**3.0**	**1.6**	**2.6**

* The bean foliage beetle, Ootheca spp., is a major insect pest of beans (*Phaselus vulgaris*)

importance of that item. The number allocated then provides a score
on a 0–5 scale, with 0 being regarded as being 'worst' or 'of no importance'. An example data set is shown in Table 6.2. The 'scores' in this
table represent farmers' own perceptions of the severity of the pest.

Some approaches to the analysis of ranked data

Below we illustrate analysis approaches to ranked data through some
situation-specific examples. There is no attempt to give a full coverage
of analysis methods, as the most appropriate form of analysis will
depend on the objectives of the study.

Whatever the objective, it is usually advisable to begin by thinking
carefully about the data structure, and then to produce a few simple
graphs or summary statistics so that the essential features of the data
are clear. Often this form of summary may be all that is needed if
extending the results beyond the sampled units is not a requirement.
However, if results are to be generalized to a wider population, sample
sizes and methods of sampling are key issues that need consideration
(see Chapter 2). Here we assume that participating respondents have
been representatively chosen.

Below we consider some data arising from a ranking exercise and
simple methods of presentation. This is followed by a brief discussion
of more advanced methods of analysis applicable to ranking and scoring
data, restricting attention largely to preference evaluations. Poole
(1997) provides fuller coverage.

> ### Box 6.1   *A descriptive summary of data originating as ranks*
>
> In a study concerning farmers' practices, experiences and knowledge of rice tungro disease, 226 farmers in the Philippines were asked to name and rank the three most damaging pests or diseases affecting their rice crop. Each pest and disease named by a farmer was given a score of 3, 2 or 1, according to whether they ranked the pest or disease as being the first, second or third most damaging in its attack on the crop. Zero was allocated to any pest or disease not mentioned by the farmer. The scores were totalled over all farmers and are shown in Figure 6.1 (below), for each of two seasons, for pests and diseases receiving the four highest overall scores. Tungro is clearly a recognized problem, but in the dry season the stem borer is identified as being the greater problem.
>
> *Source*: Warburton et al. (1998)

Simple methods of summary

The data structures that result from ranks/scores given to a fixed number of items are shown using fictitious data in Tables 6.1 and 6.2. Although the numerical values shown appear similar, there are important differences. For example, mean values for columns in Table 6.2 are meaningful summaries and give some indication of the most serious pest problem. However, producing column totals for the ranks given in Table 6.1 assumes a common distance between any two consecutive ranks. This is particularly problematic if there are missing cells in the table because some respondents have not ranked some items. One option is to give weights to each rank, for example if five items are being ranked, rank 1 is given a weight of 5, rank 2 a weight of 4, etc. In doing so, the assumptions being made by allocating numerical values to each rank must be clearly recognized – the assumption that the degree of preference for one item over the next within an ordered list is the same irrespective of which two neighbouring ranks are being considered, and the assumption that a missing value in the table corresponds to a numerical zero score (for an example, see Abeyasekera et al. 2000).

Alternative weights could also be considered on the basis of comments made by those who rank the items. For example, ranks 1–4 might be given values 9, 5, 2 and 1, respectively, if it became apparent during discussions with respondents that there is a much clearer preference for items at the top of the priority scale than for those lower down.

Allocating weights (specific numerical values or scores) to each of the ranks, while recognizing the assumptions made, provides the means to proceed with standard methods of data summary. Box 6.1 provides an illustration. Such simple descriptive summaries have a place in the analysis, irrespective of whether the study is intended for making generalizable conclusions concerning a wider target population, or is a case study in one village with just a few farmers. In the former case, the summary helps to identify statistical inferential procedures relevant for demonstrating the applicability of results beyond the research setting.

Figure 6.1 *Farmers' perceptions about four pests/diseases*

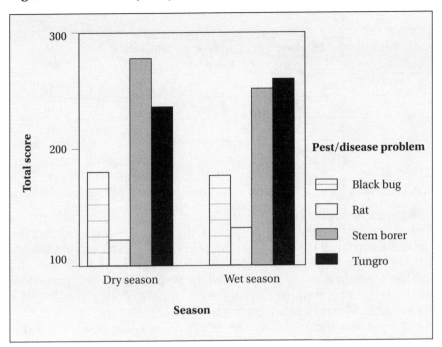

Illustrating analysis of preference evaluations

A researcher may often want to move beyond simple summaries in order to establish whether there are real differences in preferences given by respondents in the target population, allowing for confounding factors that may affect such differences. This is a situation where generalizability of study results is of primary concern. Assuming that the respondents have been sampled appropriately and that the sample size is adequate,[2] such a question can be answered by applying appropriate statistical techniques.

Consider, for example, the ranked data shown in Table 6.1, and suppose these have been allocated appropriate weights to convert them to a set of scores. Suppose the main objective is to determine whether there is a greater preference for Moringa oil[3] compared to the other oils. Although simple data summaries may suggest that this is clearly the case, the data structure may raise additional questions, such as:

- do preferences differ according to whether the woman is a wage-earner or not?
- do preferences differ across the different wealth categories?
- if preferences differ according to whether the woman earns or not, do such differences differ across the wealth categories?

There may be many other pieces of information available concerning the women participating in this study, such as the size of household or

Table 6.3 *Number of farmers giving particular ranks to different uses of water bodies*

Rank	Irrigation	Livestock consumption	Household use	Clothes washing
1	34	6	5	1
2	8	16	14	8
3	1	16	14	15
4	3	8	13	22
n	46	46	46	46

village to which they belong. Is it possible to disentangle confounding factors such as village and household size? The answer is 'yes', and a powerful statistical procedure for this purpose is the analysis of variance (ANOVA). This procedure involves statistical modelling[4] of the data and enables questions such as that above to be answered. The procedure allows relevant comparisons to be made, after making due allowance for possible effects of other confounding factors.

The general technique suggested above is quite powerful and is based on an underlying general theory that can be applied even if some data are missing or if the number of items being evaluated differ across respondents. Appropriate statistics software (e.g. SPSS, GenStat, Minitab) is available to deal with the underlying data structures and other complexities.

More advanced methods of analysis are needed when large numbers of respondents are involved. For example, the frequency of farmers giving different ranks to each of a number of maize varieties can be modelled using a proportional odds models (Agresti 1996). The interpretation of results is then based on the odds of respondents preferring one item compared to another. Some further advanced methods are described by SSC (2001).

Are non-parametric methods useful?

There is often a belief that non-parametric methods (methods that do not make distributional assumptions about the data) are appropriate for analysing qualitative data such as ranks. To illustrate the issues involved, we consider again the type of data shown in Table 6.1, assuming such data are available for a larger number of respondents or focus groups within the population targeted for research results. First, a simple summary is useful. For example, in a study in India aimed at investigating the potential for integrating aquaculture into small-scale irrigation systems managed by resource-poor farmers, 46 farmers were asked to rank four different uses of water bodies according to their importance (Felsing et al. 2000). The data summary shown in Table 6.3

clearly indicates irrigation as the primary use of water bodies. Thirty-four farmers (74 per cent) rank this as the most important use of water.

The research was, however, intended for the larger community from which the representative sample of 46 farmers was chosen. An inferential procedure is then needed to determine whether the results of Table 6.3 are equally applicable to the wider population of farmers in the community. Friedman's test (Conover 1999) may be used to demonstrate that farmers' water uses differ significantly. In this case the test demonstrated that the water uses ranked are not all perceived to be of equal importance. Further tests showed evidence that irrigation was indeed considered more important than other uses, and that there was insufficient evidence to distinguish the remaining three uses in terms of importance.[5]

Friedman's test, as well as other alternatives (Anderson 1959; Taplin 1997), is an example of a non-parametric method. Many textbooks are devoted to non-parametric procedures, but many of the methods apply to measurement data that are converted to ranks before analysis on the grounds that standard methods do not apply due to failure of associated assumptions. Their relevance is restricted to situations where testing a hypothesis is of primary concern, and this may not always be the case with many participatory reflection and action studies. The tests are also less powerful because they do not make full use of the original data. This means that differences between items being compared have to be quite substantial for statistical significance. Although many non-parametric tests exist, their use in analysing data from contextual studies is quite limited.

Other quantitative methods for qualitative data

Many other procedures are available for dealing with qualitative information that can be coded either as binary variables (yes/no, presence/absence) or as categorical variables (high/medium/low access to regional facilities; decreasing/static/increasing dependence on forest resources). If factors affecting qualitative features of the binary sort are to be explored, logistic regression modelling can be used (see, for example, the illustration given by Martin and Sherington 1997).

If a categorical variable is of primary interest, for example in exploring factors influencing the impact of programmes introduced to improve health facilities in a region, using data in the form of people's perceptions of changes in their wellbeing (better, same, worse), then methods such as log-linear modelling or proportional odds modelling come into play. These are advanced statistical techniques and if they are relevant some assistance from a statistician with knowledge of these techniques is advisable.

The advantage of using modelling procedures is that it enables the interrelationships between a wide range of other factors to be taken into account simultaneously. All too often, researchers tend to look at one factor at a time, for example when interested in factors affecting successful co-management of forest resources. The one-factor-at-a-time approach may involve using a series of separate chi-squared tests. The disadvantage in doing so is that the interactions between these factors is then ignored, whereas modelling pays attention to possible interactions.

Once the results of these modelling procedures are available, the purely qualitative features of the data become important because they give breadth and depth to the formal research findings and provide the means to explore and explain both the 'average' or 'normal' relationships and 'residual' features that emerge from the data analysis.[6]

Concluding remarks

Statistical analysis approaches can usefully be applied to qualitative data, particularly data that come in the form of ranks or scores. In situations where the sample size is adequate and the sample has been appropriately chosen to represent the target population of interest, the application of statistical methods will provide evidence-based results and greater validity for the research conclusions. We have briefly reviewed a number of techniques for describing and comparing quantified data, observing that the exact approach for a particular study will be closely associated with the study objectives and other data-collection activities. Drawing on the experiences of a survey statistician to identify the most appropriate analysis approach is likely to be beneficial. Quantification and statistical analysis should be applied to those qualitative data elements that emerge from specific research questions, not only clearing the data 'noise' from the research process, but also throwing up interesting and sometimes puzzling relationships that can be further explored and explained through more open-ended and probing qualitative research.

Chapter Seven
What do you sense? Applying analytical sensory evaluation techniques to research on development issues

QUIRIEN VAN OIRSCHOT and KEITH TOMLINS[1]

Summary

In the discipline of food science and technology, a range of methods have been developed in order to translate qualitative perceptions into data with numerical value. These sensory evaluation methods are widely used both by the food industry and by academics. The translation of qualitative information into quantitative data allows statistical analysis and more accurate monitoring of changes. This chapter considers how the framework used in sensory evaluation may find application in development research. First, an outline is given of the principles of sensory evaluation and several popular methods are described. Three case studies are presented using sensory evaluation in development research. Consumer preference testing using rating was carried out in rural Tanzania, to assess the acceptability of newly developed products. Second, an example is presented of how a semi-trained panel using scoring can monitor changes in the estimated market value of products. A study in Ghana illustrates how quantitative analysis and a profiling technique using semi-trained panels can represent consumers. Finally, some ideas are discussed on how the principles of sensory evaluation techniques could also be used to describe, analyse and understand a broad scope of development issues. These may be as, or more, abstract than food, but in a similar way consist of characteristics that bring quantitative and qualitative judgements together.

Introduction

Sensory evaluation methods used in food science and technology are designed to translate qualitative information into numerical data by applying a statistically valid experimental design and controlled testing conditions. These sensory evaluation methods are widely employed both by the food industry and by academics. Jellinek (1985) provides the following definition:

> 'Sensory analysis of food relies upon evaluation by our senses (odour, taste, colour, tactile, temperature, pain, etc.). Only by applying exact scientific testing methods can reproducible results be obtained and analysed statistically.'

In development research there is increasing awareness that the power and acceptability of participatory and qualitative research methods can be enhanced through more thoughtful and systematic combination of qualitative and quantitative methods. Participatory approaches that focus on qualitative data collection do have many advantages, such as more reflection, judgement, and comparisons, which are considered adequate for practical purposes (Chambers 1994b). Researchers have gained excellent results with participatory reflection and action methods in obtaining insights, documentation and descriptions of a situation. Participatory approaches may use ranks or other techniques to get quantifiable results, and reasonable results have been obtained using ranking. Some researchers have high-lighted the limitations of ranking and recommend scoring systems for generating more useful data. A major issue here is that ranks do not include weighted values and thus need to be interpreted with care (see Chapter 9; Maxwell and Bart 1995).

Numerical data have the advantage that they can be easily analysed statistically, and demonstrate whether there are significant effects or differences between treatments. Statistical packages for data analysis have recently become more accessible for a greater number of people, including development researchers in developing countries. Other disciplines also make use of quantitative approaches to qualitative data, with further scope for development researchers to adopt some of these methods.

This chapter considers how the framework used in sensory evaluation may find applications in development research. First, an outline is given of the principles of sensory evaluation, and several popular sensory evaluation methods are described. Then three case studies are presented using sensory evaluation in development research. Finally, some ideas are discussed on how sensory evaluation methods could be applied in development research for aspects other than food evaluation.

Principles of sensory evaluation

Sensory evaluation methods are controlled methods giving results that can be statistically evaluated. The following points need to be taken into account.

- General principles for sampling should be applied, as valid con-clusions can be drawn only if the samples tested are representa-tive of their population.
- Most test methods compare two or more samples at once. To avoid bias, the order of sample presentation should be random and the presentation consistent. Samples should look identical. Codes should be used instead of alphabetic symbols for their identification.
- A sensory panel can be compared to an instrument that objec-tively measures sensory differences or classifies the quality of a product by using a well-defined scale. A controlled environment should be used, with a minimum of distractions.

- Setting up a panel is an important part of the sensory evaluation. The number of panellists required and whether they should be experts or (trained) assessors depends on the test method used. Other considerations are the cost and the amount and type of work to be carried out (e.g. whether short or long term).
- Training of panellists will improve precision and a certain level of accuracy and reliability can be reached. Training should focus on ensuring that all assessors understand the attributes and scales in the same way.
- Questionnaires should be easy to understand with minimal possibility of misinterpretation. Alternatively, an interviewer can ask the questions and show a choice of answers on flash cards.

Testing methods

Sensory methods can be roughly divided according to their goals. For questions that ask 'Is there a difference?', difference tests such as paired comparison, triangle, duo–trio or two out of five would be most suitable, while if the question is 'What is the difference?' or 'How big is the difference?', methods using scales and profiling are appropriate. If the question involves preference – 'Which is liked?' or 'Why is it liked?' – hedonic methods or preference tests would be most appropriate.

While the first two questions (establishing difference) are often answered using a panel (trained or expert), in preference tests it is important that the assessors are representative of the users of that product or target group, and must include a large number of groups (O'Mahony 1995). Table 7.1 (overleaf) presents an indication of the required number of assessors for several sensory evaluation methods.

Difference test: paired comparison

The most sensitive and most commonly used difference test is the paired comparison test. This is a test in which samples are presented in pairs for comparison and detection of differences on the basis of defined criteria. The test determines whether there is a difference and, if so, the direction of the difference (or similarly to determine if there is a preference). The two samples in each pair may be the same or different. The assessor is asked specific, relevant question(s) referring to the difference, and to the direction of difference or preference. Within this there are two strategies: either a forced choice in which assessors must indicate which sample they find more intense or prefer even if they cannot find a difference; or to allow for no preference. Additionally, assessors can be asked how confident they are in their choice.[2]

Tests using scales and categories

Quantification of sensory data on the basis of the perceived intensity of attributes requires the use of some form of scaling procedure. Most

Table 7.1 *Recommended number of assessors for sensory methods*

Test method	Experts	Trained assessors	Untrained assessors	Consumers
Paired comparison	7	20	30	100+
Triangle	5	15	25	
Duo–trio			20	
Two out of five		10		
'A' not 'A'		20	30	
Classification	3	3		
Rating	1	5	20	50 (two samples) 100 (≥three samples)
Ranking	2	5	10	100+
Profiling (QDA)	5	5		

Source: Tomlins (2000)

detailed analysis and interpretation of sensory characteristics requires the intensities to be given a numerical value on a scale which can take the form of ranking, classification, rating, scoring or grading. Before starting the test it is important to ensure that the assessors understand and agree on the attributes or criteria to be evaluated, and have the same understanding of the ends of the scale (calibration).

Ranking

Ranking in sensory evaluation is a test where a series of three or more samples is presented to an assessor at the same time. These are to be arranged in order of intensity, degree or preference. The ranking method is rapid and suitable for the assessment of small numbers of samples (approximately six) in flavour and quality evaluations, and for a larger number of samples (approximately 20) for appearance evaluations. The recommended numbers of assessors are: two or more experts; five or more trained assessors; ten or more assessors; 100 or more consumers. Each assessor examines the coded samples in a prescribed order and assigns a preliminary ranking. This ranking can be checked and adjusted by re-examination of the samples. The assessor records the finding on a score sheet.[3] The method has a wide range of applications, and is already often used in development research.

Classification

Classification is a test in which samples are assigned to predetermined categories or classes. The classification to be applied should be clearly

---

Box 7.1 *Consumer preference testing in Tanzania using rating*

As part of a Department for International Development (DFID) project on 'Commercialization of cassava to increase incomes', the consumer acceptability of newly developed products of cassava – made using cassava-chipping equipment – was compared with traditional cassava products for making *ugali* (porridge), *udaga* (fermented cassava product) and *makopa* (dried cassava product). During group discussions it was found out that most consumers eat *ugali* as a mixture of maize and cassava. The tests were conducted in three villages in three districts, with a total number of 150 consumers. These villages were selected on the basis that a surplus of cassava was produced, which would be a requirement of commercialization. Different mixtures were tested, including *udaga*, *makopa*, and chips of sweet and bitter cassava varieties which were processed using a manual chipper. The product to test, *ugali*, was prepared by local women using a standard method agreed by the participants. The important sensory characteristics identified by the women were appearance, colour, smell, texture, flavour/taste and stickiness.

A team of four villagers were trained to help conducting the tests. They would ask the questions and mark the forms. This was necessary as some villagers would only speak their tribal language and had had either no or minimal education. The consumers were presented with three randomly ordered samples at a time, each randomly selected from the possible mixtures and served in traditional orange bowls. Consumers were asked how much they liked a particular attribute of the product, which was translated into scores: 1 = very poor; 2 = poor; 3 = normal; 4 = good; 5 = very good. The taste tests took place at a central location at the villages on market day.

The research included a number of adaptations from the standard application of rating techniques:

- assessments were written out by trained villagers who conducted the trials
- there was no use of booths or of a sensory evaluation area, but consistency in environment was created by using school benches
- the samples were tested without a sauce first and then with a sauce. This was done because Tanzanians would never eat their *ugali* without a sauce. For sensory evaluation purposes, however, the sauce might distract the taster from testing the quality of the product. Therefore adding sauce at a later stage was a useful compromise.

The analysis showed that the new cassava product was as acceptable as the traditional product, even though it was stickier and the smell was not rated as highly (probably due to differences in the fermentation process). Its appearance and colour in particular were highly rated.

See Figure 7.1 (overleaf)

---

defined and understood. Each assessor examines the samples and assigns them to one of the predetermined categories.[4] The recommended number of assessors is three or more experts or trained assessors, but this approach is less suitable to conduct with consumers.

Figure 7.1 *Summary of findings of consumer ugali taste tests conducted in one of three villages (Nyarutembo, Biharamulo)*

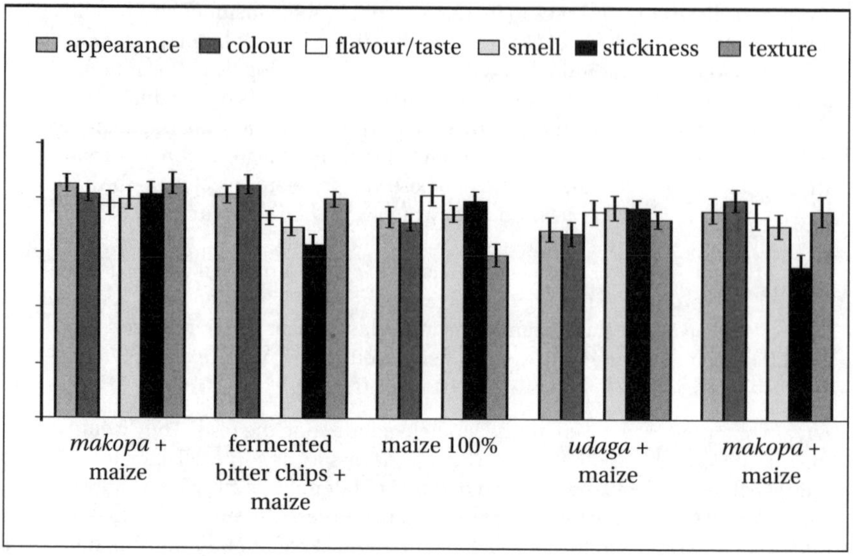

Rating

Rating is a method of classification involving categories (Box 7.1). Each category is composed of an ordered scale, with no assumption made concerning the size of the difference between the numbers. Rating can be used for evaluating the intensity of one or more attributes or the degree of preference. The recommended numbers of assessors are: one or more experts; five or more trained assessors; 20 or more assessors; 50 or more consumers (two samples); 100 or more consumers (three or more samples). If numbers are assigned, it should not be assumed that they are scores. For rating on a discrete scale with a small number of points, the results for one sample may be treated as for the classification. When the data set is large, frequency distributions are recommended.

Scoring

Scoring is a form of rating using a numerical scale. The numbers used in scoring form an interval or ratio scale (the different scores have a defined and mathematical relationship to each other). Scoring is used for evaluating the intensity of one or more attributes. The recommended numbers of assessors are: one or more experts, five or more trained assessors; 20 or more assessors. Box 7.2 gives an example of how scoring can be used in development research. The assessor assigns to each sample a value according to a predetermined scale (descriptive, line, etc.). Figure 7.2 presents a sample of a currently often used line scale, measuring 6 inches, with anchors at 0.5 inches at the ends (Stone and Sidel 1998).[5]

Box 7.2   *Using a semi-trained panel to monitor changes in the estimated market value of sweet potatoes in Tanzania by scoring*

In a component of the DFID-funded research project 'Sweet potato to generate incomes', the potential for fresh storage of sweet potato was assessed. A model using a semi-expert trained panel was applied to monitor changes in the estimated market value of sweet potato during a storage trial. The quality of the roots was assessed at zero, two, four and eight weeks of storage. Twenty randomly selected roots were taken from each store and displayed as two heaps. This is similar to the way traders display roots at urban markets. As a reference, there was a central point with several heaps consisting of roots bought at the town market. The heaps were labelled with the prices.

Ten panellists (staff at the Lake Zone Agricultural Research and Development Institute) were trained to make an assessment of the heaps and estimate the market value with reference to the standard roots. The heaps were weighted and labelled with a number and a letter.

This methodology included a number of adaptations:

- Instead of tasting food samples, the semi-trained panellists were asked to give scores only based on appearance, in the same way consumers assess the product in the marketplace. Because the assessment was simple, 20 heaps could be assessed at a time.
- The method of display was chosen to resemble the display at the market, and it was emphasized to the panel leader that it would be important to do this in exactly the same way every time. Therefore the assessment was always at the same place, using the same materials and labels.

During storage, the value of the sweet-potato roots decreased substantially (see Figure 7.3 overleaf). The greatest decrease was observed for damaged roots. Also, it appeared that the cultivars differed in their storability. While the cultivar Sinia B initially scored lower in estimated value, at the end of storage it scored higher than the other cultivars. The results demonstrated that selecting for undamaged roots is more important than cultivar.

The use of a semi-expert panel is a rapid approach for estimating the market value of stored sweet-potato roots, particularly if the station is some distance from the urban markets. By using trained panellists on-station, costs of driving to markets with samples are saved.

Figure 7.2   *Example of a line scale, six inches in length, anchored at 0.5 inches at the side, forming the ideal length for line scales*

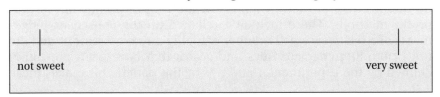

not sweet   very sweet

Figure 7.3 *Estimated market value of sweet potato in relation to storage time, cultivar and damage treatment*

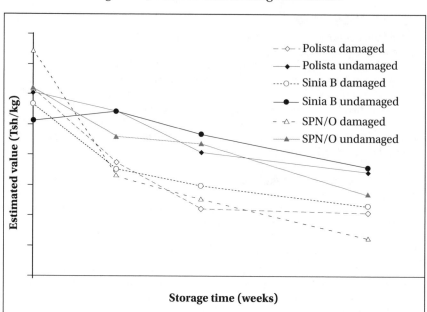

Sensory profiling

Sensory profiling methods use scales, and are the most sophisticated techniques available to the sensory analyst. Profiling aims to produce a comprehensive description of the appearance, flavour and textural characteristics of a product and to quantify the intensity of each. Hence sensory profiling techniques are often referred to as descriptive analysis techniques.

Several descriptive methods have been described, the main ones being the flavour profile method; texture profile method; quantitative descriptive analysis; and free choice profiling. The same basic principles apply to each of method: (i) verbalization of perceptions; and (ii) definition of vocabulary used to describe the perceptions.

The subjects are trained to measure this intensity with a certain level of accuracy and reliability; their assessment should be independent of like or dislike tendencies. All the descriptive techniques (except for free choice profiling) assume individual assessors have the same meaning for a descriptive term and associate with it the same perception.

The quantitative descriptive analysis technique was developed to overcome some of the restrictions of the texture profile and flavour profile methods. These include a reliance on the consensus judgements of a relatively small number of highly trained assessors, and the use of product characteristics and scales that have been previously defined by the experimenter and not by the panel. This makes these

> **Box 7.3** *Quantitative analysis of rice in Ghana using semi-trained taste panels to represent consumers*
>
> Parboiled rice produced by small-scale rural producers in Ghana is of variable quality. This study aimed to correlate sensory profile attributes used by a semi-trained panel with consumer acceptability of raw and parboiled rice. This would assist research seeking to improve the quality. The sensory panel comprised ten panellists who assessed samples in triplicate. At each of three locations in Ghana, 100 consumers sequentially scored the acceptability of six rice samples using a line scale. Consumers preferred imported parboiled rice to that produced locally. Profiling by the semi-training panel using staff at the Food Research Institute in Ghana showed that the rice samples had different profiles (see Figure 7.4 overleaf). Sensory attributes for both uncooked and cooked rice correlated strongly with consumer acceptability (see Figure 7.5 overlead). A disadvantage of using qualitative methods is that large numbers of people have to be interviewed. The use of the semi-trained panel can be used to estimate consumer acceptability rapidly, saving in cost and time, particularly in method development where, for example, the parboiling processing is being modified.

techniques expensive and time-consuming to carry out. Additionally, the flavour profile and texture profile methods are restricted to a specific group of sensory characteristics and therefore ignore the interactive effects of sensory characteristics.

Quantitative descriptive analysis has been used as an aid in product development and matching, in the maintenance or improvement of an established product, as a diagnostic tool when a product is losing its accustomed share of the market, and as a quality control measure.[6] An example of how profiling is used in development is presented in Box 7.3.

Applying sensory evaluation methods to development research

With the background of increased importance for development researchers to demonstrate the impact of our work, sensory evaluation techniques, among other techniques in other disciplines, form a framework for gathering quantitative information on issues that are qualitative in nature. We have shown through some examples how sensory evaluation techniques have been used in development research in Africa. In all three cases, the approaches were successful in that they answered the questions asked. It should be noted that two of the three case studies applied the techniques to assessing foodstuffs, while in the second case study (Box 7.2) a semi-trained panel was used to estimate market value.

We believe the principles of sensory evaluation techniques, which can help us understand the complexity of sensual experiences associated with food, can also be used to describe, analyse and understand a broad scope of development issues including, for example, situation analysis (access to markets, services or new technologies); poverty assessment; and (*ex ante* and *ex post*) impact assessment. All these

Figure 7.4 *Spider chart for most- and least-preferred rice by a*
semi-trained panel in Ghana

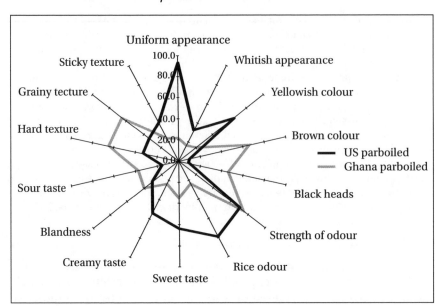

examples are as, or more, abstract than using our senses to test food. But just like the parboiled rice in the third case study (Box 7.3), each of the issues may consist of characteristics that bring quantitative and qualitative judgements together. To determine and quantify these factors, a similar approach to that described for quantitative descriptive analysis can be used.

In a current research project into the adoption of cassava-chipping equipment, for example, the baseline research indicated that the adoption of such technologies would contribute to developing the commercial potential of cassava (Van Oirschot et al. 2002). As with a piece of food that contains different dimensions of its appearance, aroma, taste and texture, people's livelihoods may contain dimensions of social, human, natural and economic issues. How can we determine what these livelihood dimensions consist of? And can we quantify them? The profiling method can be used for this, through the following steps.

- Screening and selecting of panellists: among people who have already adopted or evaluated the equipment, they need to be selected on the basis of gender, age, user of equipment, stakeholder in the marketing chain, etc.
- Developing a descriptive language ('dimensions') by panel discussion: the panellist group will identify what effects new technologies have on their livelihoods. For the cassava chipper these may include aspects of cost, water use, space, drudgery, neighbours' opinions, personal injury, marketing of the product and income. This process is in fact a form of training.

Figure 7.5   *Correlation between consumer acceptability and sweet*
taste scored by a semi-trained panel

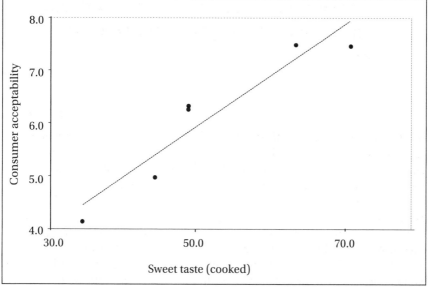

- Preparation of questionnaires or scoring sheets using the dimensions above. Line scales can be used for scoring – these are a powerful tool because they are visual and thus understandable for a large range of people. They also give quantitative data, allowing various methods of statistical analysis.
- The actual evaluation: panellists score or rate the dimensions above. For example, how much did the new technology change family income? How much did drudgery for women change after the new technology was adopted? It must be clear what the ends of the line scale mean.
- Quantified data can be taken: if line scales are used, the distances can be measured. Statistical analysis (ANOVA and multivariate methods) can be applied and data presented, usually in the form of a spider diagram such as Figure 7.4 that summarizes the data and makes relationships clear.

There are certainly many advantages to this approach. The use of line scales for scoring, in particular, is a method that is rapid and easy for people to understand regardless of educational attainment, although care is required as to the choice of line scale.[7] The scores enable analysts to quantify factors and prioritize them. Simple graphical approaches such as spider diagrams and scatter plots may assist in helping researchers interpret the results. Principal components analysis and cluster analysis may help to summarize relationships in the multivariate data. Their application could be particularly useful in areas where the adoption or impact of development programmes is assessed. Note the importance of taking baseline information if the research aim is to investigate change.

As with all research approaches, however, there are trade-offs. The use of profiling techniques in development could mean that some of the principles and rules originally applied in sensory evaluation may not apply. Note that, unlike sensory testing where the food product is in front of the panellist, scoring in development research may be by recall and has to refer to experiences that occurred maybe several days or weeks ago. This may affect how the data are distributed, which may limit the choice of analysis possible.

The sensory approach requires careful thought regarding the type of questions that can be asked; and screening, selecting and training of panellists takes time. In some ways this may be more restrictive than the typically less-structured or standardized participatory research approaches. The advantage, however, from a social statistician's perspective, is that hypotheses can be tested and detailed analyses are made possible.

Conclusions

Sensory evaluation methodology applied to measuring human perception can be a useful tool in development studies. The techniques offer a range of possibilities for translating qualitative information into numerical data. Their application is particularly useful where an answer can be given on a scale enabling a numerical value to be assigned. This allows detailed analysis and a hypothesis to be tested, which could be particularly useful in areas where adoption or impact of development programmes is assessed.

The use of semi-trained and trained panels can reduce research costs significantly and give reliable data that have been shown to correlate with consumer data. These methods can also be used in participatory research, in combination with existing frequently used participatory methods that generate numbers.[8]

Chapter Eight
Strong fences make good neighbours: survey and participatory appraisal methods in poverty assessment and poverty reduction strategy monitoring

SIMON APPLETON and DAVID BOOTH

Summary

This chapter revisits the argument for a combination of surveys and participatory appraisal methods in poverty assessment, taking into account the new challenge posed by the monitoring of national poverty reduction strategy papers (PRSPs). The two methodological traditions have different comparative advantages and corresponding limitations. The case for a combined approach rests on this complementarity. It follows that the potential for linking them in a productive way is greatest where participatory poverty assessments (PPAs) do not pretend to dispute surveys on their own terrain, and retain (along with the vocation to echo grassroots voices) as much as possible of the original rationale of rapid rural appraisal – exploratory, open-ended, holistic, sceptical and self-critical. This has not always been sufficiently recognized. As funds and ambitions for poverty reduction strategy monitoring systems increase, it becomes even more important to steer surveys and PPAs into the kinds of things they each do best.

Introduction

A decade after PPAs began to be used to supplement findings from national household surveys, the question of how best to combine the two types of method is well-trodden ground. So much has been written on the subject that it is not obvious there is any value in adding more. This chapter nonetheless does so, with two concerns in mind. One is that, in recent experience, the actual practice of poverty-monitoring efforts has not always lived up to the principles set out in typical methodological guidelines. The other relates to the rise of PRSPs as the central focus for national monitoring efforts, with the increased funding opportunities and raised expectations that this implies. The use of PPAs and surveys in poverty reduction strategy (PRS) monitoring seems to us to create both expanded possibilities for the deployment of an appropriate combination of methods, and new opportunities for getting it wrong.[1]

One of the earliest surveys of the subject, Carvalho and White (1997), provided a useful list of the strengths and weaknesses of survey-based and participatory approaches to poverty monitoring. In the first section of this chapter we revisit that treatment of the topic, underlining some points that seem to warrant greater emphasis in the light of more recent debate and practical experience.

In their 1997 paper, Carvalho and White also provided a helpful menu of ways of combining survey and participatory methods. This is a subject that has been worked intensively since the late 1990s, and we do not have space to go deeply into the question. However, it does seem worthwhile chasing one particular hare that Carvalho and White, and others writing at that time, may have helped to set running. In the following section we suggest that there is an inconsistency between arguing that methods have complementary strengths and advocating a form of integration that uses the results from one to validate or invalidate the results from the other.

We think it is worth picking up this issue because, in a country we are both familiar with (Uganda), a mistake of this kind came close to doing significant harm. Although corrected in time, there was a moment when it seemed to endanger the gains that had been made in embedding both the survey and the PPA in the national policy process. We also have a more general and forward-looking point. The level of ambition attached to both poverty-monitoring surveys and PPAs is increasing by leaps and bounds on account of the high priority given to monitoring in PRSP processes. This implies new possibilities, but also new dangers. It is important that, whether or not their contributions are closely coordinated, the two traditions should take on the parts of the monitoring task that they do best. This is the argument of the final section in the chapter.

Strengths and weaknesses revisited

Carvalho and White's (1997) overview of the strengths and weaknesses of the two traditions is presented in Box 8.1. We do not have any substantial disagreements with this summary. However, a few nuances and supplementary points seem important, particularly in the light of subsequent experience.

Survey-based approaches: strengths

A main strength of surveys is that they typically use statistical sampling in order to be able to make inferences about a general population, within margins of error that can be specified. This allows findings to be generalized, which is essential for monitoring aggregate outcomes over time – for example, average incomes or consumption, or the incidence of consumption-poverty. It also enables comparison of the findings of a particular survey with those from another, and with other data sources.[2]

Carvalho and White (1997) rightly stress the advantage of survey-based approaches in aggregation. However, survey data are also useful for permitting systematic disaggregation of results. For instance, simple cross-tabulations that answer the question 'Who are the poor in terms of household consumption?' are easily generated. This makes it

---

Box 8.1   *Strengths and weaknesses of survey-based and participatory approaches*

Survey-based approaches

Strengths:
* making aggregation possible
* providing results whose reliability is measurable
* allowing simulation of effects of different policy options

Weaknesses:
* sampling and non-sampling errors
* missing what is not easily quantifiable
* failure to capture intra-household dynamics

Participatory approaches

Strengths:
* richer definition of poverty
* more insight into causal processes
* accuracy and depth of information

Weaknesses:
* lack of generalizability
* difficulties in verifying information

Source: Calvalho and White (1997); section III, 'Strengths and weaknesses of the quantitative and qualitative approaches'.

---

possible to provide a simple statistical profile of poverty in a country – the basic element in the usual approach to a national poverty assessment. It is also straightforward to measure changes in the living standards of particular subgroups of households – the poor, those in the northern rural areas, those engaged in coffee farming, etc.

Surveys aim at standardization. Although, like everything else, this can be done well or badly, the questionnaires adopted in surveys are designed to obtain a common set of information; to fix and make transparent the nature of the interview; and to avoid possible bias arising from interviewer–interviewee interaction. Enumerators are trained and supervised rigorously to ensure consistent use of questionnaires. It is this standardization of data collection, along with representative sampling, that gives the survey approach its other advantages.

The verifiability of household survey results is also an advantage. With simple presentation of numerical results, it is straightforward to establish if the survey results support the summary of findings and conclusions derived from them. In addition, there is an increasing tendency for data to be available to other users, making the cross-checking of numerical results possible.[3]

Verifiability is not the same as not making mistakes. The findings of the household surveys about changes in consumption over time are not definitive and may be subject to considerable error. Economic data are subject to a degree of measurement error that often seems surprisingly high to non-specialists. Comparisons between surveys in some developing countries – for example, Tanzania – have often yielded dubious results, probably attributable to changes in either sampling or questionnaire design. By comparison, the wave of household surveys in Uganda since 1992 appears to have been successful in maintaining comparability, partly by keeping the sections of the questionnaire covering household consumption almost identical.[4]

It is important to use any opportunities to triangulate the results from surveys with data from other sources. This is difficult for precisely the reason that household consumption surveys are so important for monitoring economic welfare – there are few alternative sources of information about living standards. The most direct comparison is with the estimates of consumption included in the national accounts.

Survey-based approaches: some well-known pitfalls

The surveys used for monitoring poverty tend towards a behaviourist approach. That is, they limit themselves to enquiring about specific behaviours or factual matters, rather than general perceptions or attitudes. For example, rather than asking whether respondents think poverty or food availability in general has got worse, they inquire in detail about the household's own food consumption in the past few days.

Although household surveys often have a behaviourist bias, it is important to note that surveys do not observe behaviour, but at best record what respondents report about their behaviour. On some sensitive topics, more intensive research methods may be required to obtain accurate information. For example, it is argued that the National Sample Survey in India systematically under-reports the prevalence of tenancy relative to what is known from ethnographic research (Herring 2003). This is an example of what survey practitioners call 'non-sampling error.'

Under-reporting of income is widely acknowledged. Typically, income is under-reported relative to expenditure. This is perhaps because it is harder for respondents to reply 'strategically' when questioned about a myriad of small purchases, and partly because there may be less sensitivity to such mundane questions. This is one of the reasons why poverty monitoring surveys typically focus on consumption, not income, as the measure of living standards. These debates – about attitudes versus behaviour, and more direct and indirect ways of getting at the truth about behaviour – are important for survey practitioners. They are also relevant to alternative, participatory approaches.

Survey-based approaches are subject to a number of other limitations. Most important is that surveys are typically closed in form, meaning that they will not gather information that was not explicitly inquired about. An effective survey thus requires prior familiarity with the issues under investigation and the location(s) being studied. Where the survey is large-scale, covering many communities, it is perhaps inevitable that it will miss idiosyncratic but possibly important features of those communities.

Survey-based approaches are probably more suited to collecting data that are relatively simple or easy to quantify, and less suited to gathering information that is highly nuanced or covers intangibles. For example, school-based surveys may be useful for establishing whether girls performed less well in educational examinations, or whether private schools performed less well than state schools.[5] However, they may fail fully to identify the variations in parental attitudes or school ethos that explain differences in exam performance.

It is often stated that survey-based approaches to poverty analysis fail to capture intra-household issues adequately. This is a serious point. To a degree, the weakness is inherent in the use of consumption or income as welfare measures, rather than being a limitation of surveys in general, as – to a greater or lesser degree – consumption is shared and income pooled within a household. It is possible within the normal survey design to measure some consumption that is either personal or specific to a particular demographic group (e.g. women's clothes), but these often account for only a small part of overall economic welfare.[6]

Participatory approaches: some important distinctions

Not all quantitative approaches are survey-based, and not all qualitative approaches are participatory. We are concentrating on the survey-based subtype of quantitative methods. Censuses, administrative records and management information systems are examples that are clearly on the quantitative side, but do not employ sample-survey methods.

A comparable distinction needs to be made on the side of qualitative methods. The methods used in PPAs are derived from rapid-appraisal methods originally developed for project design in rural communities. Over the years, this tradition has been enriched with ideas about partic-ipation as a source of empowerment. The contemporary methodology now widely known as participatory reflection and action (PRA) is a blend of principles and techniques from these different sources. The PRA methods typically employed in PPAs are a subclass of rapid-appraisal methods, which are in turn a subclass of methods that conduct intensive local case studies using purposive samples.[7]

Strengths and weaknesses of qualitative methods in general

The strengths of participatory methods derive to a substantial extent from the case-study approach that they share with anthropological field studies and other non-survey methods of social science research. The generic advantages of such methods include:

- ability to focus closely and in depth on a case that has a number of features that are of interest from an analytical point of view, and has been selected for that reason
- possibility of being holistic – looking at a set of relationships as whole, not just a pre-selected set of attributes

- scope for paying attention – to a greater or lesser extent – to processes as well as 'snapshots' of situations
- ability to return immediately to interrogate data (with further interviews or more observations) in order to get to the bottom of a puzzling issue
- wide range of resources available for triangulation (or systematic cross-checking) by applying or reapplying different research techniques to the case.

The scope for studying process and triangulation of findings in a qualitative fieldwork context varies with the amount of time and resources that can be devoted to the case study. It may be argued that the type of case study that can be done in rapid-appraisal mode (participatory or not) is limited in both respects. The time available for the study is typically very short by anthropological standards, which means there is less scope for observation generally, and observation of processes that are extended in time in particular. Results do rely more heavily, therefore, on testimony, with the difficulties discussed above in connection with surveys.

On the other hand, the rapid rural appraisal/PRA tradition has devoted considerable ingenuity to developing a toolkit of techniques and principles for obtaining maximum results, while satisfying reasonable standards of validity and reliability, with limited resources. Opportunities for checking out the 'stories' on which inferences about process generally have to be based are provided in principle by intensive triangulation. First-time observers of PRA sessions, including seasoned anthropologists, are often impressed by the power of the techniques to generate a rich field of information in a short time.

As a result, an argument can be made that these methods provide a solid instrument for reaching an understanding of key relationships and processes. When fully applied, the principle of triangulation provides a guarantee on the robustness of findings and interpretations that is no less than that claimed for a well conducted household survey (given the different purposes of the two types of investigation). This was the case made by Chambers (1992) and others in defence of the original prospectus of PRA. Whether participatory techniques are really like this in practice is, of course, another matter.

The most obvious type of weakness of the case-study method in general is that it does not permit generalization, at least not in the ordinary sense. Sampling is undertaken 'purposively', not with a view to reaching conclusions that can be generalized to a wider population. The case-study method is not suitable, either, for providing definitive tests of hypotheses that apply to such wider populations. Case studies are typically undertaken to investigate particular puzzles that are not able to be solved on the basis of statistically representative data. Case studies often play an important role in the social sciences by generating new hypotheses or ways of conceptualizing issues that may be worth testing.

In a more practical or policy setting, a series of case studies may agree in identifying a particular problem as important – for example, child malnutrition arising from unequal gender relations within households; or unanticipated consequences of particular ways of earmarking public funds. Such findings are not generalizable, and cautious language has to be used in reporting them, taking into account the kind of purposive selection principle that has been used. The case study fulfils its proper function by drawing attention to the issues as worthy of further attention, in the form of either research or policy action. The general significance of case-study findings arises from this sort of logic, and not from the logic of statistical representativeness.

No systematic disaggregation of the sort that surveys permit is possible. Participatory poverty assessment tools usually centre on group exercises. Such groups work best when they are socially homogeneous. Each exercise is supposed to be applied to several different groups for purposes of triangulation. In practice, however, time constraints quite often lead to a situation where each technique is applied with only one group in each community. Thus, for example, matrix scoring of time trends indicates only what one group of participants regard as changes affecting their village in aggregate. Even when different groups are used (most commonly men and women separately; or better off and less well off), the procedures are not sufficiently standardized to permit results to be aggregated and compared.

Lastly, participatory and qualitative methods lack the quality of simple verifiability noted in connection with surveys. Summary reports from PPA exercises are difficult for outsiders to verify by tracing the conclusions back to the evidence. The process of analytical induction that leads from site reports to synthesis reports can, in principle, be undertaken in reverse, as McGee (2000) did for the first Uganda PPA. Efforts can be made to standardize participatory site reports in order to make this somewhat easier. But verification exercises of this sort are likely to remain time-consuming and tedious. As much of the underlying data provided by PPAs are not numerical, it is also harder to release them in a raw state.

Strengths and weaknesses of participatory methods in particular

The argument for using participatory methods, especially in the context of a PPA, does not rest entirely on the promise of better or different information. Producing information about poverty is a worthy objective. But a major problem in most countries, especially poor ones, is that available information is not used to a significant extent for policy-improvement purposes. Public officials lack strong performance incentives, and so do not have reasons to search out information. Participatory poverty assessments were introduced partly to address this problem. They drew on the experience that even quite demotivated and hard-headed officials can be powerfully swayed by well-articulated voices and other evidence from grassroots communities (Booth et al. 1998; Norton et al. 2001; Brock and McGee 2002; Robb 2002). In summary, PPAs are processes designed to influence policy, not merely data-collection exercises, and this feature of their purpose sets them apart from household survey instruments.[8]

The fact that PPAs set out to influence policy raises some genuine difficulties from the point of view of maintaining appropriate quality standards. This is not a simple issue, and it is important not to treat it simply. It is common for survey practitioners, especially those influenced strongly by the positivist tradition in social science, to be inordinately concerned about the apparent lack of guarantees of objectivity in the approach of PPAs. Because the method requires the observer to engage closely with the subject s/he is investigating, the worry is that investigator bias may fatally influence the findings.

This touches on an important issue. However, it is best discussed without too much recourse to the oversimplified and in many ways inappropriate language of 'objectivity' and 'bias'. As self-conscious survey practitioners – and researchers in the physical sciences – are aware, the mechanisms that are effective in the real world in ensuring reasonably robust results from scientific research are not primarily based on scientists being distant from and dispassionate about what they are doing. It is more complicated than that.

Putting a certain distance between the researcher and the object of research may serve certain specific purposes, as in our discussion of standardization in surveys. However, in a broader perspective scientific guarantees have relatively little to do with objectivity in this sense. They have much more to do with the 'intersubjective' relationships within a community of researchers – that is, with peer-review processes of different kinds in which errors are picked up, interpretations are questioned, and researchers' interests in arriving at particular conclusions are compensated by the different interests of other researchers.

This does not dispose of the problem. In recent decades, anthropologists have become increasingly preoccupied with the 'observer bias' problem (without necessarily calling it that). In anthropological training a stronger emphasis is now placed on what is called 'reflexivity' – a self-conscious awareness of the relationships on which the fieldwork experience is based. All findings are heavily qualified and placed in context as the result of an interaction between the researcher and his/her subject.

Participatory reflection and action is in some ways better placed, and in other ways less well equipped, to address this problem. As it is typically undertaken by a team, rather than by a single individual, there is more scope in PRA for one investigator's perceptions to be checked against those of others. The process of information generation and joint analysis in PRA focus groups is observed by trained facilitators, a process described by Chambers (1997: 159–60) as 'observable mutual checking'. In the best cases, practitioners are both critical and self-critical throughout the fieldwork process, and field reports include an evaluation of the process through which conclusions have been reached. There are also many examples of practice that falls short of this standard.

Participatory reflection and action is typically more exposed than anthropological fieldwork to the problems discussed above in connection with the handling of attitudes and reported behaviour. The pitfalls have been further increased by the recent tendency to emphasize the opinion poll role of PPAs – that is capturing 'voices of the poor', as opposed to trying to understand the situations poor people face. The fact that certain lines of questioning may elicit strategic responses is certainly as much a concern for PPAs as it is for surveys. Anthropologists are generally in the field long enough to learn about what people do, not just what they say, with the further advantage that reported actions can be checked by observation. Time constraints and other factors make the challenges greater for the PRA practitioner.

That having been said, fieldworkers are in principle always trained to be sensitive to the way testimony may be influenced by people's expectations and strategic calculations, as well as to other relevant factors (power dynamics within the group, effects of poor facilitation, etc.). Triangulation – a luxury that the survey enumerator does not enjoy – can and should provide controls on errors arising from these sources. Also, contrary to the impression that may be given by the way PPA findings are being disseminated ('voices of the poor'; 'the poor say x about y'), PRA field techniques are generally designed to achieve what behaviourist surveys do – to concentrate attention on specific points of information and not on mere opinions. The worry is not that PRA techniques are inferior in principle, but that in practice they are not always well applied. There is abundant evidence to justify this concern, at least in the context of the routine use of PRA as a project management tool (Brown et al. 2002).

In short, the PPA method has its own crop of practical issues (broadly analogous to substandard interviewing; poor cleaning of survey data; and the difference between good and bad questionnaire design). They are not deficiencies that are inherent in the particular method. On the other hand, it is important to be realistic about the probability that cost and other constraints will interact with other pressures on PPA managers to make them both widespread and difficult to root out. We return to the policy implications of this observation at the end of this chapter.

The value of combined methods

Bourguignon (2003) likens the value of combined methods in poverty assessment to the advantage of seeing a mountain from two perspectives. By considering various perspectives, one can obtain a fuller understanding of a multidimensional subject. The analogy is a good one. It is consistent with the view we want to put forward on good and not-so-good ways of attempting to combine survey and PPA approaches. The overview of this topic provided by Carvalho and White (1997) is summarized in Box 8.2.

The complementarities between survey and PPA methods are of different kinds. One kind hinges on the relationship between induction and deduction. Another is about collecting different kinds of information about poverty. Carvalho and White start from a similar conception, but we think their classification of ways of combining quantitative and qualitative methods can be improved upon. This is taken in two steps. First, we deal with a set of issues that embraces their first type, 'methodological integration', and elements of their second type, 'examining, explaining, enriching'. Then we take issue with their treatment of 'confirming or refuting'. (Integration in respect of sampling is a topic of some interest but we do not pursue it here for reasons of space.)

Using one method to inform the agenda of another

We have noted that participatory methods are more suited to exploratory research – being much more likely to uncover facts that the researcher had not anticipated. Survey-based methods are more useful for establishing or refuting simple general propositions – for example, that consumption poverty fell over time; that girls in Uganda underperform in examinations etc. They may also be used for sophisticated statistical analysis, testing models that quantify the contribution of various factors to observed outcomes – for example, the contribution of improved coffee prices to poverty reduction in Uganda (Deininger and Okidi 2003).

In UK elections and elsewhere, focus groups designed to be representative of voters (or sometimes subsets of voters, such as swing voters) are commonly used by politicians and commentators to ascertain the concerns and opinions of voters. Marketing agencies use similar techniques to discern products or advertising campaigns that would appeal to their potential customers. The results of such exercises are not used to make statistical inferences about a population, but can subsequently be subject to such testing using follow-up surveys. The fact that some insights from participatory work can be subsequently tested for generalizability using other methods means that it is not essential that the sample used in the participatory work is representative.

Examples of methodological integration of this type are not as common as might be expected in the field of poverty analysis, possibly for institutional reasons.[9] In Uganda, the welfare indicators of the National Household Survey were revised on the basis of PPA findings.[10] In the 2001 Uganda workshop, we argued that the agenda for future household surveys could probably benefit from further study of the results of the (first) PPA. Food availability, risk and alcohol abuse had been identified as important issues for poor people in the first PPA. Some of these issues – notably food availability – could be studied using existing surveys. Also, an effort had already been made to cover aspects of risk in the Uganda National Household Survey, but more work could have been done on that, particularly by extending the panel aspect of the surveys. Alcohol abuse was one issue that would be hard to study through

---

Box 8.2   *Approaches to combining survey-based and participatory methods*

Carvalho and White (1997) distinguish three major ways of combining quantitative and qualitative methods in the measurement and analysis of poverty.

1. Integrating the methodologies

- using survey data to construct purposive samples for PPAs
- using survey findings in constructing the interview guide for the PPA
- using participatory research results to determine appropriate stratification of samples for surveys
- using results of qualitative work in preparing survey questionnaires
- pre-testing new questionnaires as part of a PPA exercise
- using participatory research findings to refine the poverty indices used in survey analysis.

2. Examining, explaining, confirming, refuting and/or enriching information from one approach with that from the other

- 'examining' refers to using data from one tradition to enrich the research agenda of the other
- 'explaining' entails the use of participatory research to identify dynamics responsible for survey findings
- 'confirming or refuting' entails the use of participatory research to ascertain the validity of survey-based findings (or vice versa)
- 'enriching' entails the use of participatory research to obtain information and understanding about variables and processes not covered by surveys.

3. Merging the findings into one set of policy recommendations

This refers to the kind of joint reporting of results that was a feature of certain World Bank country poverty assessments in the 1990s.

Source: Carvalho and White (1997); section IV, 'Combining the quantitative and qualitative approaches in poverty measurement and analysis'

---

surveys, but other types of qualitative enquiry might be worth undertaking. Lastly, piloting new survey instruments in the context of a PPA exercise might yield insights that could allow the instruments to be refined before use in subsequent surveys.

A further suggestion in the Uganda discussion was that participatory research could usefully be directed at shedding light on how exactly consumption poverty fell between 1992 and 2000. This would require some refocusing of attention from the standard PPA concerns with people's existing or worsening problems, and onto their achievements and areas of progress. It would be consistent with our general suggestion that the comparative advantage of PPA instruments lies in probing the 'why' questions rather than the 'what' and 'how much' questions. Understanding what some people have done to raise their material standard of living might be useful in learning what the Government of Uganda could do to assist these efforts, and to enable others who have done less well.

A rounded understanding of poverty is unquestionably more likely if both types of method are used. In Uganda and elsewhere, PPAs have played an important part in getting recognition for the different dimensions of deprivation that matter to poor people. Participants in PPAs seldom report problems solely in terms of lack of income or consumption, instead drawing attention to a wide variety of dimensions of well-being. For that reason and others (such as the philosophical arguments associated with Amartya Sen), PPA results deserve to be taken seriously by those analysing survey results. Participatory poverty assessment findings have provided a useful counterweight to the policy biases that might otherwise have been produced by the superior measurability and comparability of consumption poverty, and the tendency of policy makers to be impressed by numbers. In the terminology of Carvalho and White, participatory work can be said to have 'enriched' the discussion of poverty trends by drawing attention to aspects of poverty and well-being that are not captured by consumption-poverty indicators.

The ability to draw attention to potentially neglected poverty dimensions does not, however, suggest that PPA methods are well suited to monitoring poverty, either mono- or multidimensionally – that is, measuring changes through time. Some dimensions emphasized in PPA reports, such as insecurity, may be very difficult to measure by any method. Deprivation of basic human capabilities will be best measured by surveys other than household consumption surveys, in which case the function of the PPA is to draw attention to the need for a range of survey resources for monitoring.[11] The suggestion that PPAs raise but do not solve the challenge of monitoring poverty trends is taken up as the next step in our argument.

Confirming and refuting

Carvalho and White (1997) identify 'confirming or refuting' as one way in which survey and participatory methods can be combined. They thereby imply that there are substantial possibilities for using surveys and PPAs to provide a check on the reliability and validity of each other's results. They are not alone in suggesting this. It was implied by other discussions of the same vintage (e.g. Booth et al. 1998) which rested the case for combined methods partly on the opportunities for triangulation between survey and PPA results.

The notion of triangulation between PPAs and surveys is not entirely misconceived, but it is open to misunderstanding. We do not think that there is substantial scope for directly comparing PPA and survey results in such a manner that they validate or invalidate each other. In Bourguignon's metaphor, both methods are ways of looking at the same mountain, but they are looking at different features, using methods that are not comparable. Therefore encouraging PPAs to develop a greater capacity to engage directly with survey results on their terrain does not do PPAs a good service.

As we have argued, participatory methods share with other case-study approaches the ability to investigate issues in an exploratory and holistic manner. When done well, this is useful for uncovering factors that were not anticipated, and in general for interrogating evidence in an open-ended way. On the other hand, even when they are done very well, participatory exercises are not well placed to confirm or refute findings from surveys. This is because the participatory method lacks the standardization which is the precondition for valid aggregation.

Trying to deal with this by introducing a greater standardization of technique into PPAs has superficial attractions. However, it is a mistake to think this is easily done and cost-free. Two examples may be given.

The first is the effort made in some early PPAs to use PRA wealth-ranking techniques to provide cross-checks on poverty-line analyses using survey data. In both the Kenya and the Tanzania PPAs instigated by the World Bank in the mid-1990s, PRA wealth rankings from sample communities were aggregated and juxtaposed with national estimates of poverty incidence from the survey, with the argument that their similarity confirmed the robustness of the results. This argument does not stand up to close inspection. There is no reason to suppose that a wealth ranking conducted at one moment in one community is comparable – in the sense that the procedure followed is 'the same' – with one carried out in another, even with the same subculture and facing similar agroeconomic conditions, at the same time. Comparing results at different times, or under contrasting social conditions, would be even less appropriate. Therefore adding up the results and comparing them with a poverty-line analysis based on an entirely different procedure is logically flawed. Wealth ranking is a means of facilitating the analysis of local stratification systems. Treating it as cut-price poverty-line analysis does not work and is a disservice to the real value of the technique.

This is not to say that information generated by wealth-ranking field exercises cannot be used to generate standardized observations that can be validly compared and aggregated. An impact assessment of the Targeted Inputs Programme (TIP)[12] in Malawi provides an example (Chinsinga et al. 2002; Levy 2003). The study used easily differentiated categories of household food-security status[13] as a proxy for poverty (food security having been identified as a key indicator of poverty in earlier participatory poverty research). Using a procedure similar to that used in wealth ranking, a small group of key informants in the sampled villages mapped their community – generating a 100 per cent sample in each site – and next used local knowledge to assign each household to a food-security status. This was then compared with data on whether they had received a TIP pack. The research found that, across the sampled villages, one-fifth of TIP recipient households were food secure.

The lesson here is that, as well as providing an instrument for in-depth understanding of local systems, wealth ranking can contribute to more standardized analysis. The vital ingredient is clarity in the research design about where local perception ends and standardized categorization begins.

The same principles apply to other PRA field instruments that have been useful for generating pictures of local trends and fluctuations – time lines, decade matrices, seasonal calendars, etc. People's perceptions of improvement and deterioration are not themselves reliable as indicators of actual changes. But perceptions are also not easily standardized, which means that aggregate conclusions about them are likely to prove perilous.

The techniques are designed in several cases to elicit specific numerical information, not just opinions. Nevertheless, their primary purpose is to permit exploration of the relationships between different changes identified at the local level (for example, between the land base of the community and out-migration). The idea is to direct attention to the processes that may underlie the more obvious changes, and help to explain them (for example, inheritance patterns and land fragmentation). It is often illuminating to reproduce the numerical results from counting, scoring and ranking exercises in PPA site reports. However, when it comes synthesizing these results at a higher level, the numbers need to be handled with extreme care. As in the Malawi case above, qualitative data can be standardized and quantified, but this needs to be done in quite a deliberate way and is least likely to apply to purely attitudinal data, including perceptions of changes in well-being.

Uganda's experience with its first national PPA did not manage to avoid confusion on some of these points. The PPA took place in 1998–9, after poverty trends from 1992–8 had been assessed using five household surveys. This sequence seemed to imply that the PPA would be well placed to confirm/refute the findings of the first five household surveys, while the survey planned for the year 2000 could be used to confirm/refute the PPA. The survey evidence for 1992–8 suggested large increases in real household consumption and substantial poverty reduction, a trend later confirmed by the 2000 data (Appleton 2001). An early report on the key findings from the PPA nonetheless concluded that – contrary to the survey results – poverty trends were adverse: 'In all communities consulted in all districts, the poor were perceived as getting poorer and the rich as getting richer' (Uganda, Republic of, 1999: 4).

This apparent disconnection between the findings on poverty trends of the Household Survey and the PPA was considered by several analysts (McClean 1999; McGee 2000). Fortunately, however, all reference to it was removed from the section on poverty trends in the PPA final report (Uganda, Republic of, 2000: 29). The section is instructive because – apart from one reference to a sense of improvement in the 1990s – it makes little attempt to establish a single aggregative conclusion about poverty trends. Instead, it limits itself to reporting trends in certain problem areas (such as food security or disease), as perceived in certain districts.

This modesty – of which we approve – illustrates the difficulty in aggregation using participatory methods. To make a single aggregative conclusion about poverty trends, aggregation would be required in at least two dimensions: across problem areas (dimensions of welfare); and across participants. By contrast, the survey-based approach simplifies matters by focusing on household consumption as the sole welfare measure (aggregating goods and services using their prices) and aggregating across individuals using a particular poverty statistic.

In the Uganda case, a potential dispute around conflicting evidence on poverty trends did not materialize, which avoided possible damage to the reputations of both types of data collection among policy makers. However, our thesis that the two methodological traditions do different things well and should be encouraged to specialize, not compete on the same terrain, is strengthened by this example.

PPAs, surveys and the challenges of PRSP monitoring

The new place of PRSPs in the policy processes of poor countries makes a difference to the above argument in two ways. First, the focus on PRSPs and their implementation brings with it renewed interest in, and hence increased funding for, the monitoring of poverty-reduction efforts and their outcomes. This is an opportunity that should be used wisely. Second, PRSP monitoring poses a whole set of new challenges. One is the challenge of setting up institutional arrangements in which monitoring information has a real chance of influencing policy and its implementation for the better. Another is ensuring that all the various levels of monitoring – from inputs to final poverty outcomes (impacts) – are adequately covered, taking into account what we know about the limitations of monitoring systems in developing countries (Booth and Lucas 2002).

Increased availability of funding, for both surveys and participatory assessments, poses dangers of inappropriate ambition. Household surveys may be pressed to adopt sample sizes and frequencies that have no technical justification. Participatory poverty assessments may become more elaborate and comprehensive, feeding the tendency to compete with surveys and further weakening the attributes of rapid-appraisal work on which its claims to rigour depend. There are already signs of both of these tendencies in some countries.

This is a great pity, not only because of the direct waste of resources that it implies, but also for another reason. Monitoring PRSPs is a broader activity than monitoring poverty outcomes. If poverty out-comes are to be improved, there needs to be effective feedback on the implementation processes and improvements in intermediate results that have been agreed in the PRSP policy process. There needs to be accessible, well communicated and robust information on whether the ambitions expressed in PRSPs and sector strategies are on the way to being realized, and on what is going right, what is going wrong and why. Although poverty outcomes do still need to be monitored, it is in some ways more important to obtain good feedback on the intermediate processes. This level of monitoring is the most useful for making timely corrections to policies and implementation arrangements, and for holding individuals and organizations responsible for their actions or inaction.

In this context it makes even more sense for surveys and PPAs to specialize in the things they do best. On the survey side, there are new opportunities for using more intensively the parts of interview schedules that give clues on matters such as use of government services. There is also likely to be a new demand for different kinds of tailor-made service-delivery surveys, which may usefully be accompanied by focus-group work assisted with PRA techniques, as in the examples cited above. Not least, PRSP monitoring should be seen as an invitation to participatory appraisal to build more consistently on the strengths of case-study methods, by becoming more focused on understanding policy processes on the ground, identifying implementation bottlenecks, and proactively investigating opportunities for change that may have been overlooked.

Participatory poverty assessments have already shown that they can do this. As well as exploring in a holistic fashion the factors and causal stories behind local situations of poverty, PPA exercises in several countries have proven adept at identifying and documenting the ways things have gone wrong in the implementation of a poverty-reduction strategy.[14] In these countries, at least, it would not take a major reorientation to apply PPA working methods more systematically to the assessment of specific policy initiatives or efforts to improve facilities or services in particular areas. The critical question in designing a PPA would, in this perspective, become whether there is something new that is worth monitoring. Participatory poverty assessments with this sort of orientation could be either sectorally focused (for example on health or crop marketing), or multisectoral.

In short, the idea that PPAs have to focus on everything that is relevant to poverty, and need to do so in a regular three-, four- or five-year cycle, does not seem appropriate any longer. The moment has surely come to turn PPA into a tool of critical policy research, with a stronger focus on more upstream issues in the causation and reduction of poverty. To the extent that new resources are available, these should be devoted to making PPAs not bigger or more frequent, but more targeted, as well as fit for their specific purpose – exploratory, analytical, sceptical, reflexive and self-critical.

Conclusions

This chapter reconsiders some well-known, but still underappreciated, points about the respective strengths and weaknesses of survey-based and participatory methods for poverty assessment. We argue that survey-based approaches are suited to monitoring outcomes in terms of readily quantifiable indicators such as household income and consumption, food availability or anthropometric status. On the other hand, participatory methods share with other qualitative approaches the ability to investigate issues in an exploratory and holistic manner. This is useful for uncovering factors that were not anticipated and, in general, for interrogating evidence in an open-ended way. The rigour of survey methods hinges on standardization, whereas that of participatory assessment depends fundamentally on internal triangulation and self-awareness among a team of investigator/facilitators. The latter applies even when (perhaps particularly when) there is an effort to handle some of the resulting data in a standardized way. In both traditions adequate time and good training are essential.

Properly understood, monitoring surveys and PPAs are highly complementary. There is a correspondingly strong argument that surveys and PPAs can enrich and/or explain each other's findings. But the thesis that they can confirm or refute each other, or provide a simple form of triangulation, is flawed. This formulation underestimates the degree to which the two methods do different things and generate findings that are not comparable. Examples have been given of instances where results were directly compared and, in one of these, significant damage to the reputability of poverty data from both traditions was narrowly avoided.

Finally, the new importance of PRSPs and their monitoring has been shown to add force to the argument in two ways. First, PPAs have played a useful role in highlighting the dimensions and proximate causes of extreme deprivation; but they have also shown that they can help in uncovering key institutional blockages and other policy weaknesses that affect poor people. The needs of PRSP monitoring will be met best if both surveys and participatory appraisals pay increased attention to this latter type of task, which means becoming more focused and specialized. Second, PRSPs have made available greater resources for poverty assessment and analysis. The new resources should be dedicated to improving quality in both traditions, not to a scale of operations that has no technical rationale.

Part III
The process of combination: democratizing research, empowerment and institutional change

Introduction
Combined research as process

In this final part we examine the use of methods that are firmly within the process of conducting development. The use of more powerful combinations of methods, and the adoption of more dynamic and explanatory analytical frameworks, are sited in a policy process in which the generation of knowledge from micro- to macro-levels, and the implementation of policy from the macro- back to the micro-level, is messy, mediated and power-infused.

Brinkerhoff and Crosby (2002) describe three generations in the evolution of policy prescription, beginning with economic models (from the 1950s through the period of structural adjustment reforms) that sought 'first best' solutions to socio-economic welfare, moving through a second-generation emphasis on institutions and political economy, with a focus on the role and capacity of the state, to third-generation approaches that see policies as dynamic processes: 'dynamic combinations of purposes, rules, actions, resources, incentives and behaviors leading to outcomes that can only imperfectly be predicted or controlled' (Brinkerhoff and Crosby 2002: 5).

A further aspiration that has emerged in recent years has been the democratization of knowledge generation through challenging the institutional exclusion of 'them' – the researched, the beneficiaries, the primary stakeholders – from development research and its outcomes. The objective of drawing a wider range of civil society actors into research processes that feed into policy chimes with the current 'good governance' agenda of political pluralism. It also fits with the increasing interest in participation in 'policy spaces' (Cornwall and Gaventa 2001; Cornwall 2002; McGee 2002) as a way of contesting, debating and improving policy reform. These policy spaces themselves, however, are politicized and politicizing, with dominant actors resisting democratizing knowledge-based debate in order to maintain their own political and ideological agendas.

These new process approaches to development and to the management of development are increasing opportunities for institutional engagement and change through research, with more and more people participating in new forms of empowering research. Empowerment, in this sense, describes a process of increasing the capacity of individuals or groups to make choices and to transform those into desired actions and outcomes (Kabeer 2000). This power transforms asset-based agency of individuals or collectives ('power within' as self-esteem and 'power to' as choice) into transforming choices ('power over') with respect to the opportunity structure in which individuals and groups are situated (Nelson and Wright 1997: 8–11). The opportunity structure comprises formal and informal institutions (social rules) that determine the allocation of resources to individuals and groups, and that legitimize and project some voices while discrediting and silencing others (Sen 1992). Where possible, local analysis should be sufficiently participatory to enable local people to map, measure and analyse their institutions, thus opening up the possibility of empowerment through institutional transformation.

Contributions

The contributions to Part III address these issues of process, politics and institutional change. Nigel Gilbert (Chapter 10) maps a 'third way' in development research which uses powerful computational models that allow new constellations of stakeholders to engage in strategic thinking on policy options. Neil Price and Kirstan Hawkins (Chapter 11) outline an innovative approach to research relating to health-seeking and sexual behaviour: peer ethnography in which peer researchers are able to explore social realities with members of their social networks and, by so doing, reverse power relations and challenge the assumptions and premises of development programmes. Andrew Dougill and Mark Reed (Chapter 12) reflect on a participatory process of developing indicators for sustainable natural resource management, and demonstrate how these data can empower communities to challenge received bio-geographical wisdom. Andrea Lampis's critique (Chapter 13) of the widespread adoption of highly technical and depoliticizing management tools, such as the logical framework, is linked to the promotion of 'open-system' tools such as the temporal logic model, in which the political and technical dimensions of project evaluation are more clearly articulated. Through case-study observations from natural resource research projects in Africa and Latin America, Kathrin Schreckenberg and colleagues (Chapter 14) emphasize the process trade-offs in management time and resources required for bridging disciplinary and methodological gaps (through joint research design, reciprocal training and frequent joint reviews) necessary for researching the interactions of people and their environment. Gordon Crawford (Chapter 15) argues that participatory methods and approaches should be employed in the evaluation of democracy assistance efforts; by so doing, he argues, the process of evaluation itself becomes a tool for democratization. Describing the design of a social policy information system in Jamaica, Jeremy Holland and colleagues (Chapter 16) show how a change in the nature and pace of information flows and a realignment of policy actors from the macro- to the micro-level can create institutional change for improved policy execution. Finally, Tanja Bastia and colleagues (Chapter 17) review a research capacity-building initiative conducted with partners in developing countries and those in transition. They observe that, at the interface of producers and users of policy-relevant information, there is a necessary trade-off between a methodological ideal and the messy reality of a policy process in which actors are not neutral to methods, data and analysis.

Chapter Nine
Quality, quantity and the third way

NIGEL GILBERT

Summary

Social scientists have struggled for the past 50 years with positioning themselves within a series of apparently crucial contrasts: positivism versus realism; quantitative versus qualitative data; etic versus emic analyses; critical versus participatory research design, and so on. While it is quite fun, and occasionally revealing, to debate the merits of these polarities, in the real world of social research there are more important issues, and more options than is sometimes noticed. This chapter reviews these dichotomies and points out that for most of them, there is a third way: methodological choices that the traditional distinctions recognize barely, if at all. The remainder of the chapter describes in more detail one such third way that is neither straightforwardly quantitative nor qualitative: the use of computational models to represent social theories and empirical data. Such models are beginning to be used both to explore abstract 'artificial societies', and to develop strategic games that can be played by policy-makers to explore policy options through interacting with other stakeholders and researchers in virtual worlds.

Conventional beginnings

Ravi Kanbur, in his contribution to a 2001 conference on quantitative and qualitative methods at Cornell University, cites Carvalho and White (1997) in defining the qualitative and quantitative distinction as follows:

> 'The quantitative approach to poverty measurement and analysis is defined here as one that typically uses random sample surveys and structured interviews to collect data - mainly, quantifiable data - and analyzes it using statistical techniques. By contrast, the qualitative approach is defined as one that typically uses purposive sampling and semi-structured or interactive interviews to collect data - mainly, data relating to people's judgments, attitudes, preferences, priorities, and/or perceptions about a subject - and analyzes it through sociological or anthropological research techniques.' (Kanbur 2001c:19).

This definition makes the important point that the qualitative/ quantitative distinction is not only about differentiating types of data, but also about approaches to analysis. One could imagine quantitative ways of dealing with qualitative data (for example, various psychometric scaling techniques) and vice versa. What is important in the debate is not whether the data are in the form of numbers or sentences, but the assumptions that underlie their analyses: the epistemological and ontological bases.

However, it can be too easy to construct some dichotomies and then place oneself at one extreme or other of the spectrum. In this chapter, I suggest that the most worthwhile and exciting way forward is to pursue an approach that does not fit neatly into any of the common dichotomies: it is both quantitative and qualitative, capable of being used in analytical as well as participatory contexts, and essentially process-oriented in a way that is still rare in both quantitative and qualitative research.

Representative samples

The main argument in favour of quantitative methods has always been that they allow one to make general statements backed by data from representative samples. They allow us to use sampling theory, not to guarantee representativeness but to quantify the probability that the sample is seriously unrepresentative. Qualitative methods, it is suggested, rarely if ever use statistical sampling techniques, and so one can never be sure that the sample is not misleadingly biased.

What is sacrificed by obtaining a representative sample is the context of the respondents. Samples are necessarily picked out at random from a population. This means that the interconnections between members are ignored. The result is a sample of people who can be treated only in isolation from their social context, in particular their social networks. One can ask John about his friends and family, but it is impossible within a random sample to ensure those friends and family are also in the sample and that data from them can be obtained. The result is that, unless the researcher is very astute, s/he is forced into a mode of analysis that treats people as atomized individuals. It is then possible to make reliable statements about aggregates, for example the percentage of people in poverty, but this almost misses the point of social science, which is to analyse social formations and institutions. We need to be able to examine phenomena located at the macro-level (the level of societies or organizations); at the micro- or individual level, and the interaction between these levels.

Using a qualitative approach, it is somewhat easier to follow social networks to obtain an understanding of a group or setting, rather than the aggregation of individual data typical of quantitative methods. However, here the problem is that the need for intensive, detailed data collection tends to require the analysis to be particularistic, and more about understanding the specific informants and their complex social situation than about typical settings and people. There is often little basis for establishing generalizations and for testing them within a deductive framework.

As several speakers at the Cornell University conference (Kanbur 2001b) observed, qualitative methods therefore usually have much less credibility with decision-makers, who look askance at the number of respondents and believe that large sample surveys are the only way to generate persuasive evidence. The response often proposed is to use some combination of qualitative and quantitative methods. For example, carry out an ethnographic study and use this to inform the design of questions in a large quantitative survey, or carry out a survey and then use qualitative methods to examine the circumstances of the 'outlier' respondents. This mixed strategy has many advantages, but there still remain some incompatibilities about the methods of analysis. Quantitative data will be analysed with statistical methods, which have almost no points of connection with the much less formal methods typically used for analysis of qualitative data.

Participatory methods

The qualitative/quantitative divide is also often aligned with a divide about political strategy, contrasting participatory with non-participatory methods. Quantitative researchers tend to focus on changing policy as their priority, and therefore their analyses are directed at decision-makers as their primary audience. Qualitative researchers are often more concerned with empowering their informants, and want to speak more directly to the people (although they too are not averse to influencing policy-makers). The different audiences are recognized to have different needs and usually different educational backgrounds, and so the ways in which research results are presented will differ greatly. But in my view this is also a misleading dichotomy.

The real question is where the power lies to set the research agenda. On the one hand, it can lie with the researchers themselves, who are able to define the research question, choose a research method and, in due course, publish the results wherever and however they please (often in the academic literature). This is the traditional model of academic research that is infrequently found in its pure form nowadays, at least in the social sciences. On the other hand, various other participants in the research process may have the upper hand in research decisions. Sometimes it is the funders, sometimes the actors who are being researched. Sometimes the other parties are closely involved at all stages of the research, with the researchers acting merely as operatives for a research agenda entirely defined elsewhere. Sometimes it is a genuine partnership. Sometimes the researchers voluntarily accede control over the research, for example for ethical reasons when they believe that the respondents have moral rights to defining the research questions; at other times researchers may do the bidding of funders because they are the paymasters, or disseminate the research findings in special ways to the respondents in exchange for access. In short, there is a parameter space in which the researchers controlling the whole process are a point in one corner, with other points in the space representing the influence of outside stakeholders controlling various aspects of the research.

In reality, the issue is still more complicated because the stakeholders may differ in the extent to which they are motivated to participate in the research process. A common situation is where the permission of some person is needed in order to get access to research data, but that person is not motivated to make a decision to grant access. Also common is the situation where a stakeholder who one thinks should be interested in the outcomes of research is in fact not so, and the research report is filed, rather than read and acted upon. Ideally, research methods need to consider explicitly the relative power and motivation of all stakeholders and should include techniques for dealing with these.

Induction and deduction

The third and final contrast is the dichotomy between deductive and inductive research strategies. Quantitative research is often associated with deduction, where one has a theory and tests it against data. Qualitative methods are often based on induction, where the data are used to generate theories. Like the others mentioned above, this dichotomy is also misleading. In practice researchers usually move from deduction to induction and back again during the course of research. The research design might aim to test a theory, but if the preliminary analyses show that the theory does not fit the data well (deduction), the data may be used to improve the theory (induction), the improved theory tested on some more data (deduction), and so on.

We hear more about the merits of qualitative and quantitative approaches and how they may be integrated elsewhere in this book. In the remainder of this chapter, I describe a third approach which is neither qualitative nor quantitative: social simulation.

A third way

Most social science research either develops or uses some kind of theory or model: for instance a theory of fertility, or a model of the class system. Generally such theories are stated in discursive English, although sometimes the theory is represented as an equation (for example in econometrics). In the 1990s, researchers began to explore the possibilities of expressing theories as computer programs. The advantage is that social processes can then be simulated in the computer, and in some circumstances it is even possible to carry out 'experiments' on artificial social systems that would otherwise be quite impossible (Epstein and Axtell 1996).

Although the simulation of social dynamics has a long history in the social sciences, the advent of much more powerful computers, more powerful computer languages, and the greater availability of data have led to increased interest in simulation as a method for developing and testing social theories (for a review see Gilbert 1999).

The logic underlying the methodology of simulation is not much different from that underlying statistical modelling (Gilbert and

Troitzsch 1999). In both cases a model is constructed (for example, in the form of a computer program or a regression equation) through a process of abstraction from what are theorized to be the actually existing social processes. The model is then used to generate expected values, which are compared with empirical data. The main difference between statistical modelling and simulation is that the simulation model can itself be 'run' to produce output, while a statistical model requires a statistical analysis program to generate expected values.

This means that social simulation is amenable to a deductive strategy in which one formulates a theory, transforms it into a computer program, runs the program, observes the output, and compares the output with data that have been collected from the 'real world'. But it is also possible to operate inductively, adapting and improving the model in the light of observations. Moreover, depending on the type of model, the data can either be quantitative (for example, the percentages of agents in various classes), or qualitative, with the agents given qualitative attributes. For instance, different agents may be programmed to use different rules of behaviour.

Some benefits of simulation

Paradoxically, one of the main advantages of simulation is that it is hard to do. To create a useful simulation model, its theoretical presuppositions need to have been thought through with great clarity. Every relationship to be modelled has to be specified exactly and every parameter has to be given a value, otherwise it will be impossible to run the simulation. This discipline means that it is impossible to be vague about what is being assumed. It also means that the model is potentially open to inspection by other researchers in all its detail. These benefits of clarity and precision also have disadvantages, however. Simulations of complex social processes involve the estimation of many parameters, and adequate data for making the estimates can be difficult to come by.

Another benefit of simulation is that it can, in some circumstances, give insights into the 'emergence' of macro-level phenomena from micro-level action. For instance, a simulation of interacting individuals may reveal clear patterns of influence when examined on a societal scale. A simulation by Nowak and Latané (1993), for example, shows how simple rules about the way in which one individual influences another's attitudes can yield results about attitude change at the level of a society; and a simulation by Axelrod (1995) demonstrates how patterns of political domination can arise from a few rules followed by simulated nation states.

Agent-based simulation

The field of social simulation has come to be dominated by an approach called agent-based simulation (or multi-agent simulation). Although other types of simulation, such as those based on system dynamics models (using sets of difference equations) and micro-simulation (based on the simulated ageing of a survey sample to learn about its characteristics in the future), are still undertaken, most simulation research now uses agents.

Agents are computer programs (or parts of programs) that are designed to act relatively autonomously within a simulated environment. An agent can represent an individual or an organization, according to what is being modelled. Agents are generally programmed to be able to 'perceive' and 'react' to their situation, to pursue the goals they are given, and to interact with other agents, for example by sending them messages. Agents are generally created using an object-oriented programming language and are constructed using collections of condition–action rules. The agent examines its rules to identify those whose conditions hold true in its current situation and then executes ('fires') the actions determined by just those rules. The effect of firing the rules will normally be to alter the agent's situation, and thus in the next cycle a different set of rules will fire.

Agent-based models have been used to investigate the bases of leadership, the functions of norms, the implications of environmental change on organizations, the effects of land-use planning constraints on populations, the evolution of language, and many other topics.[1] While most agent-based simulations have been created to model real social phenomena, it is also possible to model situations that could not exist in our world, in order to understand whether there are universal constraints on the possibility of social life (for example, can societies function if their members are entirely self-interested and rational?). These are at one end of a spectrum of simulations, ranging from those of entirely imaginary societies to those that aim to reproduce specific settings in great detail.

An interesting variant on agent-based modelling is to include people in place of some or all of the computational agents. This transforms the model into a type of multiplayer computer game, which can be valuable for allowing the players to learn more about the dynamics of some social setting (for example, business students can be given a game of this type in order to learn about the effects of business strategies). Such games are known as participatory simulations. The author has been developing such a simulation to help with making long-term strategic decisions to manage the city of Zurich's water supply (Hare et al. 2001; Gilbert et al. 2002), while others have developed games to help farmers in rural Senegal coordinate their agriculture (Barreteau et al. 2001). There are many other opportunities of a similar nature.

Conclusions

Although computer simulation can be regarded as simply another method for representing models of social processes, it encourages a theoretical perspective which emphasizes emergence, the search for simple regularities that give rise to complex phenomena, and an evolutionary view of the development of societies. This perspective has con-nections with complexity theory, an attempt to locate general principles applying to all systems that show autonomous behaviour – including not only human societies, but also biological and physical phenomena.

I began by suggesting that there are three contrasts that are often used to compare qualitative and quantitative approaches: the general-izability or context-specificity of the findings; the principal audience for the results; and whether the research adopted an inductive or deductive framework. I proposed that these contrasts are more com-plex to apply to research practice than they seem. I also suggested that for all three there is a third way, and hinted that computer modelling is a prime example of an approach that does not fit neatly into these con-ventional dichotomies. Now that I have illustrated the main features of social simulation, we can return to the three dichotomies and consider whether computer modelling should be regarded as a quantitative or a qualitative strategy, or perhaps both.

It should be clear that computer modelling can be based on quanti-tative data (as, for example, the work using microsimulation). But computer models can also be used as a formalism for expressing and working through the implications of the process-oriented, detailed and context-specific findings typically generated by qualitative research. Multi-agent models can, and often will, include a variety of agents with different attributes whose behaviour is determined by different rule sets. The level of detail required to design such agents is often available only from qualitative research, and the conclusions drawn from such models about emergent phenomena are often more similar in style to the findings expected of qualitative than quantitative work.

Computer models can be used for policy analysis, and this is the approach to modelling that is most commonly found in the literature. But as we have seen, simulations can also be an ingredient in partici-patory research, where the aim is to work with informants and stake-holders to help them understand the implications of their actions and to explore their options in possible future worlds.

Finally, computer modelling offers an opportunity additional to the classic pair of induction or deduction. Axelrod (1997) notes that:

> 'Like deduction, (simulation) starts with a set of explicit assumptions. But unlike deduction, it does not prove theorems. Instead, a simulation generates data that can be analysed inductively. But unlike typical induction, however, the simulated data comes from a rigorously specified set of rules, rather than direct measurement of the real world. While induction can be used to find patterns in data, and deduction can be used to find consequences of assumptions, simulation modelling can be used as an aid to intuition.'

So, truly, computer simulation is a third way of doing social science. It remains to be determined whether it is more enduring than its political namesake.

Chapter Ten
The peer ethnographic method for health research: methodological and theoretical reflections

NEIL PRICE and KIRSTAN HAWKINS[1]

Summary

Positivist and empiricist research methods, such as the questionnaire-based sample survey and the focus group discussion, continue to dominate social and health policy research. In relation to health-seeking and sexual behaviour, such methods have limited ability to inform about the process of behaviour change and the contexts within which different behaviours occur. This chapter outlines the principles of a new methodology, known as peer ethnography, and presents case-study material to illustrate how the method has to be adapted to meet local context and specific research needs, and how development institutions and/or programmes can be significantly influenced by using peer ethnography. One outcome of the data collection and analysis process in peer ethnography is the ensuing dialogue between the peer researchers and the programme, and between peer researchers and members of their social networks. The research process provides a basis from which peer researchers are able to challenge assumptions and premises of development programmes, but the necessary shift in power relations to enable the views of the researchers to be heard by staff does not, of course, always ensue. In this respect, the method serves to highlight the often-disempowered situation of representatives of local communities, co-opted into development programmes. Introducing into policy-making and programme implementation a truly reflexive and participatory approach that engages with the complex contexts in which health, sexual and reproductive behaviour are experienced and negotiated requires fundamental changes in the operation of institutional power, as well as in the processes by which development decisions are made, resources allocated, and policies formulated.

Introduction

Positivist and empiricist research methods, notably the questionnaire-based sample survey and the focus group discussion, continue to dominate much social and health policy research (Calhoun 1995). In relation to reproductive and sexual behaviour, such methods have been shown to be limited in their ability to inform about the process of behaviour change and the contexts within which different behaviours occur (Warwick 1982; Greenhalgh 1990; Hammel 1990; Parker et al. 1991; Hauser 1993; Baum 1995; Lockwood 1995). This chapter outlines the principles of a new methodology, known as peer ethnography

(Hawkins and Price 2000; Price and Hawkins 2002), and presents three brief case studies to illustrate how the method has to be adapted to meet local context and specific research needs, and how institutions and/or projects can be significantly influenced by using the approach. It concludes with a reflection on peer ethnography which demonstrates that, despite its limitations, the method has the potential to make a significant contribution to our understanding of health-seeking and sexual behaviour by engaging with local narratives as a political process.

Methodological context

Descriptions of the shortcomings of dominant research methods allude to the need for an actor-centred research method that enables more rigorous engagement with the realities of the everyday lives of poor and marginalized people, and which recognizes that, far from being a static set of norms and expectations, culture is continually constructed and negotiated in social interactions and everyday practice (Lockwood 1995). Investigating actors' views of their social world has largely been the domain of the anthropologist, using ethnographic fieldwork and participant observation, over substantial periods of time, to reach below the surface of reported social norms, to observe concrete actions, and to collect the discourses and narratives of people as they go about their daily lives.

The recognition by development agencies and practitioners of the limitations of positivist research methods for generating valid and appropriate information on social behaviour, and of the time constraints in conducting in-depth ethnographic research, has led to increased interest in employing rapid assessment methods (for a review see Manderson and Aaby 1992). Participatory rural (or rapid) appraisal (PRA) methods, for instance, have been used effectively by development agencies to conduct community-based analyses from an actor-centred perspective. However, experience has shown that far from being rapid, the effective use of PRA tools often requires an initial extensive input of time and resources to build relations of trust and to generate an understanding of local social contexts. Without this initial understanding of community dynamics, PRA may unknowingly favour the discourses of the powerful and elite, and promote the production of a consensus view and normative discourse (Mosse 1994: 508 ff).

Methodologies such as case study and social network analysis are increasingly being advocated for researching sexual and health behaviour (Hammel 1990; Smith 1993; Lockwood 1995; Eyre 1997; Trussler et al. 2000). The peer ethnographic approach builds on some of these methodological advances, and provides a potential approach for engaging marginalized and excluded groups in active and critical dialogue with development programmes. The method is based on gathering actors' discourses and accounts of everyday practice, while situating the accounts in social contexts in which relations of power, difference and inequality are continually negotiated. People say what they say not as a result of abstract theorizing, but as a result of their experience in concrete social, economic and political situations (Calhoun 1995). In this sense, engaging with local narratives must also be a critical and political process.

The peer ethnographic method

The peer ethnographic method is derived from the participant-observation approach characteristic of anthropology fieldwork, which emphasizes the need for trust and rapport between the researcher and the researched. The peer ethnographic method has been designed to be carried out by 'peer researchers', who are already recognized members of the community.[2] The peer researchers conduct in-depth and unstructured interviews with individuals selected by them from their own social networks. The peer researchers, in effect, become key informants by virtue of their recognized status as community members and their local knowledge (Manderson and Aaby 1992: 842). Rather than a large sample of people being interviewed once only, a series of in-depth interviews are conducted with a small sample of individuals, selected from the same social network, on the basis that data produced by intensive exploration of a few cases produce a more thorough understanding of social life than the superficial exploration of many cases (Hammel 1990: 471).

As the peer researchers have an established relationship of trust with the people they are interviewing, the fieldwork does not require the time for rapport-building typified by conventional anthropological ethnography or some PRA exercises. The approach also recognizes that social networks are not made up of consensus groups, but include relationships of conflict and distrust. The aim of the interviews is not to collect social 'facts' through individual accounts of personal experience, but to elicit the meanings that actors attribute to the social behaviour of their peers. All interviews are conducted in the third person (interviewees are asked not to talk directly about themselves, but about 'other people like themselves') in an attempt to elicit narrative accounts of how interviewees conceptualize the social behaviour of 'others' in their networks, not accounts of their own behaviour, or normative statements about how they 'ought' to behave. Consequently, differing and conflicting perspectives emerge in the narratives.

The peer ethnographic method recognizes that it is not possible to observe the behaviour or to record the narratives of others without filtering the data through an analytical framework, involving some level of meta-analysis. The peer ethnographic method is therefore structured around several key analytical issues identified by the peer researchers as central concerns of their peer group. The frameworks developed in the three case studies below consist of a set of conversational interviews aimed at eliciting perceptions of *inter alia* social identity and social networks, health and illness, sexual knowledge and sexual behaviour, and access to and quality of health services.

Conversational prompts are developed for each interview, to assist the peer researchers to initiate conversations and to follow up on key issues. Some of the prompts cover the same issue through different ways of asking, in order to allow probing and changes in conversational context. The prompts are developed by the peer researchers in an initial participatory workshop, and are intended as guides to help frame their conversational interviews, rather than as interview scripts. During their training in peer method, the peer researchers refine and modify the prompts, so that they translate easily into appropriate local language and context. The peer researchers field-test different ways to raise the same issue with different interviewees, in recognition that the way something is talked about varies even within one social context, according to the age, gender and ethnicity of the interviewee. After field testing, the prompts are refined further, so that the tools the peer researchers finally take to the field are locally specific. The peer tool is thus dynamic and flexible, continually adapted and redesigned as part of the research process. Indeed, following field testing by the peer researchers, the final version of the interview framework is often quite different to the one initially designed.

The peer researchers do not record a detailed script of each conversation or produce vast quantities of authentic conversational narrative or qualitative research data. The data collection prompts are designed to assist researchers to record phrases and/or events given most importance by interviewees during the course of the conversation. The interviewee participates in the data-recording process through confirming that phrases and events recorded are the most important ones in their narratives and explanations. The peer researchers record findings from each interview on a sheet, and during data analysis these sheets are used to show how different themes emerge in different conversational contexts.

Data analysis is carried out on two levels. The first is at the level of meta-analysis, in which the peer researchers' narratives are drawn on as a primary source of ethnographic data. In-depth interviews are carried out with the peer researchers by an experienced social researcher, over a short period at the end of the data collection process. The peer researchers become the key informants to the social researcher, and the conversational narratives they have collected provide the data for an in-depth social analysis. During this process the social researcher necessarily filters these data through an analytical framework, the theoretical background to which is made explicit in the social analysis. The second level involves the peer researchers conducting their own data analysis through a participatory workshop, facilitated by the social researcher, during which the peer researchers work as a group to identify key issues emerging from the interviews, lessons learned, and any changes to the tools for further use in research and monitoring. At this level of analysis, the peer researchers bring their own perspectives and world views to bear on the interpretation of the interview narratives.

Box 10.1   *Zambia case study*

The objective of CARE International's Partnership for Adolescent Sexual and Reproductive Health (PALS) project was to improve the sexual and reproductive health of young people, through the establishment of youth-friendly counselling corners in government clinics, and deploying trained youth educators to lead discussions with young people in the community and to provide counselling in the youth-friendly corners.

Eight PALS youth educators, who were trained as peer researchers, undertook data collection for the peer research . The researchers were a mix of female and male, students, part-time waged workers, and unemployed. They represented a number of Zambian ethnic groups, and were drawn from a range of social backgrounds. Each peer researcher interviewed around four people, with a total of 30 young people interviewed. Each interviewee was interviewed five times using conversational prompts developed for themes covering social identity, health and illness, sexual behaviour, reproductive behaviour, and access to services. CARE programme staff supervised the peer researchers over a subsequent three-month data-collection period. The data collection was carried out in three compounds in Lusaka, each served by a government clinic with a youth-friendly corner. The compounds differed significantly in terms of wealth and infrastructure, but all were ethnically mixed. The data analysis and review process followed the generic peer ethnographic method outlined above, with Kirstan Hawkins undertaking the role of social researcher.

Lessons from the field

To date, the method has been used successfully in a number of settings. This section presents lessons from three such applications of the peer ethnographic approach, in Zambia, Nepal and Cambodia. In addition to presenting some of the key findings from the use of the approach, the case studies also illustrate how the methodology has to be adapted to meet local context and research needs.

Zambia: an adolescent sexual and reproductive health programme

The first application of the peer ethnographic method was a collaboration by the authors with CARE International in Zambia, working with their Partnership for Adolescent Sexual and Reproductive Health (PALS) project in Lusaka (Hawkins and Price 2000; Price and Hawkins 2002). The data produced by the peer method allowed the peer researchers and CARE to identify a number of key lessons for the PALS project. For instance, young women engaged in commercial sex and out-of-school youth were identified as social groups not being reached by youth-friendly services. New programme approaches to reach more vulnerable and marginalized groups were identified, including utilizing peer networks to reach young people at places where high-risk sexual activity takes place (bars, night clubs and minibus stops); community-based distribution of free condoms among peer networks; use of community drama to reach out-of-school youth with information; and increased advocacy on behalf of young people on access to quality drugs for sexually transmitted diseases (STDs). Key issues and lessons learned during data analysis were used to develop indicators for subsequent PALS monitoring. These indicators included access by commercial sex workers to condoms and services; young people's ability to negotiate condom use (and associated increased condom use); young women's awareness of and access to treatment for abortion complications; and access of the client group to effective STD treatment.

A number of key methodological lessons were learned from this first use of peer ethnography. First, the interview narratives provided rich data from which to build an understanding of young people's perceptions and experiences: the data generated from the 30 sets of peer interviews were able to confirm many of the findings of a participatory learning and action (PLA) study carried out with 10 000 young people as part of the PALS design, and also provided insights and information which had been missed by the PLA (such as experiences of coerced/violent sex, and the practice of newborn baby abandonment). The method produced a sufficient and manageable quantity of data for purposes of programme monitoring, which was easily processed by the peer researchers and project staff. Following training, the peer researchers required a minimal level of support to be able to carry out the interviews. Use of the method raised youth educators' interest in finding out more about sexual and reproductive health issues. It also emerged that the method can function as a programme development tool – enabling the project to identify new peer networks and social groups with which to work, as well as potential strategies for reaching different vulnerable groups. A year after the initial use of the method, CARE was forced to scale down the PALS project as external funding was withdrawn. The PALS youth educators, in response, formed a Youth Advisory Board, independent of CARE, which continued to use the peer ethnographic approach to assess the quality of information given out by the youth educators, to assess demand for the services offered by the educators, and to find out more about the accessibility of services.

Cambodia: a sex worker behaviour-change communication programme

The peer ethnographic method was adopted in 2002 by an international NGO, Population Services International Cambodia (PSI/C) to support the development of an HIV/AIDS behaviour-change communication strategy (for further details see PSI/Cambodia 2002).

All partners in the peer ethnographic research process – peer researchers, PSI/C, local community-based organizations and the consultant social researcher – confirmed that the method elicited information that would have been difficult to generate using conven-

Box 10.2   *Cambodia case study*

Population Services International Cambodia (PSI/C) has successfully supported and promoted behaviour change among brothel-based sex workers and their clients since the early 1990s. In recognition of the challenges it faced in reaching other vulnerable groups involved in sex work, PSI/C utilized peer ethnography with two main purposes: to research the nature and dynamics of transactional sexual behaviour (specifically the meanings attached by different social groups to different types of sexual relationships, and their impact on safe sexual practices); and to facilitate the establishment of local networks in support of behaviour-change communication.

In the process of identifying and selecting peer researchers, PSI/C built collaborative relationships with community-based organizations and local and international NGOs having existing links with the target groups: involving NGO partners in the recruitment and supervision of peer researchers was necessary and important to sustain the motivation of peer researchers during the data-collection process and to ensure that peer researchers had adequate social support on a day-to-day basis.

Twenty peer researchers were selected and trained, ten from each of two target groups central to the behaviour-change communication strategy: young women who work in bars and restaurants; and male university students. The first group is highly vulnerable to HIV infection, being part of a wider group collectively known within HIV/AIDS policy discourse in Cambodia as 'indirect sex workers': women who are engaged in regular transactional sex (as part of their work, usually in the leisure industry), but who do not identify themselves as 'sex workers'. Unlike direct sex workers, most of whom work in brothels, indirect sex workers have not benefited from Cambodia's 100 per cent condom-use policy implemented in many brothels. Some of the women were recruited for training as peer researchers with the assistance of a small local NGO which runs an existing community-based health programme working with this target group. This NGO played a key role in providing day-to-day support to the peer researchers, as well as assisting in the development of the behaviour-change communication strategy among the target group. The male university students represent clients of indirect sex workers (as well as direct sex workers). Throughout the data-collection process, PSI/C's own staff worked closely with and supervised these male peer researchers to provide support and motivation.

During their training as peer researchers, both groups identified the research themes under which they would carry out in-depth interviews among their peers. The waitresses and bar girls identified work, sexual relationships and HIV/condom use; the students identified sexual relationships and HIV/condom use. Conversational prompts were developed by the peer researchers through group discussion during the training. During training it also became apparent that PSI/C supervisors would need additional support from a consultant social researcher familiar with the type of data being collected. This consultant was also involved in the final social analysis of the data. Each peer researcher interviewed between three and four of their peers. The data they collected provided an in-depth insight into how the target groups understand and talk about their sexual relationships and the social contexts in which decisions are made to use (or not to use) condoms within different types of relationships.

tional tools such as surveys, PLA and focus-group discussions. The peer research revealed that most waitresses/bar girls live in financially precarious and socially vulnerable situations, and supplement low salaries by entering into transactional sexual relationships. Social and economic outcomes are valued more highly than health outcomes, with the women trading financial returns for risk of HIV infection, for example through agreeing to unprotected sex in return for higher fees, and agreeing to not use condoms with 'special clients' such as *ta-tas* and *songsars*.[3] Some waitresses were forced to 'sell their virginity' through a broker (usually the restaurant/bar owner) to wealthy clients. Waitresses are at constant risk of violence from clients, ranging from verbal abuse to physical abuse, with reports of women being threatened with a gun. Armed men frequently force the women to have sex without using condoms. Gang rape (*baowk*) is a common experience. The research also showed that most students have multiple sex partners including brothel-based sex workers, women in other professions allied to indirect sex work, and *songsars* (usually female students). Students have extremely poor risk-assessment for transmission of HIV, and take little account of their role as vectors of disease. The practice of *baowk* with sex workers appears to be widespread among students, involving verbal abuse and sometimes physical violence.

The peer research findings have been widely disseminated to government and national media in Cambodia, as part of an advocacy campaign denouncing sexual violence as behaviour that transgresses Cambodian cultural norms. One recommendation emerging from the research and currently being discussed is for a peer education strategy for indirect sex workers, whereby waitresses/bar girls who consistently use condoms act as role models and thus agents for change (with some of the peer researchers recruited as the first group of peer educators). These peer educators will be given information on the types of services currently available for women, and a women's drop-in centre established to provide counselling, testing for and treatment of sexually transmitted infections, and rape crisis management. The research concluded that there was little to be gained from embarking on peer education with male students without first creating an enabling environment for change. One approach being considered is to develop a behaviour-change communication strategy using student role models, which mimic the students' view of themselves as 'clever' and 'modern', while exploiting this image to demonstrate that 'clever and modern men' consistently use condoms, do not abuse women, and take responsibility for their actions.

The peer method has assisted PSI/C to design community-based behaviour-change strategies for specific target groups, to facilitate networking with other community-based organizations already engaged in local-level behaviour-change strategies, and to monitor and evaluate its behaviour-change communication activities and materials from the perspective of the target group. By talking to their peers about the issues identified in the interviews, the peer researchers (especially the women) acted as catalysts for dialogue and for stimulating community-based behaviour-change strategies within their social networks. This catalytic role was enhanced because some of the peer researchers were supported by local community-based organizations.

Nepal: a safe motherhood programme

Since 2002 an adapted version of the peer ethnographic method, known as the key informant method, has been used by the DFID-funded Nepal Safe Motherhood Project (NSMP) to gain an in-depth under-standing of how women of child-bearing age perceive wider changes in the social context in which pregnancy and childbirth are experienced, and to monitor progress towards improving access to obstetric and midwifery services (a key NSMP objective). This was the first rural application of peer ethnography. Communities in rural Nepal are remote, small and highly stratified by ethnicity/caste, gender, kinship and age, which together militate against public social interaction. Young women's decision-making and behaviour in relation to preg-nancy and childbirth is influenced strongly by men and senior kinsfolk. Hierarchical power relations further discourage open communication between generations and between the sexes. This context had signifi-cant implications for the way in which the peer method had to be adapted. First, a way had to be found of ensuring representation by eth-nicity/caste within the target group (women of childbearing age). Where researchers could not be found to represent the range of castes and ethnic groups in the community, staff of local NGOs with estab-lished relationships of trust with such groups were trained and deployed as data collectors. Like the Cambodia adaptation of the peer method, the key informant method is built on partnerships with local NGOs and other community-based structures. Second, constraints on women's social and geographical mobility in rural Nepal mean there are no clearly developed peer groups or networks in the sense described above for the Zambia and Cambodia cases. Concepts of anonymity, which form the basis of the peer ethnographic conversa-tional interview techniques (such as 'tell me about others like you'), have less meaning in rural Nepal, where social and geographic mobility among women is limited, and communities are so small. To address these constraints, reference to the concept of peer was avoided in con-versational interviews: the prompts encouraged respondents to talk about 'people they know' (without identifying who they are) and 'events they have heard about or know of.' Such prompts clearly encourage responses based on gossip. However, gossip (as in the peer method) is regarded as a valid and important source of data (as discussed in the conclusions below).

An analysis of the first round of key informant data indicates findings that are likely to have been difficult to generate through questionnaire-based surveys and focus-group discussions, especially those relating to intra-community and intra-household power and gender relations and

Box 10.3   *Nepal case study*

Trained key informant researchers were responsible for data collection, and were deployed in two village development committees (the administrative level at which the Nepal Safe Motherhood Project, NSMP, operates) in each of six NSMP districts. Data collection took place over a period of approximately five weeks in each district, with the researchers receiving regular support from and debriefing by NSMP and local NGO staff. Key informant researchers interviewed a minimum of two women of childbearing age (with whom they mixed socially) using three conversational interviews to assess perceived improvements in access to mid-wifery/obstetric services, quality of care, and social mobility (for example, through perceived improvements in communication with mother-in-law and husband, to reflect improved ability to make decisions regarding health-seeking behaviour). Conversational prompts guided the interviews, which were conducted in private and at mutually convenient times. The process culminated in data analysis and dissemination workshops for village development committees and other key stakeholders.

Data analysis was in two stages (the social/ethnographic analysis in the generic peer ethnographic tool was subsumed within these two stages). At stage one, all key informant researchers from each village development committee were collec-tively debriefed every ten days by NSMP staff (who were involved in the original key informant researcher training and hence were familiar with the tool and the individual key informant researchers) along with a local NGO representative, with each key informant researcher in turn reporting on the information they had col-lected to date. The NGO representative synthesized the issues reported by the key informant researchers, and fed back the synthesis to the group who then focused on ratifying the synthesis and discussing significant similarities and differences in the data. The debriefing workshops lasted two days to allow synthesis, feedback and in-depth discussion.

Stage two of the data-analysis process was a data review and dissemination work-shop led by the local NGO, following a similar pattern to those conducted in stage one. The workshops were held at the village development committee's HQ, and designed to identify key issues emerging from the interviews, to identify lessons learned for the NSMP and wider Nepali safe motherhood programming, and to review and modify the tool for subsequent monitoring by the NSMP and village development committees. In addition to the key informant researchers, NSMP staff and the NGO (who facilitated the workshop), village development committee staff and officials, and other development agencies attended the workshops.

The first round of key informant data collection served as a social appraisal of the situation facing women of childbearing age. Once fully analysed and synthesized, the data formed a baseline against which NSMP monitors change, using the key informant research method every nine to twelve months. A short refresher training course, including conversational prompt development/modification, is undertaken with the key informant researchers before each round of monitoring starts.

their effect on decision-making and health-seeking behaviour for preg-
nant women, and to variations in indigenous health and other beliefs
by ethnicity/caste. Village development committees and the NSMP
have acted on these findings. Recognizing that women often choose
traditional healers as their first service provider, village development
committees have supported training courses for traditional healers on
the dangers of pregnancy, delivery and the postpartum period, focusing
on the need to refer quickly. An increase in referrals from traditional
healers to health facilities has followed this training. To improve quality
of care, village development committees are addressing service
providers' poor behaviour towards patients and their carers by raising
key quality of care issues at health staff meetings. In an attempt to
improve women's decision-making and autonomy (a key factor in
determining access to care), some village development committees
have set minimum female membership of 33 per cent in community
groups such as water-users' committees and forestry-users' groups. In
these and other community forums, such as mothers' groups, there is
now evidence that women's voices are being heard in relation to key
funding decisions around improving the physical infrastructure of sub-
health posts, and establishing microcredit schemes.

Conclusions

The peer ethnographic method was designed to address some of the
limitations of other applied research methods. Peer ethnography,
using limited material and human resources, and within relatively
short time frames (two to three months), can generate a sufficient
amount and quality of research data for use in the design and monitoring of development programmes. The method has also proved capable
of generating data and insights that would not have been possible
using conventional research methods (including PRA). Following
extensive field testing and application of the approach since it was
developed in 1999, some limitations as well as considerable strengths
have been uncovered.

Use of the peer method in urban settings (such as Zambia and
Cambodia) revealed the high level of diversity within peer researchers'
networks. In Zambia this diversity was further ensured by selecting
peer researchers from a range of ethnic groups and socio-economic
backgrounds, and ensuring an equal balance of male and female
researchers. One of the key lessons learned from the adaptation of the
peer method for use in Nepal relates to the nature of community and
peer networks in rural settings. The generic peer method seems to be
easier to use in urban and peri-urban settings, where peer networks are
extensive and communities large and diverse enough to generate a
sense of anonymity, and hence to allow the use of 'third-person' interviewing. In rural settings, where geographic communities are small in
population size, and where power structures and social hierarchies
limit the movement of some social groups (rural women in Nepal),

then the peer method needs to be adapted. Experience to date has, however, confirmed that with careful adaptation and sensitive piloting, the fundamental principles and methodology of peer ethnography can be applied effectively. A further limitation of the method is that peer researchers have to be sufficiently literate to be able to record the conversational interview data. This requirement may preclude the most marginalized groups from becoming peer researchers, although in Nepal this problem was overcome by training local NGO staff as researchers to interview the poor and marginalized. We consider that the approach has the potential to be developed as a purely oral method with non-literate groups, although this adaptation has not yet been field tested.[4]

One of the main concerns initially voiced by development agencies using the peer method was that the sample of respondents might be biased and unrepresentative (as peer researchers select their interviewees from within their own peer networks). The peer ethnographic method recognizes the importance of ensuring a locally representative sample, while also recognizing that it is extremely difficult to use random sampling techniques to find representative informants. Local experience is needed to know what representativeness means. Peer researchers – by virtue of their membership and understanding of the communities in which the research is undertaken – are strategically placed and able to locate a point of entry into the local social and cultural system. A further concern surrounded the need to validate the data to ensure the peer researchers were 'telling the truth'. It is at this level that peer ethnography makes its greatest departure from positivism and empiricism. A key strength of the method lies in its lack of claims to any positivist criteria for the collection and presentation of 'objective' data. The peer ethnographic method is not seeking social 'truths', as positivist methods may understand them, but an understanding of the social commentary and dynamics through which social identity is negotiated and behaviour given meaning. The main focus of the method is on analysing contradiction and difference in the discourses of social actors within a network, rather than on gathering 'social facts'.

One of the key social dynamics upon which the peer method draws is gossip (Hammel 1990). Epstein (1969: 125) expresses the functionalist view that the exchange of gossip denotes a certain 'community of interest', and that through gossip the norms of behaviour specific to a social network are expressed. However, one of the important aims of the peer ethnographic method is to highlight contradictions between the normative statements made about social behaviour and the everyday behaviours that individuals gossip about. These contradictions provide important data concerning relations of power and social context. The initial participatory training of peer researchers often serves to highlight normative discourses. For example, during the initial training in Zambia the peer researchers referred to sexual abstinence as the norm to which all their peers adhered. However, subsequent interview narratives collected by the peer researchers highlighted the contradictory nature of these normative statements and actual accounts of sexual behaviour among their peer group (Price and Hawkins 2002). Scott (1985: 282) argues that it is the act of violation of expected behaviours that makes an event worth gossiping about: the norm or rule in question often only being brought to consciousness as a result of its violation. Scott also suggests that gossip is an important form of resistance in conditions where the operations of power make open acts of disrespect dangerous. For the poor and socially marginalized, gossip may achieve the expression of disapproval, contempt and disaffection with the social order, while minimizing risks of reprisal. As such, gossip can be seen as the currency of social networks, providing valuable insights into how power operates at the local level, and into strategies employed by poor and marginalized groups in their struggle to acquire social and economic resources in highly unequal social conditions.

On reflection, one of the most important outcomes of the data-collection and analysis process is the ensuing dialogue that it generates: between peer researchers and the development programme, and between peer researchers and members of their social networks. While development agencies and programme staff tend to view the peer ethnographic method as a useful means of gathering research data, for peer researchers the approach offers the potential for greater political engagement with their peer group on issues of central importance to their lives and everyday social practice. However, while the research process provides a basis from which peer researchers are able to challenge some of the assumptions and premises of development programmes, it cannot be assumed that the necessary shift in power relations always ensues to enable the views of peer researchers to be fully heard by staff, and therefore integrated into programme design. In this respect the method may also serve to highlight the often-disempowered situation of representatives of local communities co-opted into projects and programmes. Introducing into policy-making and programme implementation a truly reflexive and participatory approach which engages with the very complex contexts in which health, sexual and reproductive behaviour are experienced and negotiated requires more than simply training peer educators or peer researchers. It also implies the need for fundamental changes in the operation of institutional power, as well as in the processes by which development decisions are made, resources allocated and policies formulated (Blackburn and Holland 1998).

Chapter Eleven
Participatory indicator development for sustainable natural resource management

ANDREW DOUGILL and MARK REED[1]

Summary

There have been few attempts to develop and apply sustainability indicators for natural resource management at farm level, and even fewer have fully consulted land-users from the start of this process. While environmental sustainability indicators need to be accurate and reliable, land-users also need them to be rapid, cost-effective and easy to use, in addition to being linked to management objectives so they can be targeted at community empowerment and sustainable natural resource management. To develop farm-level sustainability indicators that meet these criteria, a framework for participatory indicator development is provided that integrates land-user knowledge with bio-geographical information. Integration of qualitative and quantitative approaches incorporating biogeographical evaluation of land-user indicators in the context of livelihoods analyses leads to a more concise and usable list of sustainability indicators. Extension workers who are traditionally grounded in quantitative assessment methodologies can readily adopt the combined approach advocated here. Case-study material shows that Kalahari pastoralists in south-west Botswana use more than 80 sustainability indicators for natural resource management. However, indicator knowledge is sparsely dispersed and varies between different social groups. The dissemination of sustainability indicator information is ongoing, with the production of rangeland evaluation guidebooks in collaboration with the Ministry of Agriculture. These guides are designed to enable participatory assessment of rangeland condition and link this to locally applicable natural resource management advice. In this way, our research suggests it is possible to empower communities to monitor and respond to rangeland degradation in order to enhance the sustainability of natural resource management.

Introduction: sustainability indicators and participatory research

There has been much recent debate on the ability of participatory research to provide both qualitative insights into livelihood options and decision-making controls, and quantitative assessments of environmental sustainability (Abbot and Guijt 1998; Rigby et al. 2000; Morse et al. 2001). One way in which this can be achieved is to extend the qualitative, livelihoods analytical framework (Scoones 1998), to identify quantifiable indicators of environmental sustainability. Thus far, farmer-led approaches have focused largely on deriving indicators of land degradation rather than sustainability, and have concentrated on mixed and arable farming systems (Rigby et al. 2000, Stocking and Murnaghan 2001). As yet, no farmer-led studies focus on the complexity of issues and environmental changes that typify the highly dynamic semi-arid rangelands (Behnke et al. 1993) that support the livelihoods of more than 25 million African pastoralists (Lane 1998).

If sustainability indicators are to empower communities, they must be simple, rapid and inexpensive, in addition to being accurate and reliable (Pretty 2001). The majority of sustainability indicators for natural resource management have been highly quantitative. They have been identified, selected and applied by researchers, and often carry little meaning for local communities. There is no accepted framework for participatory identification, evaluation and selection of sustainability indicators that can feed into rangeland management decisions at household, community and institutional levels. A number of recent studies have taken a more qualitative approach to indicator development, eliciting indicators from local communities (Bellows 1995; Kipuri 1996; Woodhouse et al. 2000), but have been unable to ensure accuracy and reliability. By integrating qualitative and quantitative participatory methods, it is possible to combine the strengths of both approaches.

This chapter reports on research with pastoralists in Kgalagadi District, south-west Botswana. It provides a methodological framework combining qualitative livelihoods analysis with more quantitative participatory environmental monitoring research. Outputs of integrated assessments can enable land managers to monitor environmental changes either independently of, or together with, government extension workers. Participatory environmental monitoring can feed into joint natural resource management decisions informally through social networks, or formally through the establishment and support of community committees. This chapter concludes by arguing that involvement of pastoralists, extension workers and policy-makers in integrated qualitative and quantitative environmental monitoring can empower decision-makers to manage natural resources more sustainably, especially for marginalized African pastoral communities.

Background: frameworks for participatory indicator development

From degradation to sustainability indicators

The meaning of sustainability differs in time and space, and between individuals. Without a precise operational definition, eliciting sustainability indicators from local communities becomes problematic. This may explain the absence of farmer participation in the development of sustainability indicators to date. Yet operational definitions of land degradation are well established (UNEP 1997), and eliciting degradation indicators from communities is relatively straightforward (Stocking and Murnaghan 2001). As the antithesis of sustainability, degradation indicators may be reversed to derive sustainability indicators. This research advocates the integration of quantitative approaches into participatory (largely qualitative) analyses to validate and shortlist the most effective community indicators, and to involve community members in participatory environmental monitoring.

Existing sustainability indicator frameworks

A number of frameworks have been developed to classify sustainability indicators, with much emphasis on how best to integrate local community knowledge with external scientific knowledge. The most widely used frameworks employed by development agencies are the framework for the evaluation of sustainable land management (Smyth and Dumanski 1995), used by the World Bank, and the pressure–state–response (OECD 1993) and driving force–state–response (UNCSD 1996) frameworks.

Although none of these frameworks is explicitly participatory, classification frameworks like these go further than positivist, scientifically driven attempts to define indicator evaluation criteria. For example, Breckenridge et al. (1995) developed a framework in which indicators were identified by interdisciplinary teams of researchers, who evaluated them with reference to a list of predefined evaluation criteria and tested them with empirical research and then re-evaluated them. Rennie and Singh (1996) developed a similar framework in which indicators were identified by researchers; however, communities shortlisted indicators which became 'community-derived'.

The development of predefined, externally generated evaluation criteria for indicators does not acknowledge the diversity of stakeholders with wide-ranging perceptions of relevant criteria. Stakeholders' participation in the development of evaluation criteria is therefore essential for appropriate indicators to be selected. Determining users' objectives and evaluation criteria prior to the identification and selection of indicators is therefore a key step, but one that has rarely been addressed in indicator development frameworks. In the Kalahari research case study here, this is undertaken by differentiating analysis on the basis of pastoralist land tenure status. In such pastoralist societies, land tenure can be viewed as a key element of an individual's environmental entitlements.

Recent studies have taken the identification of sustainability indicators a step further towards empowering communities, by incorporating them into indicator-based management guides to assess land degradation (Savory 1988; Milton et al. 1998; Stocking and Murnaghan 2001). However, community involvement in their development and testing has been limited, and therefore empowerment negligible. Milton et al. (1998), for example, provide one of the most comprehensive suites of indicators for farm-level assessment. However, their guide was restricted to vegetation and soil-based indicators, with limited reference to socio-economic indicators that are of greater importance to individual pastoralists. Savory's (1988) biological monitoring method is more appropriate, in that it used a combination of plant, animal and soil factors as indicators of range condition, but the suggested data-collection methods were too complicated and time-consuming to achieve widespread uptake. Consideration of socio-economic variables in assessments of environmental degradation (or sustainability), together with more applicable indicators of rangeland ecological changes, are both required if more applicable indictors of environmental sustainability are to be provided for African rangelands.

Link from livelihoods analysis approaches and frameworks

The recognized need for holistic research on natural resource use matches the evolving focus of interdisciplinary livelihoods analytical approaches (Scoones 1998). This livelihoods framework designed for systematic analysis of poverty has also gained widespread acceptance and adoption in natural resource-related development projects (Ellis 2000). Consequently, the research framework proposed here for identification of sustainability indicators evolves from more general sustainable livelihoods analyses that have been employed on projects elsewhere in this region (Ashley 2000; Twyman et al. 2001).

Livelihoods approaches can be extended using a range of participatory approaches designed to provide both qualitative and quantitative information on the nature of changes in ecological communities and indicators. This information can then be used to develop indicators suitable for use by individuals or community groups to monitor changes in natural resource assets. Key methods advocated in such a participatory indicator development process include participatory mapping of different ecological resource zones (Twyman et al. 2001) through transect walks or drives with key informants. Another vital method in such dynamic rangeland systems is the use of oral testimonies or histories with elder informants who can outline significant historical transitions between ecological states (Kepe and Scoones 1999). It is thus essential that a research framework for identification of sustainability indicators integrates qualitative livelihoods analysis with appropriate quantitative elements of participatory environmental monitoring, to assess the different ecological communities across a region. It is to this end that the participatory indicator development framework proposed here was developed and applied in the Kalahari rangelands of south-west Botswana.

Research design and methods: proposed framework

Building on existing participatory research frameworks, the model proposed here stresses the need for farmer involvement at every stage in the research process (Figure 11.1). Although the simplified diagrammatic

Figure 11.1   *Participatory indicator development*
methodological framework

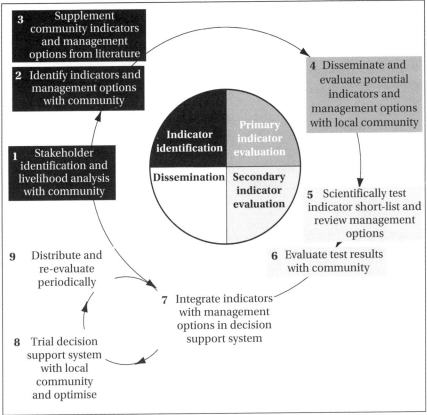

presentation suggests a series of distinct stages, the key element is the simultaneous use of the different approaches in order to integrate the qualitative and quantitative, as well as the environmental with the socio-economic.

The research framework starts by identifying relevant stakeholders and conducting a wealth ranking in order to select a representative sample for interviewing (1). (Numbers in parentheses refer to the research stages outlined in Figure 11.1). Semi-structured interviews were then conducted with pastoralists and key informants to identify the key livelihood constraints and the causes of poverty at household level, together with discussion of the objectives that different stakeholders wish indicators to meet (1). It is critical that local communities define the indicator objectives and their evaluation criteria. Much of this can be achieved using a livelihoods approach to structure the initial phases of pastoralist interviews (1). In addition, interviews were extended to include discussion of what interviewees used as rangeland degradation indicators (2). Pastoralists interviewed at this initial research stage were asked to identify objectives they would like indicators of

Table 11.1 *Indicator evaluation criteria of Kalahari pastoralists*

Indicators should:	
Ease of use criteria	**Accuracy criteria**
Be easily measured	Be reliable and robust
Be rapid to measure over space and time	Be representative of system variability
Be timely	Be scientifically credible
Make use of existing skills and knowledge	Be relevant to the system/region being evaluated
	Be diverse, encompassing a wide range of variables

rangeland degradation to meet. They were also asked to identify potential management solutions to rangeland degradation. This information was supplemented by key informant interviews, seeking innovative land-users and their innovations. Where this was problematic, they were asked to identify their main objectives for farm management, followed by an assessment of the extent to which indicators could help meet these objectives. In this way, complex environmental issues and terms are placed in the context of household decision-making and livelihood opportunities and constraints.

Consistent with accepted degradation definitions (Abel and Blaikie 1989; UNEP 1997), rangeland degradation was defined as areas of formerly productive rangeland that have declined in agricultural productivity, independently of rainfall variability. Pastoralists were also asked to identify which of these indicators they would expect to change first before a degraded state was reached. These 'early warning' indicators are process-based and are vital to improving agricultural extension advice, and to enabling individual pastoralists to adopt opportunistic management approaches capable of preventing rangeland degradation.

Interviews in the indicator identification stage of research included all pastoral groups in the region, so that wealth and land-tenure status could be assessed as factors potentially affecting knowledge and management decision-making. By differentiating the analysis of responses from different groups, it may be possible to target outputs more effectively.

Indicators cited by local communities were also integrated with indicators from the literature (3). The resulting list of parameters was evaluated in community focus groups held in four villages, as well as separate discussion groups of women and poor (classed as those who do not own livestock) to assess their accuracy and ease of use as indicators (4). A number of criteria for evaluating indicators were elicited from farmers, although 'accuracy' and 'ease of use' summarize the majority of them well (Table 11.1).

The next stage of the methodological framework involves investigation of the degradation indicator shortlist (5) using quantitative biogeographical and economic techniques (6). To achieve this, study sites were identified on a continuum from degraded to non-degraded, using economic criteria, notably herd size trends, consistent with UNEP's (1997) definition of land degradation. Trends were normalized for rainfall, and other factors influencing trends were explored in semi-structured interviews with farmers at each borehole. Degradation is inferred where declining herd size is involuntary and linked to rangeland condition. Changes in rangeland condition are gained using oral histories. Herd size trends are derived both from livestock census data and from pastoralists' records. Indicators on the shortlist are then measured at each study site using biogeographical techniques to determine which indicators best characterize the identified degraded sites. The community then evaluated the outputs of this research in further focus groups (6). In this way, the approach retains a participatory, iterative development despite the use of conventional quantitative ecological appraisal methods.

Dissemination of findings across a region should facilitate farm-level application and thus aid decision-making by individual pastoralists. In this case we propose to disseminate findings through rangeland assessment guidebooks, similar to those produced for the Karroo by Milton et al. (1998). Draft guides have been developed integrating indicators with management strategies that may prevent or ameliorate degradation (7). These guidebooks will be trialled with a representative sample of community members in order to optimize their adoption potential (8), prior to wider production and distribution through the Ministry of Agriculture (9). The process is iterative throughout, with periodic reviewing of indicator performance in collaboration with local communities (9), to ensure that guidebooks remain relevant to dynamic user objectives and assets. This will lead to rejection, adaptation and/or adoption of indicators for future guide editions. Ongoing assessment of the impact of such guides in affecting decision-making and supporting more sustainable rangeland management is a vital element of the research. This has been enabled through institutional support from the Ministry of Agriculture, and every effort has been made fully to involve their extension workers as well as the communities themselves in every stage of the research, as this will determine post-project success and dissemination of good practice.

Case-study findings

The application of the participatory indicator development framework to pastoral livelihoods research in Kgalagadi District, south-west Botswana remains ongoing and has since been replicated at two other sites in Botswana (mid-Boteti and south-west Kgalagadi). The initial findings and discussion provided here are based solely on studies in the south of Kgalagadi District, and extend a previous review of the indicator identification stages (1–3) (Reed and Dougill 2001). This chapter also discusses the findings by incorporating preliminary discussion of the primary indicator evaluation stages (4,5) and of the evaluative stages (6–9). Analysis here focuses on the methodological issues that need consideration before wider application of the participatory indicator development framework to other communities and/or environments.

Stakeholder identification and livelihoods analysis (1)

Indicator objectives were determined in two ways. Pastoralists who were able to identify objectives for indicators to meet most frequently cited improved rangeland and livestock management, as well as income generation. However, objectives were more frequently elicited through an assessment of management aims, which led to greater emphasis on increasing herd size and quality, and improved income generation.

All respondents suggested that useful indicators should be easy and rapid to use, relevant to the target area, and use existing skills and knowledge (Table 11.1). Landowners also suggested that indicators should be reliable over space and time, should encompass a diverse range of parameters, and should be possible to monitor visually on a daily basis. This indigenous evaluation information is essential to optimize the value of indicator-based management tools produced, and to ensure their widespread uptake.

As part of the initial livelihoods survey, pastoralists were asked to identify what they perceived as their main constraints to maintaining a secure livelihood. Changes and access to natural resources (both ecological and water) were the most widely cited constraint (72 per cent of those interviewed). Bush encroachment (almost entirely attributed to *Acacia mellifera*) was the most commonly cited problem, matching widespread concern over this phenomenon in the ecological literature (Dougill et al. 1999). Perceived constraints in the other capital assets were lower, with 42, 34, 32 and 15 per cent of farmers stating that they experienced constraints due to their financial, human, physical and social capital asset status, respectively.

Participatory selection of rangeland condition indicators (2)

In total 83 indicators were elicited from farmers and ranked in order of citation frequency (Table 11.2). A classification of indicators by type showed that vegetation indicators were most commonly cited (54 per cent of indicators), followed by livestock (21 per cent), soil (16 per cent), wild animals (5 per cent), socio-economic (2 per cent) and other (2 per cent) indicators. The quantity and nature of indicators were analysed according to a number of factors, notably use of fencing; herd size trends; information from other farmers and the radio; formal education status; constraints and trend lines for each capital asset; usage and attitudes towards agricultural extension; health constraints; use of

Table 11.2   *Degradation indicators ranked by frequency cited
(excluding indicators cited fewer than four times)*

Rank	Indicator	No. of times cited
1	Poor livestock condition/weight	46
2	Decreased grass cover	45
3	Increased abundance of unpalatable forbs and shrubs	34
4	Increased soil looseness	20
5	Increased abundance of unpalatable grasses	17
6	Decreased abundance of palatable grasses	16
7	Increased proportion of trees and shrubs dropping branches and leaves, or dead	12
8	Decreased abundance of palatable forbs and shrubs	11
9 =	Increased incidence of non-vegetated dunes	10
9 =	Increased incidence of livestock disease	10
10	Decreased abundance of trees	9
11	Livestock graze at increased distance from borehole	7
12 =	Decreased abundance of medicinal/edible plants	5
12 =	Decreased calving rate	5
12 =	Increased grass greyness/brittleness (less nutritious)	5
12 =	Increased abundance of harvester termites (*Makaka*)	5
13 =	Increased abundance of grasses with hollow tillers	4
13 =	Increased incidence of *nebkha* dunes	4
13 =	Increased infiltration rate in soils	4
13 =	Decreased rain-use efficiency in vegetation (poor growth despite rain)	4

savings and credit; and occupation status. Significant differences were found between different groups only as classed in terms of land ownership status. Landowners cited proportionally less vegetation (48 per cent compared with 54 per cent) and more wild animal indicators (9 per cent compared with 5 per cent), than communal farmers who relied more on vegetation (58 per cent compared with 54 per cent) and livestock (35 per cent compared with 21 per cent) indicators. Indicators that were most frequently cited by communal farmers were declining livestock condition, and decreases in both total grass cover and the abundance of important palatable forbs, shrubs and grasses.

In addition to the analysis of rangeland condition indicators by type, a functional classification was undertaken. A differentiation was made between indicators that solely described current rangeland condition, and process-based indicators that can be used as an 'early warning' of likely changes in rangeland condition (Table 11.3). Many interviewees found this distinction difficult to make, and cited only indicators of current condition. However, the extra information available in process-based indicators makes them vital in developing effective indicator-based management tools and enhancing extension advice. Early warning indicators elicited from the few indicator 'experts' are disseminated as widely as possible through the guides produced. This may facilitate more timely adaptation to ecological change by pastoralists, and feed into regional agricultural development initiatives.

A decline in total grass cover was the most widely cited early warning indicator of changes in rangeland condition. This is indicative of the increased stresses imposed on rangelands by intense grazing, especially during drought events. It is at such times that effectively permanent changes in ecological communities of the Kalahari have been predicted (Dougill et al. 1999) and therefore early warning indicators need to be tied to advice on drought-coping strategies that retain some grass cover during droughts. These indicators also tend to be capable of quantitative assessment either by individual pastoralists, or with extension staff. Consequently they offer a clear route on which to base community natural resource management discussions and decision-making.

Indicator evaluation in village-level farmer focus groups (4)

Although many pastoralists found it difficult in interviews to conceptualize criteria to evaluate what makes an effective indicator, most felt able to evaluate indicators in focus groups when introduced to the key criteria of accuracy, ease of use and local applicability. The proportion of indicators from each category obtained in these group discussions (59 per cent plant, 24 per cent livestock, 18 per cent soil) was similar to their overall proportions from individual interviews, and again stresses the need to focus primarily on indicators of vegetation and livestock change, rather than soil-based assessments.

Indicator testing and evaluation of results (5, 6)

The first stage in indicator evaluation involves the link to economic assessments of sustainability indicators (Campbell et al. 2000; Pannell and Glenn 2000). To achieve this, information on livestock herd sizes, offtake and market prices was used to identify areas that display declines in pastoral productivity independently of annual rainfall variability, and therefore can be classed as degraded (Scoones, 1995b). When economic data were not available, or were viewed as unreliable, oral histories of livestock herd size changes were conducted with key informants at each borehole to assign a degradation status to the surrounding rangeland. Following socio-economic designation of degradation status, the rangeland condition indicators were assessed

Table 11.3   *Degradation indicators ranked by number of times cited*

Rank	Early-warning indicator	No. of times cited
1	Decreased grass cover	20
2	Increased proportion of trees and shrubs dropping branches and leaves, or dead	7
3	Poor livestock condition/weight	6
4 =	Decreased abundance of trees	4
4 =	Increased abundance of unpalatable grasses	4
4 =	Increased soil looseness	4
5 =	Declining herd size	3
5 =	Decreased abundance of palatable grasses	3
5 =	Increased abundance of unpalatable forbs and shrubs	3

for each borehole using ecological and soil analyses undertaken with various community members. Preliminary environmental results validate the majority of the indicators derived from interviews showing the value of the simplified, locally applicable indicators provided by this research process.

Assessment guide discussions (7–9)

The final stage of this research framework involves further community focus groups and key stakeholder interviews with extension workers and government officials. These stages aim to enable discussion of how best to approach the dissemination of indicator information in a manner that can spread good management practice and sustainable resource management. This will be achieved through focus group discussions evaluating the range of suggested options for rangeland assessment guides and the institutional support that pastoralists feel would be beneficial in facilitating sustainable natural resource management decision-making. This stage of research will be completed in early 2004.

Discussion

Pastoralists' focus on vegetation-based indicators of degradation matches that of Milton et al.'s (1998) farm-level evaluation guide for the South African Karroo, and other less user-friendly guides that preceded it in southern Africa (e.g. Foran et al. 1978; Vorster 1982). Their downplay of soils is at variance with the focus of guides for other regions, suggesting that this emphasis may be a regional phenomenon. This is consistent with evidence that physical and hydrochemical soil degradation processes are not widely evident in the Kalahari (Dougill et al. 1999).

The absence of livestock indicators from previous farm-level rangeland evaluation guides is noticeable, as this was one of the most common types of indicator identified. With the exception of a decline in livestock condition in Kipuri's (1996) assessment of Masai indicator knowledge (defined by milk yield, fur characteristics such as matting frequency, and the colour and texture of dung), livestock indicators elsewhere in the literature tend to be relatively complex. Pastoralists here cited the indicators described by Kipuri (1996) in addition to indicators such as the distance at which cattle graze from the borehole, and increased incidence of 'long claw' (a condition where hooves become deformed due to walking on soft sand).

Factors influencing indicator knowledge in different sectors of Kalahari pastoralist societies were also assessed to help improve the targeting of rangeland assessment guides. Commercial landowners were more likely to have indicator knowledge, to rely less on vegetation indicators, and to use wild animal indicators. They were more likely to use vegetation indicators at species level rather than morphological or functional traits. Given the better educational status of this group, this may reflect a familiarity with species identification. Communal farmers, on the other hand, were likely to know fewer indicators, and to be more reliant on vegetation and livestock indicators. Although species-level indicators were approved by focus groups including syndicate and communal farmers, interview results suggest that this group may feel less comfortable with species identification. This suggests that species-level indicators should not be emphasized – something that could explain failings of traditional range evaluation methods used by the Ministry of Agriculture and outside agricultural development initiatives alike.

Work with Kalahari pastoralists has demonstrated a number of key strengths in the participatory indicator development framework proposed here. The quantity and nature of indicators collected emphasizes the importance of farmers' involvement in the development of rangeland evaluation tools. In addition, farmers' focus groups deemed these indicators easy to use. Rain-use efficiency is an example of an indicator which conventionally requires too much specialist training and equipment for most farmers, but was reported in a simplified form here as 'increasingly poor vegetation growth after rain'. Another strength of the proposed framework is consultation with farmers over the objectives of evaluation guides, and criteria that should be used to evaluate indicators. Primary evaluation objectives focused on rangeland and livestock management, however a strong link was made to livelihood strategies. The capacity of indicator-based management to enhance livelihoods should always be explicit. It was hypothesized that evaluation criteria may be useful to distinguish between farmers who may benefit from different kinds of evaluation guide. Methodologically, however, this presents a significant challenge, as different guides would need to be produced and targeted across a given area.

Recognition of the importance of pastoralist knowledge in the development of degradation appraisal tools by the Ministry of

Agriculture is positive. Through an understanding of current pastoralist knowledge, it may be possible to target extension services better towards those who have least indicator knowledge. Therefore a farmer-led approach may facilitate better outreach to those with fewer assets and provide them with locally appropriate management options. A farmer-led approach also ensures that pastoralists do not become dependent on extension services for rangeland evaluation. Due to the wide dispersion of indicator knowledge in the community, pastoralists are likely to benefit significantly from the diffusion of this knowledge through evaluation guides and informal discussions within their social networks.

The current match between community and published indicators suggests that quantitative biogeographical analyses will validate the majority of indicators elicited in this participatory study. The involvement of key informants in ecological surveys gives communities information about the relative accuracy and reliability of the various indicators, leading to the development of a more concise, usable list of the most effective indicators for dissemination in evaluation guidebooks. It also adds to the local knowledge base capable of discussing rangeland management decisions through either formal or formalized local community groups.

Conclusions

This research demonstrates the potential for using participatory approaches to gather both qualitative insights into pastoralists' livelihoods, and decision-making and quantifiable information on environmental changes. Such integrated approaches are vital to enhancing the ability of extension workers and development projects to use local knowledge in sustainability indicator identification, evaluation and selection. Consequently, it is important to train extension agents in participatory techniques in order to elicit and disseminate local expertise, and build monitoring capacity in pastoral communities. Indicators developed using the proposed framework can facilitate effective assessment of rangeland condition by non-specialists, empowering communities to conduct tasks they formerly relied on outsiders to carry out.

Case-study research in the Kalahari demonstrates that use of indicators by pastoralists differs significantly from rangeland assessment guides developed for other regions. A number of key informants were able to identify process-based early warning indicators. These are particularly well suited for the development of rangeland condition assessment guides, as they can indicate management adaptations to prevent or reduce long-term productivity declines. Indicator knowledge was differentiated by social background. The results suggest that extension services and indicator-based management tools should be targeted towards the least asset-rich, who have least indicator knowledge. It should be possible for farmers with differing capital asset status to benefit from the kind of indicators developed using this approach, diffusing knowledge more widely throughout the community, building capacity, and thus enhancing the sustainability of pastoral production and livelihoods. The participatory indicator development framework has been applied successfully in two other regions in Botswana to produce locally specific rangeland assessment guides. The need for a local, or at most a district scale of analysis is the only restriction to wider application of the participatory environmental monitoring approaches advocated here.

Chapter Twelve
Exploring the temporal logic model: a Colombian case study evaluating assistance to internally displaced people

ANDREA LAMPIS

Summary

This chapter explores the validity of a contextual approach to development research – the temporal logic model – through the presentation of a case-study evaluation of assistance to internally displaced people in Colombia. The analysis concentrates on the relationships that exist among the political and technical dimensions of traditional closed-system development research methods, such as the logical framework, as opposed to open-system tools such as the temporal logic model. The discussion of their epistemological roots leads to the conclusion that an important, and so far overlooked, question is the extent to which this relationship between the political and technical dimensions of project evaluation may produce antithetical approaches to development research and practice.

Introduction

Despite the challenge increasingly posed by innovative and participatory approaches to evaluation practices, there is still little innovation at the level of multilateral agencies. The logical framework approach is seldom overcome, and the room for real participation is restricted by factors relating to power control over processes and innovation, as well as to the inner lack of institutional and technical capacities and skills among agency personnel.

This chapter presents some reflections and findings from an evaluation process carried out for the World Food Programme in Colombia concerning their operation to assist internally displaced people. The evaluation was carried out in five different locations at the same time, and worked closely with all the actors involved. The importance of the study lies in the first use of the temporal logic model (TLM) in Colombia as an attempt to overcome the limitations of the logical framework analysis, as well as the application of a case-study approach that draws from multiple sources of evidence to gather relevant information and data. The main methodological and empirical challenge of the evaluation was to triangulate methods in generating information for the TLM, including an asset matrix, focus groups, a short questionnaire and historical documents.

Within an overall reflection of the contrasts between open and closed systems of evaluation, this chapter reflects on the internal and external validity of using participatory appraisal and evaluation techniques; the political implications of their applications within multilateral agencies' programmes; and the usefulness of techniques derived from vulnerability studies in understanding the dynamics of internal displacement. The chapter does not pretend to illustrate how quantitative and qualitative methods could or should be combined, but is a case study demonstrating what can be reasonably attempted in the context of a number of time, resource and security constraints.

Logical framework analysis: technical limitations and political implications

Within multilateral agencies, two elements appear to inform the practice of evaluation of programmes and projects. The first is a need for control and analysis of what is done and, most often, of how financial resources are spent. The second is the adoption of techniques borrowed from the array of applied social sciences, according to practical feasibility and political convenience.

Logical framework analysis (LFA) is the most widespread methodology for project design and planning.[1] As Kothari (2000) underlines, LFA is most often cited as an assessment tool, despite the fact that it was created as a planning tool. One way of seeing LFA is as the technical response of the 'community' of multilateral agencies to a 'crisis of legitimacy' that has been affecting international development over the past 10 years (Satterthwaite 2001). Within this search for demonstrable results, LFA (first explored by a team led by Leon Rosenberg: den Heyer 2001) was created as a tool to provide a clear definition of the objective of a project (NORAD 1990; Banco Interamericano de Desarrollo 1997). In turn, this tool was to provide the technical parameters against which donors, implementing teams, stakeholders and others directly involved in development could reach agreement in order to evaluate outputs and outcome.

It is interesting to take a brief look at how the literature produced by the planning or monitoring and evaluation units of international cooperation agencies presents the origins of LFA (e.g. World Bank 1996; IDB 1997; PNUD 1997). This literature stresses that LFA is a response to the lack of clear objectives in development projects, meaning the lack of a logical chain linking different levels of results (mostly linking outputs to outcomes) – but it also pragmatically skips over well-known critiques of the rigidity of LFA.

Many of the critiques applied to LFA originate within a stream of research dedicated to the exploration of alternative methods and practices to conduct development research and project implementation. The most important contribution is from Chambers (1983) and the scholars who followed his initial input (Chambers and Longhurst 1986; Longhurst et al. 1986). These authors were, in turn, inspired to a large extent by Freire's (1985) radical reading of the need for a new approach to learning and management of power relationships within the development arena.

Figure 12.1 *Logical framework planning matrix (logframe)*

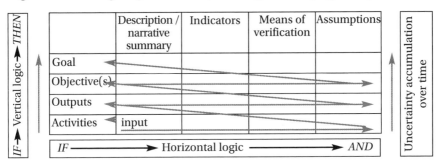

The ideological basis of this school of thought is a critique of 'official' development (Chambers 1995; Rist 1997; Pasteur and Blauert 2001). Although this chapter shares some of the main political arguments elaborated by the above-mentioned positions, it also points out the need to back them with more technical arguments. The following sections focus on two key aspects of LFA – its vertical and horizontal logic – and explore the relationship between the technical and political aspects involved in the widespread use of LFA.

The vertical logic of logical framework analysis

As illustrated in Figure 12.1, the vertical logic of the LFA organizes what appears in the 'description' column on the left, where the different implementation stages of a project (activity, outputs, objective, goal) link logistically together, according to an 'IF = THEN' mechanism. As well as serving as a pictorial way to represent how the different project components should be carried out, the LFA vertical logic has a number of other, more-or-less hidden implications.

As den Heyer (2001) points out, LFA is part of a hard-system approach to planning that mirrors social engineering. This involves an epistemological approach to development research inherited from what used to be defined as the 'hard' disciplines of physics, biology and mathematics (Wallerstein 1996). Once LFA is framed in this broader context, the above 'IF = THEN' mechanism can be seen as closely mirroring the main principle of the positivist epistemology – the explanation of natural and social life according to a series of cause–effect relationships. An interesting parallel can therefore be established between the search for laws regulating the natural world (which inspired Newtonian physics and, later, the social sciences of the eighteenth century) and the planning approaches that inherit this rather mechanical vision of the way social dynamics work. In this sense, the LFA's logframe or planning matrix (as well as the whole methodology) can be defined as a deterministic tool, or at least one having potentially deterministic effects.

In addition to this deterministic impact, the legitimation of the narrative of the LFA – the chain that links activities to outcomes through outputs – reflects the power of those that create the project narrative itself. Speech, in this context, becomes the vehicle for imposing a logic or 'meta-discourse' on competing others, legitimizing (on the basis of power) the 'correct' interpretation of things (Foucault 1998) and (in planning terms) the 'right' way according to which reality should be modified.

The horizontal logic of LFA

Inasmuch as the vertical logic tends to dominate the use of LFA, project teams, local government and multilateral agency technocrats do not pay much attention to the horizontal logic and the key role it plays in shaping the destiny of projects (Gasper 1997). This has serious implications for the chances of projects achieving their objectives.[2]

As Figure 12.1 shows, in order to move up from one level to another within the vertical logic of LFA (say from a group of activities to an output), a series of assumptions have to hold true over time. Technically, this means that the vertical logic based on the 'IF = THEN' equation is validated only when other conditions (the assumptions) are also fulfilled. The resulting equation is a sequence of 'IF + AND = THEN' prepositions that must be satisfied if projects are to come anywhere near to achieving their objectives.

One implication of this rather technical and technocratic observation is that those who plan with the LFA generally accumulate uncertainty as implementation time unfolds. This is generated by variation in the social dynamic of the context and in the broader environment. To quote White (2002b: 6): '[a]ttribution becomes harder as we move along the causal chain. It is easy to attribute responsibility for delivering inputs, and usually for carrying out activities, although external factors may play a part.'

The temporal logic model: potential and limitations

The TLM was designed as an attempt to create a planning and evaluation tool based on the principles of 'soft-system' thinking, as opposed to hard-system approaches exemplified by the logical framework:

> *'Simply defined the TLM is an evaluation tool which provides an overall pictorial representation of the program components and tracks design modifications during implementation.'*
> (den Heyer 2001: 11)

This model was first developed by a group of researchers working at the Evaluation Unit of the International Research Development Centre (IRDC) in Ottawa, Canada (see the original paper at *www.idrc.ca*). One of its principal aims is to help stakeholders understand what they are doing (or planning to do) in terms of something that is part of a broader dynamic framed within a wider open system.

Figure 12.2   *Logical statements within the temporal logic model*

A	B			
	Programme planning stages			
Vertical logic statement: *IF* these are the contextual issues that the programme needs to respond to … ↓	**Programme context**	**Target population**	**Goals**	**Assumptions**
	Horizontal logic statement 1: *IF* these are the issues for this population, *THEN* we hope to create this change based on these premises			
	Objectives | **Inputs / resources** | **Activities** | **Sustainable strategies** | **Outcomes** | **Indicators**			
… *THEN* this is the intervention designed to address it	**Horizontal logic statement 2**: *IF* this is what we want to realistically accomplish, and these are our resources to carry out these activities, and we will ensure long-term results with these strategies, *THEN* we will have this effect, which will be illustrated through these variables			
Implementation period ↓	**Instalment one: (add date here)**			
	Programme context changes	**Interim assessment**		**Modifications**
But *IF* the programme needs to be adapted… ↓	**Horizontal logic statement 1**: *IF* the programme context has changed in this manner and the interim assessment has shown this, *THEN* the programme should (or should not) adapt in this manner			
	Objectives | **Inputs / resources** | **Activities** | **Sustainable strategies** | **Outcomes** | **Indicators**			
… *THEN* this should be the modified design	**Horizontal logic statement 4**: *IF* this is what we want to realistically accomplish, and these are our resources to carry out these activities, and we will ensure long-term results with these strategies, *THEN* we will have this effect, which will be illustrated through these variables			

In her critique of the LFA, which is grounded in the greater usefulness of open-system approaches to planning, den Heyer points out that a programme is an ongoing dialogue with complex external factors. Programme design 'should change as the program adapts to a sometimes-chaotic environment, unintended effects emerge, or program assumptions are undermined. From this perspective, program management becomes more of an art form than a science' (den Heyer 2001: 2). Figure 12.2 illustrates the logical statements of the model and (see columns A and B) the two main logical chains within it.[3] The model has four lines of horizontal logic and one vertical. The horizontal logic is made up of the programme context row, programme design row, modification row and subsequent programme design rows. The vertical logic unfolds through a series of stages. The combination of the two logics is meant to convey the programme story.

Within TLM, each stage can be seen as a snapshot of the planning–implementation–monitoring–evaluation process taken over a period of time. The 'IF = THEN' statement typical of logic chain models such as LFA is here enriched and modified by an additional sentence that works like a verification question before beginning each stage of the programme: 'If these are the contextual issues the programme needs to respond to, then this is the intervention designed to address it. But if the programme needs to be adapted, then this would be the modified design' (den Heyer 2001: 10). According to the author's vision:

> *'The temporal logic model reads like a newspaper. It is comprised of two stages, with the second stage repeated throughout the program. The first stage embodies the original program vision and is referred to as the program planning stage. The program planning stage is followed by a series of monitoring stages, which record changes over the span of the program.'* (den Heyer 2001: 11)

The political implication of using TLM consists of a clear rejection of the centrality of the concept of objective planning and evaluation. This, in turn, also becomes a rejection of the 'meta-discourse' identified above as one of the main features of LFA. The TLM can be seen as an applied tool that rests on an epistemological reflection, shared by participatory monitoring and evaluation authors (Kumar 1993; Estrella 2000; Kothari 2000; Pasteur and Blauert 2000), which rejects the notion that external actors can meaningfully evaluate the actions of others.

Its epistemological roots can be traced back to the distinction between closed and open systems made by Ludwig von Bertalanffy and, more broadly, to the first elaborations of system theory dating back to the 1930s, when a deep crisis affected the scientific paradigm that had dominated science since the early eighteenth century. As Emery (1974) explains, open systems have no fixed rules or laws that regulate their functioning. The positive outcome of any adapting process depends on the specific context and the relationship a system has with its environment. Therefore adaptation is a process that has to be repeated and revalidated every time each organism or system attempts to adapt to some kind of change. The TLM transposes these principles to the logic of planning.

The main limitation of the TLM approach, however, is that it mostly works as a logic container or organizer. Its different boxes literally need to be filled up with concrete, real information and data collected through research methods. This prompts the following questions:

- is there any specific method of data collection that fits TLM better than others?
- to what extent can the blending of informal/formal methods of data collection and analysis mirror the informal/formal dynamic present within the TLM in its vertical and horizontal logic?

In the next section, we consider the use of a qualitative and participatory case-study approach to evaluation that was used to fill the TLM boxes in the context of a World Food Programme operation in Colombia.

Table 12.1   *Classification of areas of interests from the TORs according to three units of analysis*

Target group	Environment and social dynamic	Project management
People's resources	Management of risks and assumptions	Targeting
Assets and capacities	Environment	Advocacy
Land ownership	Loss or stealing of food	Quantitative results
Target group interaction with PRRO	Armed actors influence on PRRO	M&E System
Quality and relevance of 'food for work'		Role and effectiveness of contingency aid
Participation		Human resources management
Quantity, quality and acceptance of rations		Issues of security and personnel protection. Operational challenges
Sustainability and development		Mobilization and capacity to provide resources
Commitment with women		Coordination
Food security		Relationships with partners
Needs of non-displaced communities		Colombian Government efficacy

Applying the case study methodology to TLM: an evaluation of the World Food Programme's Protracted Relief and Recovery Operation

Over the past 15 years, according to 1999 data, more than 1.5 million Colombians have been displaced from their homes and had their livelihoods disrupted due to political violence. In the three-year period 1996–9, conflict created 750 000 internally displaced people (World Food Programme 1999: 2).

The World Food Programme's Protracted Relief and Recovery Operation (PRRO 6139) arose out of this context, with the following long-term objectives:[4]

> 'To cover food deficits in order to restore human capacity and enhance social cohesion.
> To support initial settlements, resettlement, and return to facilitate reintegration into society.

Table 12.2   *Arnstein's ladder of participation*

Level 1	Manipulation	These levels assume a passive audience given information that may be partial or constructed
Level 2	Education	
Level 3	Information	People are told what is going to happen, is happening or has happened
Level 4	Consultation	People are given a voice, but no power to ensure their views are heeded
Level 5	Involvement	People's views have some influence, but traditional power-holders still make the decisions
Level 6	Partnership	People can begin to negotiate with traditional power-holders, including agreeing roles, responsibilities and levels of control
Level 7	Delegated power	Some power is delegated
Level 8	Citizen control	Full delegation of all decision-making and action
		From Arnstein (1971), cited in IEG (2001)

To mitigate the impact of future crises'
(World Food Programme 1999: 8)

The immediate objectives of the PRRO were:

> 'To contribute to household food security of IDPs [internally displaced persons] during initial stages of settlement.
> To support and promote local initiatives through food-for-work activities, in order to:
>> Promote productive capacity, increasing opportunities for self-reliance.
>> Rehabilitate basic social and economic infrastructure.
>> Increase capacity building of local authorities and IDP communities through training, increased participation in PRRO activities, organization and advocacy.
>
> To promote the improvement of the diets of IDP pre-school and primary schoolchildren, and increase the coverage and attendance of these children in day-care centres and schools.
> To improve food security of the most vulnerable groups – children, the malnourished and expectant mothers, and specific ethnic groups' (World Food Programme 1999: 8)

The evaluation team for this project classified the questions to be answered according to three categories: target group; external and social dynamic; and management of the project (Table 12.1).

Table 12.3   *Case-study methodology*

Evaluation stage	Research approach	Researched variables	Involved actors*
Preliminary	Analysis of secondary & 'historical' sources	Project objectives. Project design. Targeting. Inputs. Strategy. Context. Actors and institutional dynamics	Consultancy
Workshop for analysis of parts 1–3 of country office report, plus TLT baseline	Brainstorm. SWOT matrix. Strategy analysis. TLM baseline	History of project and process of implementation according to country office, associates & national & international involved NGOs	PRRO, ICBF, RSS, PMA, Associates Consultancy
Specific fieldwork, preparation of working plan	Stakeholder analysis	Analysis of variables to be researched during fieldwork	Consultancy, World Food Programme & local actors & stakeholders
Meeting with representatives of PRRO	Brainstorm	Discussion of of objectives of evaluation	PRRO, World Food Programme & consultancy teams
Meeting with thematic UN internally displaced persons' group	Key issues analysis		
Fieldwork	See details in Table 16.4		
Data processing and analysis	Interviews transcription. Focal group results, systematization of notes. Survey coding & processing. Triangulation of evidence	All	Consultancy
Fieldwork report preparation	Qualitative analysis of contents and evidence. Basic quantitative analysis of survey results	All	Consultancy
Preliminary report preparation		All	Consultancy
Preliminary report presentation	PowerPoint	All	PRRO, World Food Programme, consultancy teams
Meeting donors, PRRO and evaluation team	Coordinated analysis according to pre-set agenda	All	PRRO, World Food Programme, donors, consultancy teams
Drafting of final report		All	Consultancy

* PRRO = Protracted Relief and Recovery Operation, World Food Programme;
ICBF = *Instituto Colombiano de Bienestar Familiar* (Colombian Institute of Family Welfare);
RSS = *Red de Solidaridad Social* (Social Solidarity Network, Colombia); TLM = temporal logic model

Fieldwork research was a substantially 'extractive' process, oriented to the collection of relevant information from different actors. Given the time constraints it would have been very difficult to create a 'deep' process of cooperative evaluation with fieldwork stages of four to five days per setting. Nonetheless, considering an ideal scale of participation (such as Arnstein's, 1971), the work realized (Table 12.2) could score on level 4 and, perhaps, level 5. People's opinions and views were highly valued and participants were both strongly encouraged and highly self-motivated.

The evaluation methodology allowed for a sequencing of methods to accommodate analysis of secondary and historical sources, along with a process of institutional engagement which allowed a broad range of stakeholders to participate in designing the research and preparing the research outputs (Table 12.3).

The case-study research activity was carried out in five geographical departments[5] in the north, north-west and west of the country. Three fieldwork teams were formed, each comprising one member of the evaluation team acting as fieldwork coordinator, one PRRO member from the national level and one regional coordinator. For security reasons, a tight schedule was organized and followed by fieldwork teams.

In order to maximize the external validity and reliability of the findings (Marsland et al. 1998), the teams applied the same pattern and sequence of research tools in each of the case studies (Table 12.4). The first step, an introductory transect walk through the settlement, sought to establish some degree of trust with the internally displaced people in that site and to acquaint the research teams with the environment.

Research activities also included semi-structured interviews with community leaders about their main concerns. These interviews were conducted on the basis of a topic guide and were designed to gather basic data on the availability of public services, the history of displacement of the community, and the main coping and income-generation strategies, and to elicit local perceptions of the programme. The use of an asset matrix was thought to be a valuable tool in order to show the World Food Programme the importance of starting to tackle the issue not only from a point of view of humanitarian assistance, but to link it up with strategies oriented towards the (at least partial) re-establishment of people's livelihoods.[6]

The same exercise was conducted with local PRRO personnel, NGOs and stakeholders, and was repeated with national teams in order to triangulate the results of both and to provide better feedback to the TLM on the issues signalled as important to World Food Programme by the terms of reference (TORs). Table 12.5 presents the very simple matrix that was used to compare results. It was essentially a content analysis, with similar matrices produced for each case study (one for each of the three main units of analysis). These were later summarized in a comparison matrix to elicit trends in the results of the evaluation.

Table 12.4   *Fieldwork schedule*

Activity	Methodology	Researched variables	Participants
Confidence-building	Introductory transect through settlement or places where targeted internally displaced persons are living	Environment. Spatial identification of key and critical areas	Target group people. Country office team members. Government agencies' team members. Consultants
General matrix of settlement	Semi-structured interview with thematic guide	Basic services. Access to public services. Population profile. Income generation. Main post-displacement activities	Leaders. Committees. People with special functions or tasks
History of community (or communities)	Focal groups	Target groups' perceptions of project implementation regarding their situation with relation to key aspects	Target groups. PRRO partners
Thematic workshops with target groups	SWOT Venn diagram Assets matrix problem tree	20 questions proposed by TORs, categorized according to closeness to: Target groups; Environment and social dynamic; Management of project	Target groups
Thematic workshop with local PRRO personnel, NGOs and stakeholders	Metaplan		
Interviews	Structured and semi-structured questionnaire		PRRO and evaluation teams to interview 20 IDPs in each settlement or locality visited for each of the five fieldwork areas
In-depth interviews with community leaders	Semi-structured interviews with thematic guide		Evaluation and World Food Programme team Interviews with local representatives of PRRO partners
Semi-structured interviews with thematic guide			Evaluation team

Table 12.5   *Results comparison matrix*

	Target groups	External actors & social dynamic	Technical aspects of PRRO	Implications and elements for conclusions
Tools				
Focal analysis with target groups				
Assets matrix				
Venn diagram				
Stakeholders' workshop				
Survey				
Project documents				
Observational guide				
Field notes				

Conceptual, technical and political reflections on the TLM approach

The application of a case-study method to TLM for the World Food Programme evaluation allowed the team to reflect on den Heyer's (2001) observations regarding the model. The evaluation confirmed her assertion that the TLM is complementary to the 'social learning process'. In other words, by recording programme context changes and interim assessment, the TLM encourages reflection on past and present activities. This can quickly become problematic, however, if project management is uninterested in information that diverts attention from the immediately understandable and quantitatively measurable. The TLM can also run up against time constraints imposed by project cycles, which prevent exploratory engagement in social learning with local stakeholders.

The second conclusion of den Heyer's is that the TLM does not have a specified time frame, in contrast to standard logic models (such as LFA) that cannot move beyond the first phase of a programme to incorporate a long-term vision. The World Food Programme evaluation suggested that this may not be the case. Certainly, standard logic models are rigid and often cumbersome to handle because of their embedded logic, yet from a technical point of view one could use the LFA matrix as a step within an unfolding story, as the TLM does. Indeed, the German agency

GTZ recommends that this should be done, with particular attention to the flexibility aspect. According to GTZ, LFA should be reformulated whenever internal or external changes make the actual matrix outdated. This is actually what TLM does on its horizontal logic (Germann and Gohl 1996).

According to den Heyer (2001), the TLM provides the flexibility to be responsive to programme context, thus facilitating the articulation between micro-theory (as an expression of the internal workings of a programme) and macro-theory (as a representation of the external changes affecting the programme and, more often than not, unpredicted by management). This possibly is the strongest virtue of the TLM, which is also strictly connected with the use of the 'goal' concept as a central one, rather than that of 'objective.' However, over a short time span (such as in a 'quick and dirty' external evaluation), or in the case of a serious lack of evidence about how the context has affected the programme, this virtue remains only a theoretical statement. In any case, targeted groups or stakeholders do not always have the knowledge or willingness to provide feedback about the changes in context.

The last point den Heyer raises is that the TLM focuses on monitoring and recording the process over input–output monitoring. This is one of the in-built working principles of TLM logic, and there is no doubt that the TLM helps people to establish some distance from the result-oriented, managerialist logic of traditional approaches to monitoring and evaluation. However, in light of the empirical work carried out with World Food Programme operation, it seems that this focus on process may be lost because the TLM is not an empirical research tool, but a logic-based tool. It organizes factors logically in a way that combines a soft-system approach (on its vertical logic) with a more formal system approach (on its multi-layered horizontal logic). The lack of physical space to record process information on a single chart creates a practical obstacle to conducting the recording and analytical work necessary for process evaluation with local stakeholders.

Conclusions

There are three conclusions that can be drawn from this chapter. The first is that adoption of different planning and evaluation approaches is not a politically neutral field of debate – as, in general, are neither science nor the production of knowledge. The chapter illustrates how the orthodox application of LFA planning is an applied case of the closed-system approach of multilateral agencies. Through the formulation of goals and objectives, it determines the likelihood of powerful political steering of the project as the main tool for development orientation. Second, there is no guarantee that qualitative or participatory research will be 'empowering' or 'non-extractive', while at the same time there are no strong arguments to confirm that quantitative research methods structurally prevent either empowerment or participant construction of knowledge.

The third conclusion is that the most relevant question here is not a methodological one, but has to do with the combination of politics, policy and techniques within development research. In this sense, the distinction between contextual and non-contextual approaches appears to be a much more promising horizon for research than the rather technical discussion on the quantitative–qualitative divide. In contextual approaches and methods, the main interest is understanding of the relationship existing among different individuals and groups, their social, cultural, natural and economic environments, and the processes of self-organization that take place through the dynamic changes affecting the system (where a system is any social process made by structures and relations). In contrast, non-contextual approaches and methods are more concerned with the determination of the behaviour of a set of variables than with the systemic relationships existing among those and other aspects of reality.

It is worrying, then, that the question of how contextual and non-contextual approaches relate to particular ideological–epistemological perspectives has so far been overlooked within development research. Practitioners must ask themselves how different world views are reflected in the practice of planning and evaluation and how these visions of reality determine the politicized use of qualitative and quantitative methods.

Chapter Thirteen
Trade-offs between
management costs and research benefits:
lessons from the forest and the farm[1]

KATHRIN SCHRECKENBERG, ADRIAN BARRANCE, ANN DEGRANDE,
JAMIE GORDON, ROGER LEAKEY, ELAINE MARSHALL,
ADRIAN NEWTON and ZAC TCHOUNDJEU

Summary

Projects aspiring to combine qualitative and quantitative research
methods face the challenge of achieving the integration of different
research methods and their results without compromising the quality
of component parts. In the natural resource field, the seasonal impera-
tives of botanical and biophysical research can restrict flexibility of
'process' projects subject to the sometimes less predictable pace of
participatory socio-economic methods. Another difficult issue relates
to how to combine methods which operate at different scales. A third
arises from the fact that many researchers specialize in either qualitative
or quantitative research. Combining the two therefore often implies a
collaborative effort between researchers from different disciplines and
organizations. This chapter draws on experience from three multidisciplinary and multi-institutional development research projects
(dealing with conservation of trees on farms in Honduras and Mexico;
domestication of indigenous fruit trees in Cameroon and Nigeria; and
commercialization of non-timber forest products in Bolivia and
Mexico) and a PhD study (on supply and demand of non-timber forest
products in Benin) to highlight some key lessons. These include the
value of jointly developed hypotheses as integrating factors, and the
need for intensive management, reciprocal training of researchers and
frequent joint reviews including interim data-analysis workshops. In
exchange for often very high management costs, the rewards for successful projects are a set of conclusions that are greater than the sum of
the separate parts.

Introduction

This chapter looks at some of the institutional challenges in combining
qualitative and quantitative approaches in development research, and
asks whether the benefits outweigh the costs. We focus on experience
from the forestry (including agroforestry) sector, specifically from the
conservation/development interface where debate is often polarized
along quantitative and qualitative lines, respectively. Our basic premise, however, is that questions relating to the complex interactions of
people and natural resources can be answered only by drawing on

some combination of quantitative and qualitative information. We also assume that this should be done without compromising the quality of data collection for any component approach. Finally, we take it as read that, in the specific context of development research, there is usually a strong emphasis on partners' capacity-building and achieving buy-in of the eventual users of the research results.

To examine the reasons why the reality of achieving these goals is often frustrating, we draw on four different development research projects, all of which deal loosely with the use by local people of trees in a more or less managed environment: supply and demand of non-timber forest products (NTFPs) in Benin; conservation of trees on farms in Honduras and Mexico; domestication of indigenous fruit trees in Cameroon and Nigeria; and commercialization of NTFPs in Bolivia and Mexico. Each involved different numbers and types of researchers and institutions, as well as representing a different combination of research approaches (see Table 13.1 overleaf). Based on the experiences of these projects, we highlight some of the key practical challenges and trade-offs (in terms of resources and time) associated with trying to bring together more qualitative and quantitative approaches.

Obstacles to integration

A similar range of problems was encountered in all four projects. Some related specifically to how to combine more qualitative and quantitative approaches in the field; some were more to do with the different worldviews of researchers working in different disciplines; and others arose from the fact that collaborating across different disciplines almost always means collaboration across institutions.

Getting the sequencing right

As outlined by Holland and Campbell (see General Introduction), the key to the effective combination of methods and data lies in the iterative relationship between descriptive (usually more quantitative) and explanatory (more qualitative) approaches. In practice, this means careful and, where necessary, flexible sequencing of methods so that the results of one strand can feed into another.

Sequencing of methods in the natural resource field is complicated by the fact that so many of them – whether qualitative or quantitative – are seasonally constrained. Phenological studies are by their very nature a record of change across the seasons. Yield studies or market surveys for fresh produce (fruit, leaves, etc.) are similarly seasonal, and farmers are more 'switched on' to discussion of domestication issues when the trees are fruiting. Botanical surveys may be restricted to the times of year when plants are in leaf but the terrain remains accessible. In the same way, much community-level and household-level work is dependent on farmer availability – affected by both seasonal migration and the agricultural calendar as well as daily work patterns.

Seasonality issues can spoil plans for integration. In the 'Conservation through use of Tree Species Diversity in Fragmented Mesoamerican Dry Forest' (CUBOS) project in Honduras, for example, our initial aim had been to have a combined fieldwork team consisting of a socio-economist and a botanist to carry out semi-structured household interviews and biodiversity inventories of the household's plots, the latter accompanied by a member of the household being interviewed. The botanical surveys were under great seasonal constraints, however, and were found to be so time-consuming that it was impossible to wait for farmers' availability to do them. We were therefore obliged to separate the socio-economic and botanical teams.

The CUBOS project also illustrates the importance of being clear about the objectives of a project when deciding how to sequence methods. If CUBOS had been only about finding the most effective way to conserve threatened tree species diversity, then we should have focused first on botanical surveys to determine the location of threatened species (which turned out to be only in Mexico and not in our other case-study country, Honduras), and then carried out the socio-economic research to see how to conserve them. The fact that the project also had livelihood objectives, however, justified the concurrent implementation of both qualitative and quantitative methods.

Sequencing can also be constrained by how experienced researchers are in different methods. The researcher's knowledge of an area is more important in determining the quality of qualitative than quantitative work (Schreckenberg 1995). In Benin, for example, the same participatory research was carried out with five groups of women one after the other, over a period of nine months. The information collected later was much more complete and reliable than that obtained from the first group of women. In the early stages we accepted too much information at face value. Later, with a deeper understanding of the area (in part derived from collecting a range of quantitative data on natural resources and markets), we were better able to recognize evasive statements or conflicting information, and to probe further. A research team new to an area may, therefore, be better off starting with quantitative work and only engaging in qualitative work at a later stage.

The greatest difficulties arise when trying to combine seasonally constrained methods with a 'process' approach in which the issues raised in early rounds of research determine the direction taken by later research activities. In the project 'Commercialisation of Non-timber Forest Products in Mexico and Bolivia: Factors Influencing Success' (CEPFOR), the main data collection tool – a questionnaire investigating various aspects of the commercialization process of NTFPs among community members and traders – was developed in a very participatory manner and took into account the results of preliminary qualitative work in the study communities. By the time it had been completed, tested and revised, however, the pressure to implement it quickly was very great if the project was to finish on time. Unfortunately, of the ten NTFPs studied several were highly seasonal, and some of the commu-

Table 13.1 Comparison of methodological aspects of four projects

	Benin PhD	CUBOS	Cameroon project	CEPFOR
Project aims	Investigate demand and supply of non-timber forest products (NTFPs) in the Bassila region of Benin	Investigate the potential for conservation-through-use of trees on-farm in the Mesoamerican dry forest zone of southern Mexico and Honduras	Investigate the constraints and opportunities for resource-poor farmers to obtain greater benefits from indigenous fruit trees	Investigate the factors that determine the success or failure of commercialization enterprises
Countries of fieldwork	Benin	Mexico, Honduras	Cameroon, Nigeria	Mexico, Bolivia
Countries of partners	Germany, UK	UK	UK, Australia	UK, Nicaragua
Languages	English, French	English, Spanish	English, French	English, Spanish
Number of partners, organization type	2 universities. 1 bilateral forestry project	1 university. 1 research institute. 4 herbaria. 2 government departments. 1 international and 2 national NGOs. 3 independent researchers	2 research institutes. 2 CGIAR organizations. 1 commercial research institute. 1 national agricultural research institute. 1 government extension service. 4 national NGOs, 1 bilateral project	2 research institutes 2 international and 3 national NGOs. 2 independent researchers
Core research team with disciplines*	1 person (social forestry)	5 people (social forestry x 2, forestry, natural resource economics, botany)	5 people (social forestry, agroforestry x 2, agricultural economics, market economics)	6 people (natural resource management, ecology, social forestry, market economics x 2, econometrics)
Time frame	1992–6 (13 months)	1996–2003 (4 years)	1999–2003 (2.5 years)	2001–4 (4 years)
Reference	Schreckenberg (1996)	Gordon et al. (2003)	Leakey et al. (2003)	Marshall et al. (2003)

* 'Core' team members are those who contributed substantially to the development of the research methods and analysis of the results. 'Other' team members are those who participated in the implementation of the research.

	Benin PhD	CUBOS	Cameroon project	CEPFOR
Methods used, listed in order of those producing the most quantitative data through to those producing the most qualitative data	Tree inventory around 3 villages to measure density of NTFP species. Fortnightly phenological study of 11 NTFP species. Yield studies for 2 species. Weekly market surveys at 2 markets. Household surveys of NTFP use in 4 villages. Focus groups on women's income and expenditure patterns. Focus groups on uses of main NTFP species. Participant observation of NTFP harvesting and processing	Botanical surveys of species occurrence in different land-use types in 8 communities. Economic studies of benefits of on-farm trees in 2 communities. Community-level participatory work in 8 communities. Semi-structured household interviews in 8 communities on tree management and use practices. Focus groups on particular tree products and production systems	Biophysical measurements of fruit of 2 species. Phenological studies of same 2 species. Monthly NTFP market surveys at 11 markets. Inventories of fruit trees on farms in 6 communities. Community-level participatory work. Household interviews in 6 communities	Household surveys in all 17. communities. Trader surveys along market chains for 10 NTFPs. Market reports for 10 NTFPs. Community-level participatory work in 17 communities. Background policy study in each country
Sequencing of methods	Phenological study and market surveys carried out simultaneously with focus groups. These provided background for development of a very specific household survey instrument applied at end of study period. Timing of inventory and yield studies determined by seasonality	Community-level work provided general context for selection of households for household interviews. Timing of botanical surveys constrained by seasonality and need for land-use information from the household interviews. Results from household interviews and botanical surveys fed into design of economic study. Information from household interviews later cross-checked with focus groups	Community-level work provided context for selection of households for interviews and farm inventories. Biophysical and phenological work constrained by seasonality. Market surveys carried out independently of other work but in nearest markets to study communities	Community-level work provided context for selection of households for surveys and for identifying market routes and traders to be interviewed. Together with policy studies, community-level work helped identify the issues to be addressed in the household survey
Existence of explicit research themes	No. Methods used to explore general research hypotheses	No. Some implicit in project document but never explicitly amended in the light of emerging findings and changing donor priorities	No. But some developed as research progressed	Yes. 6 hypotheses, each with about 10 research questions, were developed at first project meeting
Number and types of meetings held	None between all partners. Few others. Most consultation by post	All project partners only brought together for final project 'maturity' meeting. Core team met about once a year	Inception workshop with training of whole team. Interim monitoring workshop. Data analysis workshop. Maturity workshop. Writing workshop. UK-based team met twice a year	4 workshops for core team. 2 inception workshops in Bolivia and Mexico. 2 market training workshops. 2 whole project data analysis workshops. 1 dissemination workshop. Quarterly meetings of UK-based team
Reference	Schreckenberg (1996)	Gordon et al. (2003)	Leakey et al. (2003)	Marshall et al. (2003)

nities were accessible for only part of the year. Implementation of the questionnaire in some communities was therefore substantially delayed, with knock-on effects on the timing of data analysis.

This raises the issue of how to squeeze research, of whatever type, into a conventional project cycle. Even a slight delay in starting a project can lead to the boat being missed on some seasonally constrained activities and, in turn, require a change in the overall sequence of methods. Sequencing is further complicated by the need for development research projects to keep an eye on the policy process, producing briefings for specific events. Donors' requirements for interim policy outputs also put increasing pressure on interdisciplinary research projects, which may need to draw on several strands of research (each with its own timetable of analysis) to come up with integrated recommendations.

Reconciling sampling strategies

Sampling strategies (and the resulting recommendation domains) are without doubt one of the most difficult issues to resolve within a multidisciplinary team. The first issue relates to sampling over time. Many quantitative approaches in the forestry sector are dependent on the vagaries of nature (e.g. phenological, yield and market studies) and should be carried out over several years to enable the team to learn (test and amend methods) in the first season, and to allow for year-to-year variation in fruiting (which may impact on prices etc.). In the Cameroon project, for instance, many of the trees that had been selected for observation did not fruit in the year we were working. This need to carry out fieldwork over several years may be difficult to combine with qualitative approaches (community-level participatory reflection and action in the Cameroon case) that hope to provide rapid feedback to communities.

It may also be necessary to compromise over spatial sampling. In Cameroon the fact that the 'biophysical' team (who were measuring variation in fruit characteristics) needed to access trees of particular species meant that one of the four case-study villages was selected for its abundance of a particular species, even though it was not typical of the area in many socio-economic respects. Furthermore, although we wanted to carry out the biophysical work on the trees observed in the farm tree inventories, this was not possible because the biophysical study required a minimum number of trees and these could not be found within the 20 households involved in the farm inventory (and sometimes not even within the village selected). So the biophysical sampling strategy had to be adapted, and we were unable to test some of the hypotheses (e.g. that various farmer characteristics were linked to particular fruit characteristics) that would have required socio-economic and biophysical information to be collected for the same trees/owners.

Collaborating across disciplines

Modern researchers tend to undergo increasingly specialized disciplinary training. Bringing together qualitative and quantitative approaches therefore requires not just a multidisciplinary team, but also a multi-person one. This means that projects need to deal with the relative requirements of the methods as well as of individual researchers and their parent institutions.

Trying to meet several individual research agendas may 'inflate' projects beyond what is necessary to answer the central questions. How willing individuals are to compromise depends greatly on how well they understand, and are interested in, the different project components. This kind of mutual respect and common focus on project goals may take time to develop. In the CEPFOR project, for example, although the core team decided early on to take a participatory approach to developing the research methods, the implications of what this meant in practice were not explicitly discussed or agreed by all team members. As a result, the inception workshops in each country were primarily devoted to collecting a specific subset of data from participants to enable an early trial data analysis. But this meant that methodology development had to be pursued by email in a manner that was very time-consuming and did not result in immediate ownership of the overall approach by all partners.

Ideally, trust should be established when sampling strategies and data quality issues for each research strand are being discussed, as these issues can usually be understood across disciplines. Data analysis, however, may be beyond all but the relevant specialists. Having confidence in each other's conclusions therefore depends on the trust built up early on in the project.

One of the problems of a multidisciplinary team is that it is often large, and few researchers are likely to be working on the project full-time. Budget constraints simply make it impossible to fund a large number of specialists for the duration of the project. Instead, each one is paid for short periods, sufficient to carry out their research component, but rarely sufficient to cover the interaction time required to facilitate integration between disciplines. When all a project's researchers are dividing their time between several activities, it is difficult enough to schedule fieldwork, let alone cross-disciplinary project meetings. Successful integration of qualitative and quantitative approaches therefore almost inevitably extends the length of the project.

Collaborating across institutions

Given that many institutions specialize in a particular type of research, achieving multidisciplinarity often requires working with several institutions. This introduces many complications that, although only indirectly the result of combining qualitative and quantitative approaches, can prove a serious obstacle to integration.

All institutions have different ways of working, including the extent to which they insist on strategic versus operational planning of research agendas. In some cases research must be included in annual work plans, in others it can be planned more quickly and informally. Differing financial years can complicate budget management, as can varying flexibility in an institution's ability to transfer funds between years and budget lines. Together these factors determine how likely an organisation is to be able to support a process project in which qualitative and quantitative approaches are sequenced in response to results of earlier data collection.

Different institutions typically have quite different goals, which can impact greatly not only on how research is carried out, but also on what forms of dissemination are expected. Thus academic institutions are interested in testing research hypotheses, and researchers are judged on the basis of peer-reviewed publications. Others are more interested in achieving policy impact. Development NGOs, on the other hand, usually want immediate results for the study communities. The Benin PhD study was a typical example of the problem of having multiple taskmasters – the university required 'innovative' work; the bilateral donor required standardized data; and the host project sought practical advice – resulting in the need to collect sufficient data to satisfy all three and produce several types of output. In such a situation, it is essential that all stakeholders agree exactly who needs what at an early stage.

Three of the projects worked with local NGOs, most of which had either a strongly qualitative development focus, or a more quantitative conservation focus. While this caused some difficulties with respect to how receptive they were to multidisciplinary approaches, a more fundamental issue was their lack of experience in carrying out rigorous research. In the CEPFOR project, it became clear that this was particularly problematic for qualitative data collection. We had selected various participatory reflection and action tools precisely because our NGO partners were experienced in using them, but it turned out to be impossible to convince partners that these needed to be employed as rigorously as our quantitative data collection tools if we wanted data that were comparable across the 17 study communities.

The Cameroon project represents an ideal case in which the national coordinating organization, in this case the World Agroforestry Centre (ICRAF), itself has a mandate to work in an interdisciplinary manner and therefore had a good understanding of the methodological and consequent logistical needs of all the research strands.

Making it work: the costs

Over the course of the four projects it has become clear that compromise and sufficient resources of time and money can help overcome many of the obstacles discussed above.

Joint development of hypotheses

Jointly developed hypotheses can be an excellent way of focusing all project partners on the key thematic questions. They are particularly useful in determining the relative contributions of qualitative and quantitative approaches, and how they can be integrated most effectively.

It pays to state hypotheses explicitly, unlike in the CUBOS project in which hypotheses resided primarily in the heads of the original project planners. They were therefore not 'owned' by the new field team that took over just after the inception of the project. As a result, for justifiable logistical and methodological reasons, this team dropped some of the more quantitative elements of the household interviews and botanical surveys. Some of the analysis originally foreseen was therefore not possible. The lack of guiding hypotheses was compounded by low-intensity management (split between two institutions with very different worldviews), and a lack of project reviews which might have enabled the team to identify and remedy data gaps at an early stage.

The CEPFOR project took the decision to invest time in developing six fairly general hypotheses, each supported by a set of more specific research questions. Based heavily on the international literature, these turned out to be an excellent way of introducing national partners to this body of theory. More importantly, they were an essential tool for ensuring that different components of the research focused on the same issues and fed into each other's analysis (see Table 13.2, page 201).

Many research projects compromise on their methodology to keep within budget and time. The existence of a clear set of hypotheses can be very helpful in determining just how much it is possible to compromise before the project loses its focus. In the CEPFOR project, for example, it was impossible to carry out a detailed quantitative market analysis for all the NTFPs studied, and decisions about which to drop were based on how much each product could contribute to the understanding of the project's hypotheses. This also illustrates that it is often not necessary for all research methods to be implemented across all case-study products or communities. The Cameroon project found that it was more effective to focus qualitative community-level work in Cameroon only, while some of the more quantitative tools were also used in two Nigerian communities. Although less complete, the Nigerian data provided a good balance to the Cameroon data and greatly enriched the overall results.

Reciprocal capacity-building

Ravallion (2003) argues that the main barriers to mixing qualitative and quantitative methods lie in the resistance of practitioners to stepping outside the traditional boundaries of practice. To get around this, both the Cameroon and CEPFOR projects invested heavily in capacity-building for their partners.

The Cameroon project began by training biophysical, market and socio-economic researchers in participatory methods and community-level work. In addition to generating a broad understanding of the aims of the project, the training course was a fun way for the diverse research team to get to know each other and appreciate each other's skills and disciplinary perspectives. At the time, we considered it less important to train the whole team in the more quantitative (and seemingly more straightforward) biophysical and market research techniques. In retrospect this was a missed opportunity for the biophysical team, in particular, to influence elements of the market and socio-economic work.

In addition to providing cross-disciplinary training, the CEPFOR project illustrated the need to train NGO partners in general research best practice, including consistent standards of data collection, recording and management. It also showed that ongoing capacity-building was vital not just for the field staff, but also for the core planning team to ensure that they understood and respected each other's approaches. This was achieved through frequent team meetings and mini-seminars by each specialist, enabling participants to begin to understand each other's disciplinary languages and appreciate both the potential and the limitations of different analytical approaches.

Early joint analysis

Meetings to trial analysis at an early stage of the project are an essential part of capacity-building for partners, who are much more likely to collect data well if they understand how they are going to be used. Such meetings also provide an early opportunity to determine whether data type and quality are sufficient to meet the project's needs. In Cameroon, for example, very simple information such as 'plot age' was not recorded on the inventory forms, as the collectors did not realize the importance of this particular information for linking different data sets. Delays between data collection and analysis meant it was then impossible to go back to the same plots to complete the data.

In the CEPFOR case, conclusions based on early analysis of the quantitative data were challenged by the qualitative information, and further inspection revealed an error in the original data. Parallel analysis of the different strands also highlighted which of the project's hypotheses and research questions were not being sufficiently tackled by any strand.

Joint analysis at an early stage of the project has the added advantages of focusing the minds of the mainly part-time research team; providing a deadline for work components to be completed by; and, where necessary, helping to bring the different research strands back into step with one another.

Inviting selected disciplinary experts to some of these analysis meetings can be very rewarding. In the CEPFOR project, for example, an external statistician facilitated an important discussion about the limitations of our varied research approaches and the implications for the project's recommendation domains.

Table 13.2   *How the CEPFOR project used hypotheses and research*
questions to determine data source and type of analysis

Hypotheses and research questions	Data source	Analysis methods	Who?
Hypothesis: changes in trade in non-timber forest products (NTFPs) have a greater impact on the poorest producers, processors and traders			
Research question: are the same individuals involved in production (collection and cultivation), processing and trade?	1. Survey question 1.1 2. Community reports sections 7.5 and 7.6	1. Regression against measures of success 2. Tabulation by products and communities	1. DWtV 2. EM and KS
Explanatory note: Each of the project's six hypotheses was broken down into several research questions	Explanatory note: For each research question we determined which data sources would provide relevant data	Explanatory note: This column indicated what kind of analysis would be carried out	Explanatory note: Here we assigned responsibility for different parts of the analysis

Intensive management, frequent reviews and long-term commitment

A full-time research coordinator is always a benefit, but particularly so in multidisciplinary (and multi-institutional) projects which require additional work to ensure that all collaborators work towards the same goal. It is important that this person understands the research requirements of all partners and can mediate fairly between different research strands as necessary, for example if compromises on sampling strategies are needed, or delays in one component cause problems in another. In a comparative project, at least one person from each discipline should know most, if not all, the fieldwork sites in order to be able to evaluate the quality of the data collected in them.

It is almost impossible for a project crossing disciplinary, institutional, and usually national boundaries to have too many opportunities to feed ideas from one research team/component to the other(s). As much as email has revolutionized communications, crossing disciplinary boundaries requires a great deal of trust between collaborators which can best be fostered through frequent face-to-face meetings. In the CEPFOR project meetings built rapport and enabled all collaborators to question, doubt and explore issues directly with other partners – fuelling learning curves, increasing transparency, and reducing any potential confusion, misunderstanding or resentment in achieving joint project goals.

In addition to the more intensive management required and greater number of cross-project meetings, a project combining qualitative and quantitative approaches is likely to need more time simply to allow for the complexity of sequencing, particularly if seasonally constrained quantitative methods are being integrated into a process project.

The rewards

Carvalho and White (1997) discuss three ways of combining the best of qualitative and quantitative approaches:

- **integrating** the quantitative and qualitative methodologies
- **examining, explaining, confirming, refuting and/or enriching** information from one approach with that from the other
- **merging the findings** from the two approaches into one set of policy recommendations.

Each of the four case-study projects attempted to achieve some or all of these in different measure. The Benin PhD study deliberately kept each methodological approach quite separate to avoid compromising quality. The fact that all were undertaken by a single researcher, who could determine sequencing to suit the needs of the research rather than being constrained by the availability of disciplinary specialists, meant that the separate methods were used in a flexible and iterative manner. As a result, even though the research was carried out during a single year, a combination of information about agricultural practices, how women earned their livelihoods, and patterns of tree densities (from tree surveys) allowed for a complex understanding of how NTFP use was changing over time.

The original aim of the CUBOS project was to integrate the botanical and socio-economic methodologies. In the event this was not practical, but the two teams at least overlapped in the same communities for some of the time and ended up providing different but complementary types of information. In comparing biodiversity in Honduras and Mexico, for example, a good grasp of tenure issues and their relation to biodiversity was vitally important to understand why some areas might have rare species and others not. By merging the findings from the two approaches, it was possible to derive rich policy recommendations that spoke to both conservation and livelihoods worlds.

In Cameroon, there was no direct integration of methodologies. although each took into account the other's needs when determining sampling strategies, and used the same villages. The location of the project within a permanent research institution with ongoing work in the study areas also made it possible for some iteration to take place and additional research to be carried out. The merging of the findings from the qualitative and quantitative strands was important not just in the development of high-level policy recommendations, but also at a very practical level in helping farmers select trees for domestication. This requires not only an understanding of people's varied preferences (e.g. for large kernels or tasty fruit; for low trees to facilitate harvesting; or for aseasonal production to meet local market requirements), but also an understanding of the existing biophysical variation within a particular species or tree population, and how different characteristics are linked. For the individual researchers the greatest benefit of the multidisciplinary collaboration was the personal understanding and experience they gained, which has benefited their subsequent work.

The CEPFOR project made the greatest attempts to achieve methodological integration. Its research hypotheses were framed in such a way that they could have been investigated only with a combination of qualitative or quantitative approaches. Based on qualitative work at community level, the project developed a survey tool that provided data for econometricians, market analysts and socio-economists, and for use in the development of Bayesian belief networks. The process was much more time-consuming than if the research approaches had been pursued separately, and also led to some loss of quality in the data collected. The benefits were in the establishment of a truly inter-disciplinary team, from field-based researchers to office-based managers, who shared a fuller understanding of the project objectives and achievements, and in a comprehensive and multifaceted approach to commenting on the project's hypotheses.

Overall, the projects suggest that there are many benefits of combining qualitative and quantitative approaches:

- more complex understanding of the issues being researched leads to more meaningful and often more precise recommendations
- drawing on different disciplinary approaches ensures a broader policy impact as recommendations are taken seriously by policy makers from both quantitative and qualitative schools
- reciprocal capacity-building within the team opens researchers' eyes to the potentials and pitfalls of different approaches
- working within a multidisciplinary team means researchers are constantly being challenged to justify their approach and conclusions, ensuring that only the best is taken from each
- the continuing challenge and opportunity to learn from colleagues leads to much greater researcher satisfaction.

Conclusions: is it worth it?

This chapter began with the premise that natural resource management questions can be answered only with some combination of qualitative and quantitative data. These data could be obtained through two or more separate single-discipline projects, with an additional project to integrate the results. Depending on when, and how well, the separate projects were planned, the integrated results may or may not respond precisely to the questions being asked. Another option would be to design a single integrated project from the start. The lessons of the projects presented in this chapter are that this latter option is worthwhile not only because it produces a set of rich and layered results that are more relevant, useful and adoptable at the level of the ultimate (farmer) beneficiary, but also because it ensures buy-in from varied stakeholders and has the added benefit of achieving high levels of researcher capacity-building and satisfaction.

We should not, however, be under any illusion that, simply because we are dealing with one project instead of several, a project integrating qualitative and quantitative approaches will be a cheaper or faster option. The costs are primarily in the form of more project meetings and capacity-building to ensure mutual methodological acceptance, the time needed for iteration of methods (particularly if some are seasonally constrained), and the intensive management required to keep a multidisciplinary (and usually multi-institutional) project on track. If we face up to these resource implications, then qualitative and quantitative approaches can be combined to great benefit.

Chapter Fourteen
Evaluating democracy assistance: the inadequacy of numbers and the promise of participation

GORDON CRAWFORD

Summary

Democracy assistance entails the promotion of democratization by international donor agencies. Over a decade after its introduction, evaluation of its impact and effectiveness has become crucial, yet faces considerable methodological challenges. In this chapter, the limitations of conventional evaluation methodologies are explored, notably those of the logical framework approach, with reference to recent evaluation studies in this field. Four main shortcomings are examined: a project rather than a programme focus; applicability to 'hard' rather than 'soft' data; inward rather than outward orientation; and a problematic emphasis on causality and quantitative indicators. An alternative methodology is proposed that involves a participatory political process. A participatory approach entails greater emphasis on qualitative methods, although quantitative methods can usefully be combined, for example by converting qualitative evidence into quantitative scores. Two advantages of the proposed methodology are claimed. For donor agencies, past and current efforts are subjected to more critical examination. For participant evaluators, knowledge of processes of political change is enhanced, strengthening local action for democratic reform. Thus the act of evaluation can become an act of democratization. Such arguments are at variance with current practice, however, and a wider aim of this chapter is to encourage a shift in development agency practice in evaluating democracy and governance assistance.

Introduction

During the 1990s, the promotion of democracy and governance (DG) emerged as a major field of activity within international development cooperation, with significant amounts of aid funding now allocated to this area. After more than a decade of such activities, the question of evaluation has become a crucial one, essential to assess the achievements of DG assistance as well as to learn lessons and improve its future effectiveness.

There are considerable challenges to evaluating DG assistance. This chapter examines the relative merits in this field of two competing methodological approaches: conventional evaluation and participatory evaluation. The chapter is in four main parts. First, this introduction briefly examines the challenges and problems associated with DG evaluation, notably in assessing the impact of external assistance on national-level political change. The second part then examines the application to the DG sphere of conventional evaluation methodology – logical framework analysis and related results-based approaches – by a number of development agencies, with shortcomings emphasized. Third, the application of a participatory approach to DG evaluation is discussed, with advantages highlighted. Finally, the conclusion briefly summarizes the evidence and argument, reasserting a twofold advantage of a participatory approach to DG evaluation – for development agencies, a more critical appraisal of their role, better informed by local perspectives; for participant evaluators, knowledge of processes of domestic political change is further enhanced, thereby building local capacity to press for democratic reforms.

Challenges in evaluating DG assistance

The inherent difficulties in evaluating DG assistance are at their most acute when conducting an impact evaluation at national level, that is, assessing the contribution of external assistance to democratization in a particular country. Six main issues are identified, focusing on problems of attribution, which leave a number of unanswered questions.[1]

- The **multiplicity of actors and factors in complex political change**, and the difficulties of differentiating the contribution of a single actor. How can the contribution of internal and external actors, and of individual donors, be distinguished?
- **With and without scenarios and issues of counterfactuality** – how is it possible to gauge what would have happened anyway, without external support? At best it may be possible to show some correlation between the nature of external assistance and such developments.
- **External–internal relationships** – in attributing perceived developments partly to the activities of external actors, have the interrelationships between internal and external actors been sufficiently addressed? External efforts may depend on local support, for instance. Alternatively, countervailing forces in the particular country may undermine external actions.
- The **overall political context** is an important determinant of programme impact, either conducive or unfavourable to democratic reform, depending on the relative strength or weakness of pro-democratic actors, as well as structural factors such as patterns of economic development.
- **Time scale** – how possible is it to evaluate the impact of projects and programmes that have only recently been completed, given that democratic change is a long-term process?
- **Unintended impact** – external intervention involves a dynamic, interactive process and can have unintended side effects. Does the search for positive impact ignore the possibility of negative impact?

How do different methodological approaches respond to these challenges, and what are their relative strengths and weaknesses in doing so? These are the main questions addressed here through the examination of conventional and participatory approaches to evaluation.

Conventional evaluation: the 'false dream of science'?[2]

Logical framework analysis (LFA), including the closely related results-based approach, represents the application of the conventional evaluation paradigm in the aid sphere, including its implementation in the DG sector by key development agencies (see Box 14.1 below and overleaf). Its continued wide appeal requires that it be examined seriously. A brief introduction to LFA is provided here, followed by an assessment of its adoption in the DG field by four official development agencies: the Canadian International Development Agency (CIDA), the US Agency for International Development (USAID), the Swedish International Development Co-operation Agency (Sida) and the European Commission. A final section offers an overall critique of LFA, highlighting its shortcomings and limitations as a means of evaluating DG assistance.

Logical framework analysis entails the application of the 'experimental approach' to evaluation, itself based on positivist social science, with evaluation methodology based on a theory of causality (Rebien 1996: 19–21; Pawson and Tilley 1997: 4–8). The logframe approach rests on tracing causal connections between project inputs (or activities), outputs and objectives, with the latter divided into immediate objectives (or project purpose) and wider objectives (or

---

Box 14.1   *Development agencies and the evaluation of democracy and governance*

CIDA and USAID: results-based approaches

In the mid-1990s, both CIDA and USAID introduced a modified, logframe-related approach to monitoring and evaluation on an agency-wide basis, known as 'results-based management' and 'managing for results', respectively. For CIDA a 'result' is defined as 'a describable or measurable change ... that is derived from a cause and effect relationship' (CIDA 2000a: 12), in other words, attributable to resource inputs. Results-based management entails a typical logframe approach with the construction of a performance framework and a performance measurement framework. The performance framework provides the anticipated cause-and-effect relationships from the level of activities (inputs) upwards to strategic goals, including assumptions and risk assessments; the performance measurement framework provides a systematic plan for measurement and verification through (mainly quantitative) performance indicators and data collection requirements (CIDA 2000a: 32).

Box 14.1   *Development agencies and the evaluation of*
(continued)   *democracy and governance*

Sida: the 'Evaluability of Democracy and Human Rights' projects
– a logframe-related assessment

Sida introduced the logical framework approach as a standard part of its project cycle management in 1996. The evaluability of democracy and human rights assistance by means of logframe methodology was given specific consideration in a study conducted for Sida jointly by a private consultant, ITAD Ltd, and the Overseas Development Institute, London (Sida 2000). Findings were negative overall, with only two out of 28 projects assessed as meeting the evaluability criteria and thus suitable for logframe evaluation. The conclusions drawn, however, are not that the logframe approach is inadequate or flawed and that alternative methods should be sought, but that low evaluability can be remedied through improved project design in logical framework terms. Two assumptions appear to underpin this study. One is that a wider impact evaluation is not feasible given that 'most D/HR interventions are small-scale relative to the complexity of the problems addressed' and that it is 'over-optimistic to count on significant progress towards wider objectives from donor financed D/HR activities' (Sida 2000: 6). Thus 'the evaluation of outcomes [is] generally more feasible than the evaluation of impact' (Sida 2000: 6). The second assumption is of the superiority of logical framework analysis, hence a reluctance to examine other possible approaches to evaluation in this area, despite the terms of reference that the study 'analyse and possibly also propose alternative impact evaluation approaches' (Sida 2000: 24).

European Commission: methodological ambiguity

The logframe approach has been adopted in two recent evaluations of European Commission democracy and human rights programmes, that of the Mediterranean Democracy Programme (MDP) (European Commission 1999), and of 'positive actions in the field of human rights and democracy' (1995–9) in the African, Caribbean and Pacific (ACP) countries (European Commission 2000). Both studies are basically aggregates of project evaluations, with logframes used to assess the relevance, efficiency, effectiveness, impact and sustainability of projects. Interestingly, although the terms of reference require the application of LFA in both instances, the evaluators differ in their responses. The ACP study enthusiastically adopted the logical framework 'as the cornerstone of its methodology', describing it as 'the most widely accepted planning tool' and a 'useful quality assessment tool' (European Commission 2000: 18). In contrast, the MDP study expressed reservations as to the appropriateness of the logframe approach, emphasizing that political programmes have 'many "soft" components with regard to project results, objectives and impact ... very difficult to measure in terms of the logical framework' (European Commission 1999: 15). Intriguingly, and notwithstanding the terms of reference, the MDP study cites support for this viewpoint from the Commission itself, quoting the statement that 'human rights projects are quite different from infrastructure construction programmes, and the evaluation and selection criteria should therefore be based on a different approach' (European Commission 1995, cited in European Commission 1999: 15). It would seem that little progress has been made, or attempted, in formulating that alternative approach.

programme goal). A logical framework matrix is initially prepared at the design stage of project cycle management, inclusive of the above dimensions, plus performance indicators and their means of verification, along with a statement of the risks and assumptions involved (Cracknell 2000: 108–12). This provides a means of monitoring and evaluating progress towards achievement of stated objectives, one that is essentially quantitative in nature, although the use of qualitative indicators is allowable. Logical framework analysis provides a seemingly rigorous evaluation methodology, although limited to tracing the realization of declared objectives. It is generally acknowledged, however, including among supporters of LFA, that it is best suited to evaluating lower-level project objectives and 'less well adapted to tracking performance of programmes and policies at a higher level' (Cracknell 2000: 116).

Within the sphere of development assistance, USAID and CIDA originally introduced the logical framework approach in North America in the early 1970s as a means of project management, inclusive of evaluation. Subsequently, it has been widely adopted by many European agencies, notably by GTZ; the UK Department for International Development (DFID) in 1985; more recently by the European Commission and Sida; and additionally by the World Bank (Cracknell 2000: 101–6). Thus, although LFA has faced increasing challenge in the 1990s from participatory approaches (Rebien 1996; Cracknell 2000), its popularity and appeal among development cooperation agencies is evident. But is it a suitable methodology for evaluating DG assistance? Danish International Development Assistance (Danida), part of the Ministry of Foreign Affairs, notes that LFA has been recommended for use in the human rights and democracy field by the influential Development Assistance Committee of the Organization for Economic Cooperation and Development, yet Danida's own view is that LFA and political analysis 'are not particularly compatible' (Danida 2000: vol. 1, 66).[3] The application of logframe-related evaluation to the DG sphere by four agencies – CIDA, USAID, Sida and the European Commission – is examined here, highlighting its limitations and questioning its appropriateness.

Logical framework analysis: a technical solution to a political problem?

Logical framework analysis is an approach that has generated considerable controversy, focusing on its notions of causality and its reliance on quantitative data. Partly stemming from the general critique of positivist approaches to evaluation (Guba and Lincoln 1989), LFA within aid evaluation has come under increasing pressure from alternative approaches that emphasize participatory and qualitative dimensions (Rebien 1996; Cracknell 2000: 178), seen as especially valuable for evaluating social development projects (Marsden and Oakley 1990; Marsden et al. 1994). A review of such general debates is not possible here, and the critique offered in this research focuses specifically on the shortcomings and limitations of LFA as a means of evaluating DG assistance. Four main problems with LFA are briefly highlighted: its project not programme focus; its applicability to 'hard' not 'soft' data; its inward not outward orientation; and its problematic emphasis on causality and quantitative indicators.

The logical framework approach is narrowly geared towards evaluation of projects, most appropriately where clear outputs can be achieved within a specific time span and where hard quantitative data are more readily available – blueprint-type projects such as infrastructural projects. It is less appropriate for evaluation of wider programme goals. This is especially true for DG, a soft area of programming in which institutional relationships and culture are the subject of reform, where time frames are hard to predict, and change is difficult to measure (CIDA 2000b).

Logical framework analysis is inward-orientated, inverting evaluation towards predetermined project objectives. In contrast, evaluation of political interventions requires an outward orientation, able to capture the political context in which such interventions are implanted. This is particularly important given that the overall context is itself a significant factor in influencing the success or otherwise of external donor interventions, for instance the relative strength or weakness of domestic pro-democratic actors. Thus the nature of democratization, and of programmes intended to assist such processes, are not appropriate to logframe-type analysis: LFA 'cannot anticipate and capture the political dynamics in which local actors will make their decisions' (Danida 2000: vol. 1, 66). Indeed, the logframe approach tends to assume the idea of progress, being designed to accompany a process of positive change. Two problems emerge, however. One is that democratization is not a linear process of positive and gradual change, rather it is an irregular process following a non-linear pattern, with progressions and regressions. In the case of regressions, LFA becomes obsolete. The second problem is that the combination of inward orientation and assumed progress means that LFA is unable to countenance negative, unintended effects of DG assistance, one of the challenges noted above.

Such criticisms can be broadened to reject more paradigmatically the 'inadequacy of numbers' and the 'false dream of science' with regard to the emphases on causality and quantification, as with Carothers' (1999) forthright critique of USAID's 'managing for results' system. He perceives that the 'core problem is that democratization in any country cannot be broken down neatly and precisely into a set of quantitative bits' (Carothers 1999: 291). In other words, there are difficulties both with the division of whole, complex processes into a series of fragments, and with trying to quantify them. Using such 'informational bits as criteria of success without grounding them in sophisticated, deep-reaching analyses of the political context produces superficial and dangerously misleading pictures' (Carothers 1999: 291). Carothers cites the example of Cambodia in 1997 as evidence, where USAID reported that 'progress against indicators exceeded expectations' with regard to its democracy programme, 'almost surreally' oblivious to the recent coup that had derailed the democratic transition (Carothers 1999: 291–2). As regards quantification, the problem is that:

> *'In most cases, numbers tell very little, and what they do tell is unclear. Reducing large elements of democracy ... down to two or three extremely narrow quantitative indicators does irremediable violence to those concepts.'* (Carothers 1999: 293)

Given the complex nature of democratization and the variety of factors involved, both structural and agency-related, the establishment of plausible linkages between donor interventions and political change may be the best that can be hoped for.

In sum, LFA is rejected here, as are results-based approaches, as inappropriate for evaluating DG programmes. Such instruments of conventional evaluation offer little to resolve the challenges of evaluating DG assistance. They are narrow in focus, more pertinent to the limited functions of project cycle management, with little or no consideration of the range of factors involved in complex political change. They are oriented to providing an immediate assessment of newly completed projects, largely blinkered to negative, unintended effects, and less able to trace medium- to long-term impacts. The (pseudo-)scientific approach, largely based on quantitative methods, is unable to cope with the dynamic political context in which DG activities are embedded. Logical framework analysis offers an inappropriately technocratic solution to a political problem. It is concluded that evaluating DG assistance is more art than science.

Participatory evaluation: an alternative approach?

The dismissal of LFA as inappropriate still leaves many questions unanswered, not least the considerable difficulties associated with DG evaluation. Here we propose an alternative approach to such challenges, one that is essentially **participatory** and **qualitative** in nature. In doing so, our aims are twofold: one relatively pragmatic, the other more political in nature. The first is to contribute to resolving the methodological difficulties encountered in this field and therefore to provide a more accurate assessment of democracy assistance activities. The second aim is to shift the notion of evaluating democracy assistance from one that is perceived as a technical exercise to one that involves a participatory political process, thereby becoming an integral part of democratization itself.

Participatory evaluation: absolute or relative concept?

Participatory evaluation (PE) is not a new concept within development discourse,[4] but has attracted increasing interest and attention in discussions of aid evaluation (Cracknell 2000). Such trends can be problematic, however, with Rebien (1996: 65) observing that 'participatory evaluation has inherited some of the basic weaknesses of the participation concept itself'. Most commonly, a 'participatory' element is included into an evaluation study in order to integrate beneficiaries' opinions into the report. Essentially, this is an instrumental use of 'participation,' a means of improving data collection by supplementing other sources with beneficiary views, yet with stakeholders remaining as **objects** of the evaluation. In contrast, a genuinely participatory methodology entails stakeholders becoming the **subjects** of the evaluation process, themselves determining the nature of the investigation, not mere sources of information for a donor-led inquiry. In this truly participatory form, participation occurs throughout the evaluation process, from design and planning stages onwards. Such an absolute concept of PE is far less compatible with conventional evaluation. Indeed, Cracknell (2000: 333) acknowledges that 'The participatory approach, in its full rigour, is clearly incompatible with the traditional approach.' It is this genuine form of participatory evaluation that is advocated here as an alternative approach.

Participatory evaluation and DG assistance: congruence and compatibility

Although PE is not a new concept, it has not been applied in the field of DG assistance, at least not in its absolute or genuine form.[5] Nevertheless, it is asserted here that a genuinely participatory approach to evaluation is appropriate and beneficial in evaluating DG assistance, for three reasons.[6]

First, PE addresses some of the key challenges of evaluation in this area, as outlined above. These challenges lead to a number of subsidiary 'what', 'how' and 'who' questions, as follows.

- Given the significance of political context, what means can be engaged to determine the main opportunities for, and obstacles to, democratic development in a particular country, and to assess the relevance of external actors' efforts within that context?
- Given the multiplicity of actors and factors involved in political change, how can these be untangled and the specific contribution of external assistance be specified?
- Given the need to disentangle external–internal relations, who is best placed to ascertain the extent to which perceived donor success depends on local support or, conversely, the extent to which countervailing, internal forces undermine donor efforts?
- Given the issues of unintended impact, who can best assess the full impact of external activities, both positive and negative?

It is proposed here that these difficult subsidiary questions can be most satisfactorily addressed by the reflections and analysis of a repre-sentative group of well-informed national actors, engaged in a collective

Box 14.2   *Undertaking a participatory evaluation of DG assistance*

How might a participatory approach to DG evaluation be undertaken in practice? Four key stages in the PE process have been identified: planning; data gathering; data analysis; reporting and dissemination of findings (Estrella and Gaventa 1998: 28). A preliminary or pre-planning stage can be added to these, in which evaluators are selected.

Selection of evaluators: issues of inclusion and exclusion

How are the evaluators selected? Who is included and who is not? Two selection criteria are proposed. One is based on the notion of stakeholding, but broadened to include those who are affected both directly and indirectly by the interventions under examination.[7] This brings together a wider variety of perspectives from both government and non-government contexts, not restricted to those who have a direct (financial) stake in the programme. It is crucial that the evaluation group should contain representatives of indirect stakeholders, providing more independent and critical viewpoints, given that direct beneficiaries of democracy assistance funds could be disinclined to 'bite the hand that feeds them'. The other selection criterion relates to democratic values, that is, evidence of a positive engagement in democratic procedures, with a manifest commitment to frank, open and transparent discussion, including respect for the viewpoints of others. By such criteria, those groups unlikely to make a positive contribution would exclude themselves.

Planning

An initial forum can enable agenda-setting, with participants negotiating the key issues for research and investigation. The two main tasks are establishing objectives and selecting indicators (Estrella and Gaventa 1998: 28–9), with a large initial workshop as the most likely mechanism. Establishing objectives amounts to determining the terms of reference of the evaluation. A limited number of indicators will need to be agreed through negotiation, with discussion likely in thematic groups. Guidance could also be sought from the candidate indicators generated by development agencies, especially the qualitative indicators forthcoming from USAID.

Data collection

Research commences in earnest in this phase in working groups. A variety of tools and techniques are available, and guidance on the most suitable can be sought from the handbooks and manuals on participatory monitoring and evaluation (Estrella and Gaventa 1998: Appendix 2). Many of the tools are drawn from participatory development methods more generally, notably participatory reflection and action, and one challenge is to select and devise methods that are appropriate to the political sphere. Another is to ensure that gender-sensitive techniques are included, enabling gender analysis to be undertaken.

Data analysis

Data processing and analysis is undertaken by all evaluation participants, not an elite few as is traditionally the case. Initially, participants would largely remain in thematic working groups, with critical reflection along the lines of investigation posed at the planning stage, such as the successes and shortcomings of the programme, and understanding the impacts of activities, including unintended effects. Findings on the various evaluation questions can then be presented for further discussion at a whole-group workshop.

Box 14.2   *Undertaking a participatory evaluation of DG assistance*
(continued)

Reporting and dissemination
This final task entails clear documentation of the processes undertaken, the information gathered, the knowledge gained and lessons learned from the evaluation, stated in a manner that is clear and accessible to all possible users. While specific lessons for external actors will be one key outcome, the participatory nature of the evaluation means that donor agencies do not hold exclusive rights over the product. Rather it becomes a tool for use by all actors engaged in efforts to promote democratic change, one means by which the evaluation process can become an integral part of democratization itself.

Role of facilitator
An experienced facilitator of participatory processes is often invaluable and critical to the success of a participatory evaluation. The multiple roles and skills required of the facilitator are outlined by Estrella and Gaventa (1998: 43) and by UNDP (1997: part 4). A key role is to act as a catalyst, encouraging participation and sharing of ideas by all, directing and guiding the process to constructive outcomes without controlling it.

process of dialogue and negotiation. This is precisely the type of forum that would be established to undertake a participatory evaluation, as mapped out in Box 14.2. By such means, answers to the above questions would be elicited through the collective analysis of data gathered by local participant evaluators, with findings enriched by their knowledge of and active involvement in democratization processes in their country. Although prescription is contrary to the nature of PE, the completion of a political context study as background information is a likely prerequisite of the participant evaluators. This could be commissioned out to local academic specialists, potentially making use of democratic audit methodology, itself having a participatory dimension (Beetham et al. 2002). A political context study would provide the necessary data for evaluating how far progress (or otherwise) in democratization can be attributed to donor agencies and their use of aid as DG assistance.

Second, the principles of PE relate closely to the principles of democracy. Estrella and Gaventa (1998: 17–27) define the four characteristic features of PE as: participation, learning, negotiation and flexibility. All four are closely associated with the principles of democracy. Participation itself is clearly central to democratic processes. The democratic principles of popular control and political equality (Beetham 1999) are realized precisely through political participation, minimally in electoral processes, as well as more substantially through a variety of democratic practices, both to influence policy-making and to hold government to account, from local community level upwards to national level. Regarding the other principles of PE, there is a clear resonance with democratic values. Democracy is precisely about resolving differences and taking decisions through negotiation, dialogue and compromise, in contrast to rule through coercion and control over the means of violence. In democratic processes and practices, the need for flexibility and the degree of learning are both at a premium.

Third, the process of PE is akin to the process of democratization itself. There is general consensus that democratization is essentially an internal process to which external agencies can, at best, contribute some support. Likewise, PE provides a nationally based evaluation that is embedded in local knowledge and analysis of the changing circumstances of the political context. Processes of democratization and PE are also similar insofar as reflexivity and dialogue are crucial to both. Within political movements, social actors gain a critical awareness of the success and limitations of their efforts to engage with, and change, current social realities through reflection and dialogue, thus stimulating further action for change. Similarly, PE entails collective reflection by and dialogue between a range of domestic actors in order to appraise the efforts of external agencies. The outcome of such participatory evaluation potentially links back to the democratization process, with learning for all. For development agencies, their past and current efforts are subject to critical assessment, enabling objectives to be revisited and strategies refined, enriched by internally generated proposals for democracy assistance activities. For participant evaluators, knowledge of processes of political change is enhanced, in turn informing and strengthening local action for democratic change.

Participatory evaluation: issues and challenges

Despite the above discussion on conducting a participatory DG evaluation, it is unlikely to be a straightforward and trouble-free undertaking, and possible challenges and difficulties are anticipated here. As a relatively new approach, PE in general is itself engaging with a number of such issues and concerns (Estrella and Gaventa 1998: 37–48; Estrella et al. 2000), with two challenges of particular significance to evaluations of political programmes. These are examined here.

Issues of power

It is recognized that 'complex social dynamics and power relations' underlie the practice of PE (Estrella and Gaventa 1998: 37), particularly as regards processes of negotiation. There are issues of power both within and between the range of social groups engaged in the evaluation process, given unequal social relations and differences in social status. Between groups in a DG evaluation, differential power could arise between actors located at different institutional levels, for example between officials of 'high-level' government agencies and civil society activists. Within social groups, social divisions can lead to differential influence, for instance by gender. A key dimension concerns the planning stage and the question of who influences the selection of evaluation criteria and indicators (Estrella and Gaventa 1998: 38, citing Rubin 1995: 39).

Resolution of power issues is not easy. As a prerequisite, recognition and awareness of such issues are clearly essential, with the facilitator potentially playing an important role. The involvement of a critical mass of non-government and non-élite actors in the evaluation group, not just tokenistic and isolated representation, could help to identify and challenge power issues. The participation of a significant proportion of women is similarly important to ensure gender aspects are addressed. In addition to such specific measures, there are more general grounds for optimism that power issues may be addressed in a forum evaluating DG assistance. Power is a political concept, with democratization aimed at achieving greater popular control over both governmental and economic power. As discussed, PE itself is closely related to such processes, aiming to redress power imbalances, and a failure to address power differentials in the forum itself would be incongruous.

Issues of conflict

Following Guba and Lincoln (1989), collaboration and consensus are key aspects of a participatory approach. Yet the articulation of different views, concerns and interests can also lead to disagreement and conflict, especially where such differences are seen as embedded in existing social institutions of inequality, with the potential to paralyse the PE process (Gaventa and Blauert 2000: 234). Guba and Lincoln's lack of attention to the potential for conflict in negotiation processes appears to have been replicated in much participatory evaluation, with the acknowledgement that 'conflict and mechanisms for resolving conflict is seldom explicitly discussed in the literature' (Estrella and Gaventa 1998: 39). Yet the potential for conflict is probably greater in evaluations of political matters. First, politics in general, and democratization in particular, involves competing interests and struggles over power, likely to be reproduced to some extent in the evaluation context. Second, the involvement of multiple stakeholders from different institutional levels increases the diversity of views and interests. Seeking resolution to different stakeholder interests is not an uncomplicated or undemanding task. Frequently there are real, existing differences that emerge out of social inequalities. They are not going to be simply negotiated away, as imagined in Guba and Lincoln's (1989) approach. Nevertheless, the process of participatory evaluation does provide a forum for democratic dialogue that is precisely aimed at addressing such differences, with the potential for compromise and agreement on how to tackle key issues within a democratic framework.

Summary

The advantages of a participatory approach to evaluating DG assistance are manifest. An extended role is given to well-informed national actors, with the evaluation benefiting from their expert knowledge of political processes in their own societies. Donors are provided with findings that can potentially improve the relevance, effectiveness, impact and sustainability of their DG support. A basis for more genuine ownership and partnership, ostensibly much sought after by donor agencies, can thus be established. Such findings can also feed back into local organizations, at both government and non-government levels, through their representatives who were involved in the evaluation study. The learning process is thereby transmitted into wider society, contributing to those pressures and movements for democratic change, albeit in a minor way, on which depend not only the success of external efforts, but the prospects for sustained democratization as a whole.

Conclusions

This chapter addresses the methodological challenges of evaluating DG assistance. It stresses the inappropriate nature of logframe-related evaluation in the political aid field. Aside from the inadequate nature of quantitative indicators and the 'softness' of data in a sphere in which institutional relationships and culture are the subject of reform, a key criticism concerns the inability of a logframe approach to impart or to take into account the political context in which DG projects and pro-grammes are embedded. Logical framework analysis is inward-orientated, inverting evaluation towards achievement (or not) of predetermined project objectives, whereas evaluation of DG assistance requires an outward orientation, able to capture the dynamic political context of which it is part. It is argued that the application of LFA and other quan-titatively based methods in this field demonstrate the inadequacies of a technical approach to evaluation of political processes. One related outcome is the dearth of critical analysis of the role of external actors, with evaluation solely of donor agencies' own objectives, compounded by relationships in which consultant evaluators and beneficiaries of assistance are behoven to the funding agencies, producing predictably positive findings.

The challenges in evaluating DG assistance remain, however, 'more pronounced than in the assessment of other types of development assistance' (Danida 2000: vol. 1, 10). In rethinking evaluation methodolo-gy in this field, as advised by UNDP (1998: 27), we turn to the alternative of participatory evaluation. It is argued that a participatory approach to DG evaluation is both appropriate and beneficial. Its suitability is claimed on the basis of congruence and compatibility, sharing many of the characteristics and principles of democratization itself. Further, the potential for a synergistic relationship between participatory evaluation and democratization is asserted. The anticipated outcome is a learning process for all. For donor agencies, their past and current efforts are subject to constructive criticism, enabling objectives to be revisited and strategies refined, better informed by internal perspectives. For participant evaluators, knowledge of processes of domestic political change is further enhanced, building local capacity and, in turn, strengthening local action for democratic reform. Thus the act of evaluation can become an act of democratization.

Chapter Fifteen
Monitoring social policy outcomes in Jamaica: combined methods, democratic research and institutional change

JEREMY HOLLAND, STEADMAN NOBLE,
ANDY NORTON and KEN SIGRIST

Summary

The Government of Jamaica has designed a national Social Policy Framework that will be monitored in selected parishes throughout the country. Innovative methods are being designed that encourage local people to monitor progress towards improved social outcomes. These monitoring methods need to be sufficiently robust to generate representative and credible data; sufficiently flexible to allow the emergence of both nationally comparable indicators and contextually relevant indicators of social policy improvement; and sufficiently process-based to stimulate institutional transformation for improved performance at different levels of policy-making and implementation. This chapter maps out the method being adopted, and argues that shrewd combinations of methods and data types can create the institutional ownership, engagement and transformation necessary for sustained improvement in social policy outcomes.

Introduction

This chapter documents the methodology presently being developed to monitor and improve social policy in Jamaica. Designed as a key component of the Jamaica Social Policy Evaluation (JASPEV) process (initiated and led from within the Cabinet Office, with support from the UK Department for International Development (DFID), the methodology seeks to embed a combination of methods within a participatory process of institutional change at different levels of governance.

The JASPEV process is part of a broader emerging paradigm of 'democratizing' research, based on the proposition that broad ownership of the generation and analysis of evidence will lead to more effective and sustainable policy process. The process is influenced by methodological traditions with contrasting ideological roots but complementary objectives and methods: new public management approaches emphasizing outcome-based diagnosis and institutional transformation; and participatory monitoring and evaluation, with its roots in project and community development. Under JASPEV, the Jamaican Cabinet Office is promoting a system of locally generated but nationally comparable benchmark indicators that it is hoped will encourage mutual learning and institutional change.

Background: the Jamaica Social Policy Evaluation project

Social indicators in Jamaica have traditionally been very good for a middle-income country, especially in health, but there is an increasing concern as to whether these high levels are being eroded in recent years. The JASPEV process was designed to address a range of specific concerns about the management and implementation of social policy. Primary among these were: a perceived lack of mechanisms for achieving policy coherence; a lack of mechanisms for establishing and updating strategic priorities; the constrained situation in terms of public resources for social policy; and the perceived lack of a culture of evaluation and responsiveness to users in the delivery of public services.

The two key outputs of the JASPEV process in its first phase have been a Social Policy Framework (Government of Jamaica 2002) covering the period up to 2015, and a five-year Action Plan (2002–7). Taken together, these documents seek to provide:

- a vision for the kind of society Jamaica aspires to being and achieving
- a set of key policy goals that sum up a range of concrete outcomes or results representing progress towards realization of the vision
- a set of goals and objectives for changes in institutional systems and relationships that support the achievement of the policy goals
- a framework for assessing progress over time towards the goals
- an Action Plan outlining a five-year programme of measures to strengthen the design and implementation of social policy, with a view to achieving progress in relation to the outcome and process goals outlined.

The key goals identified in the document *Jamaica 2015* (Government of Jamaica 2002) are grouped as outcome and process goals, each with accompanying frameworks of benchmark indicators. The relevant parts of the document are summarized in Box 15.1.

The process goals listed are intermediate – it is through the improvements proposed at this level that it is hoped to influence the outcome goals listed in Box 15.1. The Social Policy Framework outlines the overarching vision and goals, while the Action Plan is intended to strengthen the policy, strategic planning and implementation capacities of the social policy community in Jamaica. A key element of the Social Action Plan is the development of five thematic prototypes, the first identified as 'youth inclusion', addressing specific priority themes that cut across functional boundaries in the public sector, as well as the boundary between the public sector and the rest of society.

Monitoring social policy: the inheritance

Monitoring at national and local levels becomes a key tool for ensuring progress towards fulfilling social policy goals. In some contexts this

Box 15.1   Jamaica 2015: *social policy goals*

'To realise the vision of a better Jamaica, Government commits itself to achieving progress towards the following key goals, constantly assessing our progress, reformulating our policies and strategies according to the best analysis and information available, and reporting back to the Jamaican people on the progress that has been achieved.'

Key outcome goals

1 Human security
A peaceful and mutually respectful society with increased safety, security and freedom from fear in the home and in public spaces.

2 Social integration
An inclusive and non-discriminatory society which respects group and individual rights, promotes social justice, accepts diversity, builds trust and communication between all groups.

3 Governance
More effective, complementary, accountable and transparent government structures, seeking to move decision-making closer to the people.

4 Secure and sustainable livelihoods
Widened, higher quality livelihood and employment opportunities for all Jamaicans, with particular reference to those disadvantaged in the labour market.

5 Environment
Improved environment for quality of life, for Jamaicans living and as yet unborn.

6 Education and skills
An education which facilitates life-long learning and acquisition of social and life skills for all.

7 Health and physical well-being
Enhance the broadly defined health status of the population.

Key process goals

1 Policy process
Strengthening coherence, timeliness, ownership, participation and quality in the formulation of social policy.

2 Strategic planning and resource allocation
Strengthening the integration and effectiveness of planning and budget processes through enhanced prioritization, collaboration across ministerial and other boundaries, realism about available resources, reliability of delivery of budget allocations and flexibility of resource allocation.

3 Responsiveness and institutional learning
Promote the development of a more responsive, people-oriented and innovative culture in Jamaican social policy institutions.

4 Monitoring of social trends and outcomes
Promote enhanced effectiveness of social information systems in shaping the development of policy through improved timeliness, relevance, richness, presentation and participation.

Source: Government of Jamaica (2002)

function can be fulfilled by third parties, such as public sector auditing bodies. Yet in many countries independent public sector watchdogs do not exist, and have little chance of being established and accepted by civil society in the short term. In these cases NGOs can play a very effective monitoring and social auditing role (Zadek et al. 1997) by developing a consensus on what should be monitored, and establishing a process for placing information in the public domain. Methods have been designed and adapted for this purpose, with report cards a good example of a tool used successfully to audit service providers (see, for example, an unpublished paper by K. Gopakumar and S. Balakrishnan of the Public Affairs Centre, Bangalore: 'Citizen's feedback and state accountability: report cards as an aid to improving local governance', *www.pacindia.org*).

An alternative to third-party monitoring is for community actors themselves to benchmark outcomes, and then work backwards to policy and other outputs (e.g. from identifying a more peaceful community as an outcome, to identifying frequency of public telephone vandalism as an outcome indicator, and from there designing social policy and other interventions). Importantly, this process prompts local diagnosis and action, often involving new forms of institutional alignment and forcing a higher level of accountability among participating agencies or duty-bearers.

One local government initiative in the USA, the 'Oregon Shines' programme,[1] has demonstrated this powerful process in which (locally owned) information generation drives institutional change. The Oregon initiative reflects a tradition of thinking about institutional learning and change that can be traced through management thinking. It builds on familiar elements of 'new public management' approaches, including an emphasis on improving coordination, joined-up government, innovative partnerships between the public, private and voluntary sectors, flexibility and orientation to outcomes in the management of public policy. The Oregon model adds to this a strong emphasis on local-level engagement in the definition of benchmarks and the organization of appropriate local-level action to tackle identified issues and problems.

A quite separate, but latterly converging, stream of thinking about change is that rooted in participatory development. A draft paper (Francis 1999) notes the convergence of ideological strands of thinking on participation and highlights the radical tradition of participation in Latin America with its emphasis on (empowering) process (Freire 1970; Fals Borda 1988); the participatory reflection and action tradition emerging from agricultural research in the south (Chambers 1994a); and the more functional management and organizational thinking of the USA, with its emphasis on improving efficiency and outcomes.

Participatory monitoring and evaluation has emerged from this process tradition to challenge the instrumental use of highly quantified input–output indicators to measure project progress, usually as part of what is seen as a tyrannically positivist logical framework project management tool (see Chapter 13). Participatory monitoring and evaluation reflects the principles of participatory development by stressing the **process** of assessment, reflection and action that overrides extractive concerns with data collection by project 'outsiders' (see Chapter 14; Guijt and Gaventa 1998; Estrella et al. 2000).

It is this emphasis on process that brings the institutional learning approach of new public management together with participatory research's interpretation of reflection and action. This convergence provides new opportunities to move the process beyond a managerialist concern with systems based on checks and balances, and to move upstream from a participatory reflection and action focus on community or project. It also provides an exciting new opening for pluralism in the use of methods and data sources, as discussed below.

Monitoring social policy outcomes in Jamaica

The methodological challenge for those seeking to improve policy outcomes in Jamaica is threefold, to:

- establish more effective institutional links between the providers and users of policy-relevant information so that the information generated is timely and relevant, resulting in powerful, evidence-based policy analysis
- combine more effectively data sources and methods for social policy analysis allied to increased appreciation of the comparative advantages of a different methods
- embed policy research in a continuing process of institutional transformation and empowerment at different levels of governance.

Recognizing these challenges, the JASPEV task force has developed an organizational arrangement, allied to a social policy information system, that aims to stimulate the institutional connections and methodological innovations necessary for improved social policy design, delivery and outcomes.

The driving force behind the system is the process of benchmarking indicators at the local level. Community members across different localities identify their own benchmarks, and voluntary teams measure and monitor progress against these benchmarks and in comparison with other localities (see Figure 15.1 overleaf). Assessment of outcomes and process against a particular social policy theme will be shared with a group of technical specialists (chosen on the basis of their expertise and their institutional capacity as change agents) in that thematic area, and with a group of three policy-makers (cross-party MPs and junior ministers) whose departments link to that theme. This triangular institutional set-up forms the basis for a continuing loop of assessment, diagnosis, design and delivery of social policy. At the same time, the process will create institutional space at the local level for new alliances of civil society and state actors to mobilize resources towards increased accountability and improved outcomes.

Figure 15.1   *Evaluating social policy at the local level in Jamaica*

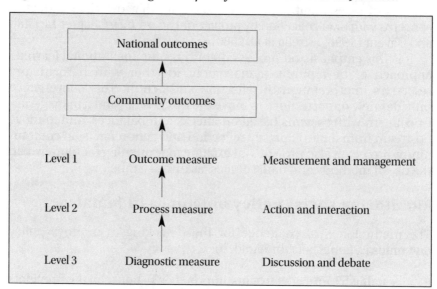

For the monitoring instrument to be useful for analysis and action, it needs to have three types of measure: diagnostic, process and outcome.

Diagnostic measures (Figure 15.2) refer primarily to those questions that elicit information which provides a context for understanding the existing reality while driving debate, discussion and diagnosis about the outcome.

Process measures (Figure 15.3) refer primarily to those questions that help local people take immediate action to advance progress towards the desired (benchmarked) outcomes. These measures tend to be intermediate, and to assist the community in developing a plan of action. They reveal aspects of attitudes, perceptions, behaviours, relationships and resources which, if re-ordered, could lead to significant progress towards the outcome. At best, these measures drive local action and re-order how people relate and interact with each other with a view to achieving outcomes.

Outcome measures (Figure 15.4) are those questions that indicate progress towards achieving the stated outcomes. These measures tend to be more long term, and are very crude in measuring the outcomes. If measurement of the outcomes shows that progress is not being

Figure 15.2   *Example of a diagnostic measure of youth inclusion*

What would be the main reason for preventing you taking a job if one was available now?

Nothing (would accept)	Awaiting promised job	Pregnancy	Amount of pay	Have to stay with relative/ children	Home duties	Do not need a job	Illness	Other (specify)
1○	2○	3○	4○	5○	6○	7○	8○	9○

Figure 15.3   *Example of a process measure of youth inclusion*

What efforts have you made to get a job? (multiple responses allowed)

Applied in writing	Applied in person	Registered at employment agency	Advertised on radio or newspaper	Asked friends	Tried to get a loan	Other (specify)
1○	2○	3 ○	4○	5○	6○	7○

achieved, then the assumptions, diagnosis and actions will have to be revisited.

It is generally felt that whereas outcome measures are not likely to see any change in the short term, it is best to use process measures in the interim and check outcome measures at an appropriate time when those data are more likely to be available. For example, data on level of educational attainment are not likely to be generated until the end of an academic year; but the desire for further studies, or level of enrolment in education and training programmes, could be intermediate proxies of the outcome that could register change.

The data generated by participants will fit different purposes. A core of indicators will need to be quantifiable and standardizable so that progress can be compared across time and locations.[2] A further set of indicators can be more contextual and more qualitative, allowing research participants and the consultative network to generate their own narratives, analysis and action for change.

In order to accomplish this result, significant questions and challenges face the JASPEV task force. These include:

- what is the correct balance between local and policy demand for information?
- what are the 'right' questions that communities need to ask that will lead to institutional and policy action?
- how much information do communities need to collect in order to influence the institutional and policy processes?
- what measures are appropriate for ongoing monitoring that tells us something about how overall efforts are taking us closer to outcomes?

Figure 15.4   *Example of an outcome measure of youth inclusion*

What were you doing for most of the time over the past month?

Working	Has job but on leave	Looking for work	At home	Trying to start a business	In a formal or informal training programme	At school full-time	Other (specify)
1○	2○	3○	4○	5○	6○	7 ○	8○

Conclusions

This chapter briefly outlines an innovative approach to community-based monitoring that seeks to inform and provoke change in the design and implementation of social policy in Jamaica. The approach adopted in the JASPEV process is highly ambitious in its attempt to combine technical innovation in the collection and flow of information with institutional transformation at different levels of governance.

The risks associated with the process as it moves into implementation are likely to revolve around the threat of a lingering credibility gap in the data generated, and continuing scepticism towards an institutional change agenda. The first risk is more easily dealt with. At the macro-policy level, faced with the mindset of an empiricist, survey-dependent establishment, credibility comes through the mutually reinforcing power of quantitative and qualitative data generated using a range of more-or-less contextual research methods[3] and delivered in a timely fashion through a social policy information system that functions well. At the local level, ownership of the data generation and analysis process has been shown in the Oregon model, as elsewhere, to generate a common perception of trustworthiness among local actors.

The institutional challenge is more serious and poses a far greater risk to the success of JASPEV as a process. The politicized nature of institutions in Jamaica, the role of hierarchy and patronage, and the prevalence of 'turfism' within and between political parties are widely recognized and criticized by a cynical and weary civil society. The challenge faced should not be understated, yet the set-up of JASPEV, while managerialist in tone and influence, does create political space for institutional change through its emphasis on the interaction of nodes of local and national processes. Ultimately, it is on the democratic generation and ownership of information that emerging systems of accountability and delineation of responsibility for the delivery of social policy will stand or fall.

Chapter Sixteen
From development research to policy change: methodological learning from a research capacity-building project

TANJA BASTIA, ELEANOR FISHER, JEREMY HOLLAND
and DUNCAN HOLTOM

Summary

Although there may be widespread recognition of the need for social research capacity-building in developing countries, studies capturing capacity-building experiences underline the difficulties of this undertaking. It is relatively easy to increase the quantity of individual or institutional outputs, but this does not ensure quality, nor does it ensure sustained improvements in long-term research capability and strengthened connections to an evidence-based policy process. This chapter reviews the experience of implementing one such initiative – the Social Development Research Capacity-building (SDRC) project, funded by the UK's Department for International Development (DFID) and implemented with four partner countries between 1997 and 2002. The chapter briefly describes the project design and strategies for building social research capacity. The discussion then considers how the project was taken forward in each country context and the methodological issues that emerged. The chapter concludes with a reflection on lessons learnt from the experience of capacity-building around the development of new methodological skills.

Introduction: social research capacity-building issues

Within the social sciences there is a history of application of social research to practical issues in developing contexts (e.g. Mair 1957; Brokensha 1966). This legacy fed into the emergence of social development as a sphere of professional expertise in the 1980s and 1990s (Cernea 1995; Rew 1997; Eyben 2003). The focus on poverty reduction as a central development goal of the past decade (e.g. see the UNDP's Millennium Development Goals, *www.undp.org/mdg*) and the development of new ways of understanding and analysing poverty (e.g. Sen 1981; Chambers 1989; Narayan et al. 2000), coupled with an emphasis on the need for evidenced-based policy-making (Nutley et al. 2002), has given new impetus to demand for social research skills in development arenas.

New thinking on poverty and poverty reduction interventions – such as participatory poverty assessments, anti-poverty reduction frameworks, poverty and social impact assessments, and an emphasis on governance and human rights – suggests a need for new methodological ideas and innovative methods for researchers to draw on. These include methodologies that combine qualitative and quantitative socio-economic methods, capture the experiences and understandings of different groups of people, and incorporate stakeholder consultation processes. This can be seen in Africa, for instance, in the case of poverty reduction strategy papers which necessitate extensive consultation and use of contextual data (Newman and de Haan 2001).

Despite increased demand for locally generated and 'owned' research data, countries differ in their institutional capacity for generating, absorbing and using research-based knowledge, particularly in the social sciences. Indeed, the existing unequal distribution of knowledge between rich and poor countries, and within countries, may well be widening (RAWOO 1997/98: 9; Netley, undated). This puts an onus on governments and funding institutions working in the development field to help enhance research capacity in order to contribute to more effective knowledge generation and uptake (Killick 2001; RAWOO 2001; Surr et al. 2002).

Development of new methodological skills is clearly a part of this process, one held to be valued by southern partners (Earl and Smutylo 1998; ITAD/ODI 2000; RAWOO 2001). Donors such as DFID recognize the importance of research-based knowledge in development (DFID 1997; see also Surr et al. 2002). Social research, specifically, can be a means to generate insights concerning how people are affected by, or excluded from, social change.

Although there may exist widespread recognition of the need for social research capacity-building in developing countries, studies capturing capacity-building experiences underline the difficulties of this undertaking (Ryan 1999a,b; West and Shackleton 1999; ITAD/ODI 2000; Puchner 2001; RAWOO 2001; Weber and Mujica 2001; Toye 2002). It is relatively easy to increase the quantity of individual or institutional outputs, but this does not ensure quality, nor does it ensure sustained improvements in long-term research capability.

In this chapter, we review the experience of implementing one such initiative – the DFID-funded Social Development Research Capacity-building (SDRC) project. Between 1997 and 2002 the Social Development Division of DFID financed this capacity-building initiative in four developing or transitional countries – Bolivia, Tanzania, India and Uzbekistan.[1] Below we briefly describe the project design and strategies for building social research capacity. The discussion then turns to consider how the project was taken forward in each country context and the methodological issues that emerged. We conclude with a reflection on lessons learned from the experience of capacity-building around the development of new methodological skills.

Table 16.1 *Capacity-building issues and strategies proposed*

Capacity-building issue	Strategy	Country
Networking between research institutions	Focal point institution(s) with high capacity	Bolivia (CERES) Uzbekistan (CER) India (Orissa and West Bengal – NCCDS/CSSSC/ISED)
	Focal point institution with conditionality linked to appraisal	Tanzania (REPOA)
	Develop network through initially strong external inputs	India I (Udaipur and Tamil Nadu)
	Target junior researchers	Tanzania, Bolivia, India (Orissa and West Bengal)
Training: concepts, methods, and policy analysis	Training for research audience beyond SDRC programme	India I (Udaipur and Tamil Nadu)
	Introduce international trainers with in-country experience	Uzbekistan, India I (Udaipur and Tamil Nadu)
	Use experienced local and regional researchers	Tanzania
	Field-based research training for practitioners already working in given areas	India I (Udaipur and Tamil Nadu)
	Interdisciplinary training teams	India I (Udaipur and Tamil Nadu)
	Post-research workshops reflecting on methodological issues learned	Bolivia
Strengthening links to and building demand among policy makers	Identify research institutions with good existing links to policy audiences	Bolivia, India I (Udaipur and Tamil Nadu), Uzbekistan
	Early briefing/discussion/ stakeholder workshops	Tanzania, India I (Udaipur and Tamil Nadu)
	Consultative group meets periodically	Bolivia
	Dissemination: workshops and other audience-targeting media (newsletters, bulletins, journals, websites)	All
	Create networks with thematic focus, bringing together policy makers, researchers and donors	Uzbekistan, India I (Udaipur and Tamil Nadu), Tanzania
	Integrate research and practice at local sites of development	India II (Orissa and West Bengal)

The strategy for capacity-building within the SDRC project

Contextualizing capacity-building strategies

Having different capacity-building strategies was recognized to be important at the start of the project if SDRC was to flourish in countries with contrasting traditions of social research and policy-making. Therefore it was proposed that process issues should be emphasized over and above the need to follow one particular model. Three concerns were highlighted: first, the need to build capacity in terms of network strength among social development research 'suppliers' or 'doers'; second, the need to inject effective training components into SDRC implementation; and third, the need to create and improve links between research and policy, building demand among policy-makers and commissioners of research. This led to the identification of the key issues and strategies set out in Table 16.1.

The country projects

This section describes each country project, touching briefly on methodological issues that emerged.

SDRC in Uzbekistan

In Uzbekistan, a transitional country of the former Soviet Union, social research has a history of being driven and closely controlled by the government. In the late 1990s links between research and training, and between research and social policy formulation, were held to have 'ruptured' due to a breakdown in planning and data collection apparatus, decline in public sector research and training, and a 'brain drain' to private institutes (Kandiyoti 1998). A technocratic tradition among bureaucrats had firmly embedded the idea that quantitative methodologies were a 'scientific' means of analysis, as opposed to 'unscientific' qualitative methods, of which there was little experience. Macro-economic and statistical analysis inherited from the Soviet period dominated information on social policies and social trends. By implication there was a strong bias towards quantitative information, with little expertise present for the generation and analysis of qualitative data, which was considered vastly inferior by a sceptical policy audience.

The SDRC project was therefore confronted by the need to develop not only the capacity to utilize different methodological frameworks and methods, but also the need to support a process in which a shift in values could take place, without qualitative research or combined methods being dismissed out of hand either by members of the research community or by policy-makers. Two key challenges were identified (Kandiyoti 1998). The first was the need to help establish a body of social knowledge that did not use a planned economy or administration as its starting point; the second was the need to introduce new methodologies for examining poverty that drew on participatory thinking and combined methodologies (translating and using, e.g., Booth et al. 1998).

The thrust of the SDRC project in Uzbekistan was on developing capacity-building related to the introduction of new methodologies. In many ways SDRC was in the right place at the right time: demand for new ways of examining poverty was coming from government in association with international donors, and researchers were very open to new ideas because of this demand. Despite this, the project was still confronted by difficult hurdles, both in terms of data gathering and analysis still being dominated by quantitative techniques and rationales, and in terms of gaining acceptance from policy makers and a wider research community for the qualitative data generated. Nevertheless, a window of opportunity was opened with further scope for development of new methodological skills.

SDRC in Bolivia

The SDRC context in Bolivia was very different and more fragmented than in Uzbekistan. Although there were similarities in the reliance of the public sector on quantitative and aggregated statistical data, the generation of these data was located within the public administration, with both universities and NGOs having separate research traditions. From the start the project, seeking actively to strengthen linkages between policy-makers and researchers in Bolivia, fell on complex political terrain, with some researchers and research institutions clearly being linked to party politics and others trying to distance their research

---

Box 16.1   SDRC in Uzbekistan

The Centre for Economic and Social Studies (CER) in Ferghana Province coordinated the Uzbekistan component of the SDRC project. The CER proposed to take the project forward in four ways: first, to address a key policy issue, poverty alleviation, through the use of new approaches and methodologies; second, to activate a network of researchers based in Tashkent and Ferghana cutting across university, private and public sectors; third, to provide training in qualitative and participatory methodologies; and fourth, to promote the 'mainstreaming' of participatory methodologies in policy work.

The proposed capacity-building strategy of CER came in the context of the Uzbekistan Cabinet commissioning it to develop new methods and indicators for income assessment, linked to World Bank financing of a living standards measurement survey. It was felt that a focus on a single issue was likely to achieve the greatest impact for capacity-building as the need for the development of new methodologies was explicitly recognized within government and donor policy circles. Engagement with a social development research agenda was seen as an entry point to work with international development institutions.

from political agendas. This raised questions of how to build bridges between the research and policy spheres, a general opinion being that a stronger academia would make a stronger impact on policy-makers in the long run.

In contrast to Uzbekistan, the idea of social development research was by no means new, although it was characterized as 'human development.' This implied that researchers held established ideas about what social development research entailed and the methodologies involved, which social development capacity-building needed to build on.

For the many private research institutions and NGOs that exist in the country, participatory methods had become common, particularly in organizations engaging with donor-oriented research agendas. In contrast, among university departments within the context of very low levels of primary data gathering, the tendency was towards expertise in quantitative data collection methods. These two methodological traditions were not necessarily well integrated.

A mixture of methods was used for the different pieces of research commissioned as part of SDRC in Bolivia, driven less by an integrated design process than by the researchers' established methodological repertoires. Research on education and young people's perceptions, for instance, held scope for making greater use of qualitative methods, but the local researchers chose to place greater emphasis on a survey-based methodology. In contrast a project on social mobility did use qualitative methods in the form of life stories; however, there was a sense that this was somewhat imposed and their use was not fully embraced.

In terms of policy influence, the project process threw into relief the importance of siting a technical research methodology within a more fundamentally political terrain. It is telling that a separate initiative – the Urgent Social Development project,[2] which was based on consultation workshops rather than on conventional research, and had a far more immediate policy influence – was the component that was least research-oriented, being based essentially on consultations.

SDRC in Tanzania

Although evidently a very different context, Tanzania did share some common ground with Bolivia in terms of the level of research capacity, its distribution between different research institutions, capacity-building needs, and levels of methodological skills. Like many other African countries there is very inadequate funding for tertiary education, with poor institutional capacity to conduct social research or focus on social policy and poverty issues (cf. West and Shackleton 1999; Toye 2002).

Methodological skills were unevenly distributed, with generally inadequate levels of methodological training and a bias towards empiricist enquiry where training did exist. In the context of poor funding, the university sector was dominated by traditional skills and training in quantitative social science research. Against this background, there had been an institutional shift in the location of social development

---

Box 16.2   *SDRC in Bolivia*

The *Centro de Estudios de la Realidad Economica y Social* (CERES) in Cochabamba acted as the main coordinator for the Bolivian component of the SDRC Project. CERES was identified as a potential champion for social development research, building capacity among smaller research groups. Hence CERES sought to 'regionalize' SDRC and to involve research teams drawn from other research bodies, with particular emphasis on junior researchers.

Four pieces of research were conducted: (i) a questionnaire survey, combined with in-depth, open-ended case-study interviews of pupils and their teachers, exploring young people's perceptions of the education system's influence on their values and their knowledge about democracy and citizenship; (ii) a study of territorialism and indigenous use of natural resources, emphasizing the use of a participatory methodology and participatory reflection and action techniques; (iii) a quantitative study of decentralization; and (iv) a study of upward social mobility that applied a life story methodology.

---

research away from university centres towards independent research agencies or to individual freelance consultancy work.[3] In Bolivia and Tanzania, high-profile academics and researchers were found to operate on a freelance basis while maintaining their university posts. This shift had been prompted in particular by a long-term decline in public funding for social science research, coupled with new opportunities arising from donor and government demand for development research; in effect this fostered small pockets of research capacity within the (semi-)private sector.

In terms of outcomes, the quality of research outputs linked to the SDRC project was mixed. One feature that became apparent was that training in methodological skills was not well integrated with support for individual research outputs. So, for example, the same individuals might not be involved in the two activities.

Because the Tanzanian NGO REPOA (Research on Poverty Alleviation) supported research of potential policy relevance, and because the Director had a high-level policy role, there was the possibility that REPOA had a good 'entry point' to policy circles. Initially it was proposed that the project would influence policy makers through three mechanisms: getting practitioners to review research proposals; hosting a national stakeholder workshop; and conducting a stakeholder meeting to establish a network to review and discuss research reports. In addition, a conduit for introducing research results into the policy-making process was held to be through REPOA's position on major policy forums.

SDRC in India

India presented a situation very different from the other country contexts: it is a vast country, has a well developed tertiary education sector, with good social research capacity, and good links between the research

---

Box 16.3   SDRC in Tanzania

The Tanzanian NGO REPOA (Research on Poverty Alleviation) acted as the SDRC partner in Tanzania. Prior to SDRC, REPOA had already been supported by donor funding (from the Netherlands) very much concerned with building capacity for research on policy issues. SDRC funding was channelled through a 'second window' for research grant making, which was organized around four core themes: (i) the impact of social policy on poverty; (ii) rural policy and poverty; (iii) urban poverty; and (iv) the measurement and definition of poverty and income distribution. Research was intended to be multidisciplinary and to incorporate different methodologies. Linked to this was the organization of training workshops to introduce new methodologies (emphasizing qualitative, participatory methodologies), particularly for younger researchers.

REPOA's research funding was predicated on a peer-review and mentoring process, needed for the assessment of research applications and support for the research. For the mentoring process, there were two categories of researcher in the programme. The first group were the junior researchers mentored by more senior researchers associated in some way with REPOA, with the latter forming the second group. However, there was only a very small pool of busy senior researchers to draw on, and the approach was severely constrained by this lack of human resource availability.

---

community and policy makers, at least in certain domains. There was some polarity between research NGOs whose work was based largely on qualitative data collection using participatory methodologies, and research institutions conducting non-participatory and typically quantitative social research. However, there was also a well-established tradition of ethnographic research, based on the use of qualitative (non-participatory) methods.

Despite this flourishing social research tradition, some concerns were identified regarding the relationship between research and policy making. These concerns were particularly linked to the demands of the international donor community, in which there is a particular conception of 'social development' skills which were not being met by local researchers or research institutions.

SDRC India was organized into two linked initiatives: state-level capacity-building (in Orissa and West Bengal), and NGO network strengthening (in Rajastan and Tamil Nadu). The two parts each linked together a series of networking activities, workshops, training courses, small research projects and dissemination activities. During the process of SDRC India Phase 2, a National Implementing Agency and National Advisory Committee were established to try to integrate different components of the project and achieve greater national-level ownership of all the separate activities. Towards the end of the project a standing conference and coordinating group, *Jibika Vikas Samaj Gavesna*, was established within the eastern India component for dissemination and network strengthening. With support from CDS (Centre for Devlopment Studies), *Jibika Vikas Samaj Gavesna* produced

---

Box 16.4 *SDRC in India*

The SDRC NGO network-strengthening initiative in Rajastan and Tamil Nadu was designed to bridge the gap between three constituencies: NGOs/researchers, policy makers, and bureaucrats. The core of this component focused on the creation of institutional capacity among well-established NGOs, enabling them to run a programme of research training, and to support field research. These NGOs were Seva Mandir located in Udaipur, Rajastan and the DHAN Foundation (Development of Humane Action) located in Madurai, Tamil Nadu; through the programme of activities they then linked to a larger network of NGO research and training centres.

The SDRC state-level capacity-building component, based in Orissa and West Bengal, focused on 'Poverty Awareness in State Action Networks Development', aimed to increase the ability of Oriyan and West Bengali state governments to understand the contributions that can be made to poverty reduction at state level through social development assessment and knowledge. The component was implemented through three independent research institutions: the Nabakrushna Choudhury Centre for Development Studies, the Centre for Studies in the Social Sciences, and the Institute for Socio-Economic Development, all independent research institutes. The key activities were think pieces on poverty themes discussed at state-level workshops, together with downstream research commissioned as a result of issues identified at the workshops.

---

a resource book on SDRC process and results (CDS 2002) to serve as a guide to the complex network of institutions, human skills and social capital formation created through the SDRC intervention.

Discussion

One of the difficulties in drawing any firm conclusions regarding SDRC's contribution to capacity-building and learning on new methods is that the time involved was simply too short.[4] Nevertheless, SDRC provided individuals and institutions with opportunities to forge new links, develop research ideas and learn new methodological skills, which may well have not taken place outside the project. Whether any of this contributed to sustainable capacity-building is an open question, but it did contribute to some – albeit limited – human resource development.

Methodological skills and methodological bias

As regards strengthening of methodological skills specifically, this met with some successes and raised many issues along the way. Arguably, the most notable success was the way the project was used as a vehicle for methodological learning in Uzbekistan, but significant individual skill development also took place for junior researchers in each country context.

Discussion of capacity-building in methods prompts the question of what methodological traditions social development researchers are drawing on. These traditions vary not only within countries, but also between different types of institutions and individuals. Indeed, one of the key learning points from the project was the way that certain methodologies are part of a domain occupied by researchers from different backgrounds. Broadly, academic social scientists working in university contexts tended to be most at home with quantitative social research techniques – found to be the case within certain institutions in India, Tanzania, Bolivia and Uzbekistan – while participatory research methods are more firmly within the domain of NGOs – as in Bolivia, Tanzania and India.

These biases are rooted in a historical background in which public administrations have tended to favour quantitative methodological techniques from which statistical information on social issues can be generated. Historically, universities have produced the researchers who have serviced this demand. In contrast, cutting across this background are the newer constituencies that favour information generated through participatory consultations and techniques, largely serviced by NGOs.

Qualitative and participatory methods are very much part of the social development portfolio and were implicitly favoured within the SDRC project. An important question is how to encourage researchers to bridge a methodological divide, and to introduce new ideas. In the case of Uzbekistan, SDRC could clearly contribute expert inputs on qualitative methodologies, but this was not always the key issue for researchers or policy-makers. In India, for example, NGOs involved in advocacy work were very adept in the use of participatory methods, but might find themselves at a loss when it came to using quantitative methods in ways that generated powerful statistics for advocacy and to challenge official figures.

Theory and method

There is a tendency for social development in the UK to be process-based and open-ended, seeking to capture diversity and understand complexity. However, good quality social development research places this emphasis on process within a grounded understanding of conceptual issues and theoretical ideas drawing from selected social science disciplines. For researchers drawn into social development work, such a background should endow them with a capacity to be methodologically innovative, with the ability to use tools and frameworks in flexible ways depending on the context, issues they are confronted by, and questions posed for research.

A narrow focus on social development methods without a theoretical grounding can carry the danger that researchers bypass the crucial steps of identifying an appropriate social development conceptual orientation and research agenda, and of refining suitable research questions. Otherwise, one may find methods introduced as part of a discrete training package – as in the case of Tanzania – without being fully embedded within a research process from which individuals could learn the most, endowing them with experience against which they can experiment and respond to new challenges as and when they arise.

Research to policy

In the context of debates about the role of knowledge in policy, there is renewed interest in bridging the divide between research and development policy (Lindquist 2001; Nielson 2001; Crew and Young 2002; Nutley et al. 2002; Ryan 2002; de Vibe et al. 2002).[5] Through critiquing 'lineal' and 'incrementalist' models of the policy-making process, these overviews congregate around conceptual models that view policy processes as multifaceted and non-linear, situating researchers in relation to a multitude of other actors with influence on this policy process. To do so they draw on conceptual frameworks that emphasize the idea of policy networks and knowledge communities (e.g. Grindle and Thomas 1991).

Given the centrality of bridging the gap between research and policy making for the promotion of social development, during the course of the SDRC project some of the researchers involved suggested that it might also be useful to think of the strategies developed in order to reach the aim of policy influence as part of the social development methodology. For researchers to be able to influence the policy-making process, this process itself needs to be known to the researcher. In some cases a lot of time and energy was spent finding out how the not-always-transparent policy-making process worked, and who precisely was to be targeted within the body of people involved in this process.

The hegemonic hold of quantitative data

A desire to be innovative and to use different types of methods appropriate to different contexts conflicted with the way in which data were differentially valued. Put more starkly, quantitative data still prevails as the most valued type of social data in many public policy circles. This was strongly experienced in Uzbekistan, where there is extreme scepticism within policy circles regarding qualitative data, but also in India, Bolivia and Tanzania, where statistics are highly valued even when of dubious quality. Moving beyond quantitative data to the use of qualitative methods, or even towards the integration of methods (following Carvalho and White 1997) can be a long path to tread.

Much of this comes down to creating an environment that is conducive to social development research and experimentation with new methodological ideas, as well as to the uptake of findings that are generated. These are fine words in principle, but in contexts where research capacity in general is extremely poor and where research may have little influence on the policy process, this is no easy or short-term matter. A bottom line is that reliability and quality are important. Systematizing and discussing experience is crucial for mutual learning, ensuring that experience is not simply lost – but this is not easy under time, financial and ideological pressures.

This also brings a further set of problems in the context of innovation and creativity, in that reliability and quality matter only if recognized. This is why capacity-building support needs to be long term, why new methodological ideas need to be embedded within wider innovative conceptual thinking, and why capacity-building needs to incorporate sustained contact between government, academic, donors and civil society actors – building good relationships over time is likely to lead to increased effectiveness.

Conclusions

This chapter reviews the experience of supporting research capacity-building initiatives in four developing or transitional countries. The comparative experience confirms that there are methodological, analytical and process challenges to strengthening the supply and fostering demand for social development knowledge. Visions of innovative and shrewdly pluralistic combinations of methods are met with the reality check that prejudices prevail, and that knowledge generation should be 'fit for purpose' rather than measured against absolute standards of rigour and pluralism. Concerns with strengthening the use of methods also need to be checked by a reassertion of the importance of the theoretical and conceptual frameworks within which data of any sort are fed. Yet most important, perhaps, social research that satisfies academic standards of quality is of itself no guarantee of its use by policy makers. Lineal or rational–comprehensive models of policy making fed by apolitical 'evidence' are nothing more than a normative ideal, and research capacity-building work that has only focused on enhancing pure research skills will continue to yield disappointing results in terms of embedding research in the policy process. Nevertheless, 'knowledge' remains at the heart of the new models of policy processes, and social research that satisfies academic standards of quality is still needed for effective social development policies. The need for an ever-widening range of actors to generate (and use) policy-relevant knowledge suggests not only a traditional process of research capacity-building, but also that an understanding of policy-making processes and the capacity to form new relationships and linkages across institutional boundaries have to be built.

Glossary

anthropology The study and analysis of the origins and characteristics of human beings and their societies, customs and beliefs.

behaviourist approach An approach limited to enquiring about specific behaviours or factual matters rather than general perceptions or attitudes.

bias An inclination to favour one attribute or characteristic more than another; a partiality that prevents the objective consideration of an issue or situation.

capability The power or ability, perhaps not made full use of, that enables a person to function – to be and do in a way that is of value.

complementarity A context in which research methods from different traditions are combined and sequenced in a way that improves the quality of the research and its outputs.

confidence (degree of) Measure of probability by which a statistical score, such as a sampling result, may be considered reliable.

constructivist Referring to a school of approaches to research that stress an interpretive nature of knowledge construction, recognizing that different interpretations of 'reality' exist, so that data lose their independence and individuals construct their own perspective of the world based on their unique knowledge and experience.

contextual methods Methods that sacrifice breadth of coverage and statistical generalizability for an in-depth exploration of issues within the social, cultural, economic and political environment of a specific (geographical or social) locality.

cost benefit analysis An economic appraisal of a project that compares its costs against the benefit it provides, and includes social costs and benefits.

covariant A relationship in which two variables respond.

data Information or facts obtained through observation, experimentation and research.

deductive Reasoning process in which the researcher begins with a theory and then gathers evidence, or data, to assess whether the theory is correct; generally used with quantitative research methods that produce data that can be statistically analysed with the aim of measuring, aggregating, modelling and predicting behaviour and relations based on what can be observed and independently verified; works from the more general to the more specific.

emic Expressing the views, concepts, categories and values of insiders (Chambers 1997).

empiricist Referring to the gaining of knowledge through experiment and observation (rather than theory).

empowerment A process of increasing the capacity of individuals or groups to make choices and to transform those into desired actions and outcomes.

entitlements The totality of things (e.g. goods or capabilities) that a person can have by virtue of, and dependent on, his or her rights in relation to others and others' rights in relation to him or her (Sen 1992: 347–8).

epistemology The philosophical theory of knowledge, and especially the critical study of its validity, methods and scope.

ethnography The detailed study and representation of people and their interaction in their cultural or subcultural groups that provides scientific description of individual human societies.

etic Expressing the views, concepts, categories and values of outsiders (Chambers 1997).

externalist see **etic**.

extractive Research that is used to elicit information from a research community to benefit 'outsiders', without consideration of how the research process can be used locally for reflection and action.

functionalist Referring to the theory that all elements of a culture serve to satisfy culturally defined needs of the people in that society or requirements of the society as a whole.

hedonic The hedonic function is used in regression analysis to adjust for differences in characteristics between varieties of a good.

hegemonic The preponderant influence of one state over another.

hermeneutics The science and practice (principles, rules and methodology) of interpretation and explanation.

hierarchical (multi-stage) sampling The process of selecting a sample by division of a population into primary sampling units, only some of which are sampled. Each of those selected is further subdivided into secondary sampling units, and so on, providing a hierarchical subdivision of sampling units. Usually primary units are selected on a judgement basis, and ultimate sampling units should be sampled in an objective way. This enables contextual, in-depth research that produces both qualitative and quantitative information, in sites and with groups that are representative of larger populations.

ideology The ideas, beliefs and values which form the basis for a social, economic or political system; a system of normative opinions, beliefs and values held by a person, social group, society or nation.

impact Any change, positive or negative, intended or unintended, that occurs as a result of an activity or an action (e.g. project, programme or policy)

indicator A specific, observable and measurable quantitative or qualitative factor, variable or characteristic that provides a simple and reliable basis for assessing achievement, change or performance.

inductive Reasoning process generally used with qualitative research methods in which data (e.g. judgements and perceptions) are gathered and examined, with space created to analyse complex and often non-quantifiable cause-and-effect processes and the meanings people impute to these processes; hypotheses are formulated and theories developed in response to what the data reveal; works from specific observations to broader generalizations and theories.

interpretive Subject to interpretation.

inter-subjectivity The process of people coming to know a common phenomenon, each through his or her subjective experience, through the mutual sharing of meanings, behaviours, activities and events in interactive situations.

iterative A term used to describe a process in which some operation is performed repeatedly.

learning organization An organization that behaves flexibly through systems, mechanisms and processes that encourage and facilitate the continuous learning and capability enhancement of its members in order to continuously transform itself and improve outcomes by empowering people.

livelihood Comprises the capabilities, assets and activities needed as a means of living.

logical positivism A form of empiricism which holds to scientific method as a means of establishing objective reality (Chambers, 1997).

longitudinal trends Trends in the data associated with a specific population over a given time period.

method A way of doing something, especially a systematic way with an orderly and logical arrangement and sequence.

monitoring and evaluation Management and learning tools that involve the periodic collection of data (monitoring) and systematic analysis of data (evaluation) in order to review and assess the progress of a plan against timelines and objectives, and the impact of the implementation of a plan, so that learning can occur.

non-contextual Methods that sacrifice in-depth exploration for breadth of coverage and statistical generalizability.

normative Fitting with an accepted or most frequent value or state.

objectivity Refers to the extent to which multiple observers can agree on a phenomenon and is ensured by removing the influence of the researcher (i.e. background, previous experiences, interests, motivations, expectations and preconceived ideas) on the research process.

ontological   Relating to the principles of pure being, with the nature and essence of things.

participation   The process through which stakeholders are involved in, influence, and have control over the development process (including priority setting, policy-making, resource allocation and access to public goods and services).

participatory research   Research that emphasizes a philosophical commitment to respect local knowledge and facilitate local ownership and control of data generation and analysis, in order to enable local people to establish their own analytical framework and to be in a position to challenge 'development from above' (Mukherjee 1995: 27) through public and collective reflection and action.

perception   A person's view of something arising from their selection, organization and interpretation of information.

plurality   The state of being plural; a large indefinite number.

positivist   Of, or relating to, positivism, a form of empiricism that bases all knowledge on perceptual experience (not on intuition or revelation) and holds scientific method as the means of establishing objective reality.

purposive selection   The selection of a sample population on purpose rather than using probability-based (random) sampling.

qualitative research   Qualitative research tends to produce data that are stated in prose or textual forms, and seeks to explain difference rather than standardizing to describe the norm.

quantitative research   Quantitative research prioritizes descriptive analytical breadth of coverage and produces data in the form of numbers that can be aggregated and analysed to describe and predict relationships.

random (probability-based) sampling   The process of selecting samples at random from a complete list of a given population, so that each member of the population has an exactly equal chance of selection; sample selection is objectively based on known chances of inclusion in the sample, and is determined in an objective way, not influenced by personal preferences.

reflexivity   A self-conscious awareness of the relationships on which the fieldwork experience is based. All findings are heavily qualified and placed in context as the result of an interaction between the researcher and his/her subject.

reliability   The extent to which each repetition of the same instruments will yield similar measurements.

representativeness   The degree to which a given sample accurately represents the total population from which it was taken.

rights   Claims to social arrangements and relationships that protect people from abuses and deprivations and provide the freedoms necessary for a life of dignity and fulfilment.

rigour   The quality of being logically valid.

sampling   The process of taking a subset, or portion, of a population from which data can be collected in order to make generalizations back to a population.

sampling error   The degree to which a sample differs from population characteristics on some measurement.

social learning   A process that encourages reflection on past and present activities.

stakeholders   The various individuals, groups, communities or institutions who are affected by, can influence the outcome of, or have an interest in a given project, programme, policy or any other issue.

standard segments   Segments refer to submodules of a research instrument that share the same design characteristics.

subjectivity   Refers to the degree to which a researcher uses interpretive research processes and judgements based on individual personal impressions and opinions, rather than external facts, to make the subject of the interpretation meaningful.

survey   A system for collecting information to describe, compare or explain knowledge, attitudes and behaviour.

theory   An organized set of ideas that explain how or why something happens in some domain of inquiry and can be used to predict future observations.

triangulation   The use of multiple perspectives by combining multiple data sources, observers, methods, analyses or theories to derive and substantiate an assessment or conclusion in a process of cross-checking and cross-validating, in order to reduce the bias that comes from single-informant, single-method, single-observer or single-theory studies.

trustworthiness   The quality of deserving to be believed; the degree to which a representation of reality is believable.

validity   The degree to which the results of a study are likely to be true, believable and free of bias; achieved when the measurement does what it is intended to do and is related to truthfulness or accuracy in measurement.

vulnerability   A dynamic concept concerning the changing state of being of individuals, households and communities relating to their survival, exposure to risk and stress, defencelessness, self respect and ability to invest in or draw down on a range of assets in the face of internal or external shocks, cycles and trends.

List of contributors

Savitri Abeyasekera is Principal Statistician in the Statistical Services Centre at the University of Reading. Her interests, mainly in relation to developing countries, include many aspects of data management and analysis, and mixing qualitative and quantitative approaches.

Simon Appleton is a Senior Lecturer at the School of Economics at the University of Nottingham. His research interests focus on human resources, labour markets and poverty in developing countries, especially Africa and China.

Adrian Barrance is an independent consultant based in Tegucigalpa, Honduras. His main area of work is the formulation of integrated rural development and conservation projects.

David Booth is a Research Fellow and Coordinator of the Poverty and Public Policy Group at the Overseas Development Institute in London. A sociologist with an interest in African and Latin American policy issues, he was formerly Professor of Development Studies at the University of Wales Swansea and a lecturer at the University of Hull.

Tanja Bastia is a PhD student in Development Studies at the University of Wales Swansea. Her research focus is on migration, gender and ethnicity in Latin America. She has also conducted related advisory work for DFID and the ILO.

Jutta Blauert works as a researcher and consultant in Mexico and is teaching at a Masters Programme in Development Cooperation at the Instituto Mora, Mexico City. She previously worked at IDS, University of Sussex. She works in the areas of participation and development, sustainable rural development and natural resource management, organizational learning and participatory monitoring and evaluation.

Jenny Briedenhann has over 20 years experience in the tourism field in South Africa. She has recently joined the London-based New Economics Foundation. Her research interests centre on the development and management of rural and community-based tourism.

John R. Campbell is an anthropologist in the Department of Sociology and Anthropology, School of Oriental and African Studies, University of London. He has worked in Ghana, Tanzania and Ethiopia, and undertaken development consultancy in Ethiopia, Kenya, Tanzania and Botswana.

James Copestake is a Lecturer in Economics and International Development at the University of Bath. His research interests include microfinance, rural development and management of development, drawing particularly on experience in Bolivia, India, Zambia and Peru. He is currently a member of 'WeD' (ESRC research group on wellbeing in developing countries) and 'Imp-Act' (Ford Foundation funded action research into the impact of microfinance on poverty).

Gordon Crawford is a Senior Lecturer in Development Studies in the School of Politics and International Studies at the University of Leeds. He specializes in issues of democratization in developing countries, including the role of international actors in democracy promotion.

Ann Degrande is a socio-economist working with the World Agroforestry Centre in Cameroon. Her main interests are in participatory tree domestication.

Andrew Dougill is a Lecturer in Environment and Development at the University of Leeds. His research focuses on assessments of land degradation processes and their links to the underlying socio-economic root causes of environmental suffering. His experience focuses on the links between environmental changes, farmer decision-making and livelihoods in the Kalahari rangelands in Southern Africa.

Eleanor Fisher is a Lecturer in Development Studies at the University of Wales Swansea. She is a social development specialist with particular interests in poverty and vulnerability analysis and in rural sustainable livelihoods, and with research experience in Eastern and sub-Saharan Africa.

Nigel Gilbert is Professor of Sociology at the University of Surrey. He has long been involved with social simulation as a method and its application to a variety of domains, including the management of environmental resources.

Jamie Gordon is a Postgraduate Researcher at the Department of Geography, University of Durham. He works in Mexico and Central America on forest management, biodiversity conservation and the functioning of NGOs.

Alejandro Guevara is a development economist, focused on social and environmental issues and head of the Department of Economics, Universidad Iberoamericana in Mexico.

Kirstan Hawkins was formerly a Lecturer in Anthropology and Development at the University of Wales Swansea, and is currently Director of the Peer Ethnographic Unit at Options Consultancy Services Ltd. Her research interests are in HIV/AIDS and reproductive health.

Jeremy Holland is a Lecturer in Development Studies at the Centre for Development Studies, University of Wales Swansea. His research interests include poverty analysis, rights-based approaches, social policy and participatory and combined research methods, with field experience in the Caribbean, West Africa and the Middle East.

Duncan Holtom recently graduated with a PhD in Development Studies at the University of Wales Swansea. His research focus was on power and political discourse in Tanzania.

Michael Jennings is a Lecturer in Development Studies at the University of Wales Swansea, with research interests in politics, governance and civil society in sub-Saharan Africa and in the history of development processes and interventions.

Susan Johnson is a Lecturer in Institutional Economics and Developments at the University of Bath. Her research interests include gender, financial markets and NGO management, drawing particularly on East African experience. She is currently a member of 'WeD' (ESRC research group on wellbeing in developing countries) and 'Imp-Act' (Ford Foundation funded action research into the impact of microfinance on poverty).

Andrea Lampis is a Researcher at the Faculty of Human and Social Sciences of the University Externado of Colombia, where he coordinates the Sociology Programme. He also works as a consultant in participatory evaluation and planning for a number of development cooperation international and national agencies. He is reading for a PhD in Social Policy at the London School of Economics.

Roger Leakey is Professor of Agroecology and Sustainable Development and Director of the Agroforestry and Novel Crops Unit at James Cook University in Cairns, Australia. He is particularly involved in the development of domestication techniques and strategies for indigenous trees within agroforestry practices, for the purpose of poverty alleviation, environmental rehabilitation and social welfare.

Elaine Marshall is a Senior Programme Officer at UNEP-WCMC, where she manages a DFID-funded Forest Research Programme on non-timber forest products, bringing together the fields of sustainable use, socio-economics and marketing. She has particular interest in social forestry, gender impacts and poverty alleviation.

Adrian Newton is a Senior Lecturer in Conversation Science at Bournemouth University. He has been involved in a number of multi-disciplinary research projects focusing on the conservation and sustainable use of forest biodiversity.

Steadman Noble works for the Government of Jamaica in the Office of the Prime Minister as a member of a team coordinating the Jamaica Social Policy Evaluation (JASPEV) project. He has a background in community development and participated in the recent 'Consultations with the Poor' participatory research process in Jamaica.

Andrew Norton is Head of Social Development at the UK Department for International Development. He has formerly worked for the Overseas Development Institute, the Centre for Development Studies at the University of Wales Swansea and the World Bank. He is a social anthropologist by background with experience of applied development and social policy practice in Africa, the Caribbean and South Asia.

Quirien Van Oirschot is a food scientist and post-harvest technologist, based at the Natural Resources Institute, University of Greenwich. She has overseas research experience in Tanzania, Uganda, Kenya and Colombia.

Neil Price is a Senior Lecturer at the Centre for Development Studies, University of Wales Swansea. He has undertaken ethnographic field-work in Cambodia, the Caribbean, China, Kenya and Zambia. His main areas of advisory expertise are in social, policy and institutional analysis in the health sector, and in the appraisal, monitoring and evaluation of HIV/AIDS and reproductive health programmes.

Mark Reed is a Research and Teaching Fellow at the University of Leeds. He is approaching completion of a PhD on 'Participatory Indicator Development and Environmental Monitoring in the Kalahari, Botswana'. This work has linked closely to the UN-funded Indigenous Vegetation Project that has adapted his research for wider dissemination to study communities across Botswana.

Kathrin Schreckenberg is a Reseach Fellow at the Overseas Development Institute, London. Her principal interest is in understanding how farmers can obtain greater benefits from the trees on their land, both individually and through community forestry.

Ken Sigrist is a consultant on institutional and governance issues, and is currently working as strategic adviser to the prime minister of Romania on public administration reform. He was a senior economist at the World Bank for many years, but latterly he specialized in organizational development and institutional design issues.

Zac Tchoundjeu works for the World Agroforestry Centre in Cameroon where he is Regional Coordinator for the African Humid Tropics. He is a forester specialized in vegetative propagation and working with farmers to domesticate agroforestry tree species.

Keith Tomlins is a food safety and quality scientist at the Natural Resources Institute, University of Greenwich. He has been involved for many years in project management, research and consultancy throughout Africa on issues of food safety, with expertise in sensory evaluation and consumer acceptability (preference mapping).

Eugenia Wickens is a Reader in the Faculty of Leisure and Tourism at Buckinghamshire Chilterns University College. Her research interests are cultural tourism, tourist motivations and experiences, tourism development and educational tourism.

Ian Wilson works as Special Adviser at the Statistical Services Centre, University of Reading. His interests include sampling and surveys, mixing qualitative and quantitative approaches, and longitudinal studies, mainly in relation to developing countries.

Katie Wright-Revolledo is an ESRC-funded Post-doctoral Researcher at the University of Bath. Her research interests include gender, microfinance, identity and migration, drawing particularly on Peru experience. She is currently currently a member of 'WeD' (ESRC research group on wellbeing in developing countries) and 'Imp-Act' (Ford Foundation funded action research into the impact of microfinance on poverty).

Gil Yaron is an economist working on natural resource and development issues. He is a director of the consulting company GY Associates Ltd and, with his colleagues, works with communities, NGOs, international agencies and policy makers in the UK and many developing countries.

Endnotes

GENERAL INTRODUCTION

1 We are grateful to Eleanor Fisher, Duncan Holtom and an anonymous reviewer for comments on this general introduction.

2 These concerns were raised at a Conference on Combined Methods in Development research at the University of Wales Swansea, July 2002.

3 Shaffer (1996), for example, argues that epistemological differences between income-based and participatory approaches to poverty assessment cannot be resolved by a technical fix because they are neither right nor wrong, just different.

4 There is not a clear binary distinction between types of methods and types of data; Figure a.1 shows these two elements as spectra.

5 However, surveys are not always non-contextual – they can be designed to collect quantitative data but within a more contextual methodology, e.g. Lanjouw and Stern's (1991) implementation of a contextual village survey in Palanpur, India.

6 Inspection of two recent issues of the *American Journal of Sociology* found that two-thirds of the papers used regression-based statistical analysis, or similar (White 2002a).

7 Wilks (2003: 162) quotes Heilbroner and Milberg (1995: 126): *'Economics must come to regard itself as a discipline much more closely allied with the imprecise knowledge of political, psychological, and anthropological insights than with the precise scientific know-ledge of the physical sciences. Indeed, the challenge may in fact require that economics come to recognize itself as a discipline that follows in the wake of sociology and politics rather than proudly leading the way for them.'*

8 This is a particularly important comparative advantage as many household surveys take the household as a single unit of analysis.

9 Commenting on the post-Soviet Central Asian policy shift to targeted social welfare, for example, Kandiyoti (1999) argues that the donor-driven restructuring of information systems to provide externally compatible survey-based data in the region cannot provide the type of information – on the nature of household composition and coping strategies – necessary for sound policy analysis. Moser (1998), through her call for social policy to complement household strategies in post-apartheid South Africa, reaches similar conclusions.

10 Feminist research, for example, has emphasized the social construction of reality by men, with women's experiences and interpretations consistently marginalized (Roberts, 1988; Ruth, 1990; Letherby, 2003). In this way, gender becomes a 'category of social thought', leading to 'particular kind(s) of social and historical experience' (Kelly-Gadol, 1987: 18).

11 Lincoln and Guba (1985) originally used the label 'naturalist' but later preferred 'constructivist' (Guba and Lincoln, 1989).

12 Since we do not have unmediated access to the world, our accounts cannot reproduce, but only represent the world (realities). Therefore researchers' accounts will inevitably highlight some aspects and suppress others, depending on the researcher's own discursive construction of the world, and hence what is considered relevant and what is not. Thus 'there can be multiple and non-contradictory and valid explanations of the same phenomena', each highlighting different aspects of the same phenomena (Hammersley 1998: 74).

13 Two decades ago, Miles and Huberman (1984: 20) observed:
    'It is getting harder to find any methodologists solidly encamped in one epistemology or the other. More and more "quantitative" methodologists, operating from a logical positivist stance, are using naturalistic and phenomenological approaches to complement tests, surveys and structured interviews. On the other side, an increasing number of ethnographers and qualitative researchers are using pre-designed conceptual frameworks and pre-structured instrumentation, especially when dealing with more than one institution or community ... we contend that researchers should pursue their work, be open to an ecumenical blend of epistemologies and procedures, and leave the grand debate to those who care most about it.'

14 The notion of objectivity is fundamental to the empiricist tradition, and indicates that 'the meanings and conditions of subjects' lives are independent of those subjects' (Servaes, J. and Arnst, R., Universities of Nijmegen and Antwerp, 'Does it make sense? Validity and evaluation in quantitative, qualitative and participatory approaches to (communication) research', unpublished paper), and therefore that they can be isolated, measured and tested.

15 Herring (2003) refers to the 'Chai stall error' in survey research from the case of a rural credit survey in Pakistan in which questioners made up answers on the basis of conversations at the local tea shop, rather than visiting the sampled households. In other areas when implementing the same survey, questioners, fearing their personal safety, stayed away from many areas but still felt compelled to fill in the forms anyway.

16 Recent debates about poverty in Jamaica became highly charged in the wake of published poverty trend figures that showed poverty falling during a period when people perceived a decline in their economic wellbeing (Carlton Davis, Cabinet Office, Government of Jamaica, personal communication).

17 White (2002a) compares data mining in participatory research with econometric research in which a model is first derived and the data fitted to that model: 'There is a saying that "if you torture the data long enough [they] will confess". In the famous case of Burnside and Dollar's (2000) paper on aid effectiveness, quite small changes in model specification could change the results to make them inconsistent with the arguments advanced in the paper.

18 The issue of reliability and validity of data has been the subject of considerable attention (e.g. Silverman, 1993; Bryman, 2001). We strongly suggest that readers look at this literature, which is only tangentially addressed by Lincoln and Guba.

19 The Millenium Development Goals were approved by the General Assembly of the United Nations in 2000. They represent a continuation of the International Development Targets codified by the Development Assistance Committee of the OECD in 1996.

20 Reviewing the World Bank's poverty assessments in sub-Saharan Africa, Hanmer et al. (1997) concluded: *'we would go so far as to suggest that there is nothing of policy relevance to be learned which is dependent on the notion of a poverty line as deployed by the World Bank in the Poverty Assessments.'*

21 To the point where McGee (2003: 132) comments: *'Much confusion could be avoided if we could reach a consensus that income poverty should be referred to as just that, and that when "poverty" is discussed it means a lot more than that. Some would say that agreement has already been reached on this, but in practice "poverty" is still often used to refer to income poverty.'*

22 The 'Voices of the Poor' participatory study for the World Bank's *World Development Report 2000/01* (Narayan et al. 2000) crystallizes this new approach in the manner in which elements of powerlessness and ill-being were brought together in one 'many-stranded web'. Similarly, the sustainable livelihoods approach (Scoones 1998) provides an analytical framework for understanding poverty that has been adopted in varying forms by UNDP, DFID and international NGOs such as CARE and Oxfam.

23 The United Nations Development Programme has been instrumental in bringing the rights and entitlements agenda within development agency discourse (UNDP 2000); the Organisation for Economic Co-operation and Development notes the importance of a rights approach that 'links empowerment to international agreements on human political as well as economic social and cultural rights' (OECD 2000); and the *World Development Report 2000/01* (World Bank 2001) promotes a form of material empowerment that exceeds what Moore (2001) calls the 'cheap talk' of community empowerment.

24 Sen's (1999) characterization of 'development as freedom' perhaps most aptly captures the mutually reinforcing relationship between rights and development: without freedom, there is no development; with freedom, development as a process of uplifting personal wellbeing is enhanced.

25 These include tensions in the production of poverty reduction strategy papers by heavily indebted poor (HIPC-eligible) countries, and the recent round of poverty and social impact assessments that have sought to identify, *a priori*, the impact of macro-policy triggers on poverty outcomes (Evans et al. 2003).

26 Several participants at the Cornell Workshop (Kanbur 2001a) noted a disconnection between qualitative and quantitative disciplines in development, referring to 'unconnected worlds' (Kanbur 2003b) in which practitioners pursue their own research agenda using their familiar methodologies and in their own language. The main point, concludes Kanbur, is that 'practitioners do not seem to talk to each other as much as they ought to ... given (their) ... common objective(s)'. Others noted, more worryingly, an inequality between development disciplines and their methodologies of choice. Wilks (2003) referred to the danger posed by an econo-mistic disciplinary stranglehold. McGee (2003), citing reviews of methodologies used in World Bank poverty assessments (Carvalho and White 1997; Whitehead and Lockwood 1998), notes that '"equality in difference" remains elusive', with qualitative find-ings in mainstream poverty literature 'still subject to questions which are not commonly asked about quantitative findings, the use of which is seen as "natural"'. She concludes that 'when brought together, the two approaches rarely have similar status.'

27 There are parallels here with concerns within participatory research about what Guijt and Cornwall (1995) call the 'manual mentality'.

28 These two constellations had been starting to merge, largely through the rhetorical support for process and participation by World Bank President James Wolfensohn and ex-Vice-President Joseph Stiglitz.

29 Many economists claim that income inequality is good for growth because it strengthens incentives to effort and risk taking (Wade 2001: 1437).

30 Chambers' (1997) critique of 'normal development professionalism' suggests that institutionalized power produces institutionalized ignorance fuelled by a positivist science. He argues that this pervades development practice from macro-policy through sector policy and planning to development projects.

INTRODUCTION: PART I

1   White (2002a) gives the example of the potential for qualitative research on labour exchange options to improve the content of rural labour market surveys in Africa.

2   A powerful example is the use of qualitative research to explore perceptions of social capital in Tanzania and, from these percep-tions, to generate weighted indicators with cardinal scores for econometric testing (Narayan 1997). A similar process was fol-lowed in the construction of indicators for participation in water projects (Isham et al. 1995).

3   This comparative analysis might address, for example, whether stratification according to the household survey is matched by the results of rankings drawn up by local analysts (Booth et al. 1998: 60).

4   Croll (2000), for example, uses ethnographic methods to explore the statistical relationship between sex and infant mortality in India and China, and develops a thesis on daughter discrimination

that highlights the economic status of women. White (2002a) points out that these arguments have subsequently been incorporated into economic models of the household.

5   Hanmer et al. (1997) argue that by establishing the ability of qualitative approaches to collect data normally gathered from more expensive techniques, verification plays two important roles: data users will gain the confidence to use the results from qualitative investigation in advance of receiving results from formal sample surveys; and for some uses it should, in time, become accepted that the formal survey is not required at all – here they draw a parallel with the difficulty proponents of sample surveys had in initially having their methods accepted.

6   Demonstrated, for example, in their application to gender in the Zambia poverty assessment, and to social capital in the Tanzania participatory poverty assessment (Booth et al. 1998: annexes 4 and 5, respectively).

7   Booth et al. (1998) recommend the use of multidisciplinary research teams as a means of reducing bias and improving trust-worthiness through triangulation.

8   Shah (1993), for example, describes a participatory method of 'visual interactive questionnaires' used by villagers in Gujarat, India, whereby quantitative questionnaire variables and categories were generated through collective reflection.

9   Variables for this comparison have to be contained in the larger survey, and have to be easily, if informally, recordable in the case-study community. The profile of that community then has to be carefully compared with the larger survey. A community may be found to fit the poorest quintile of a larger survey according to most variables (e.g. rooms per household; utility access), but may have a relatively high educational level. Because of the potential impact of this outlier variable on outcomes such as employment, conclusions from this study about employment and livelihoods will probably not be representative of other communities (Booth et al. 1998: 59).

10   Random stratified sampling is a technique that divides the population into different groups or classes called strata, then draws a sample from each stratum at random.

CHAPTER TWO

1   Substantial parts of the work reported in this chapter were carried out by the author as part of DFID NRSP (SEM) Project R7033 under a grant held jointly by the Natural Resources Institute, University of Greenwich, and the Statistical Services Centre, University of Reading.

2   Hierarchies are not unique, for example, there are different representations of a community other than the holder of an officially defined post. However, it is important to recognize that

information exists at different levels and to think systematically about linking them.

3   In statistical parlance, the standard terminology refers to multi-stage sampling, but that term is avoided here as it carries a good deal of baggage irrelevant to our purpose as well as misleading overtones of multiple time points.

4   In these cases, the sample contained two primary sampling units and some hundreds of secondary units (households). Our main objection to such designs was that the sampling at the level of primary units was poorly conceptualized and poorly justified – no attempt was made to demonstrate where the two sites were in relation to other places; and a sample size of two was (beyond doubt) unable to represent the larger reality about which DFID or Government might usefully have been informed. In one case, at least, the two primary units were chosen within a large and important agro-ecosystem – fine, but the main feature recorded in the final technical report was that several other sites were rejected because they did not have the 'right' combination of features, indeed that the chosen sites were of a type that was quite hard to find. So what did they represent? There were no confirmatory studies where conclusions from the two main study sites were even briefly calibrated against the realities of other places. Note that the work done within sites was argued to be of wider general relevance – to be research, rather than being defended as locally relevant empowerment, for example.

5   This question has remained with the author for 38 years. Working briefly as a statistician in a marine biology laboratory, he was told, while helping a struggling scientist, 'only one crab in 100 is typical.'

6   For a start, the sample size of primary-stage units (e.g. number of subdistricts) would have to be very large. A sample of two subdistricts is still a miserable little sample size of two, regardless of how many households are interviewed in each one.

7   For example, if 11 children had to be approached to obtain the sample of size ten to which child Reddy belonged, that has a different evidential implication than if ten children could be assembled only by approaching 60. If the hit rate is a lot less than 100 per cent, good practice demands some attempt at characterizing the misses, and the impact on the conclusions of their omission or non-compliance.

8   The number of communities and the number of EPAs should be the same - as the method description indicates - but of course four is just an example.

9   The original idea concerned a standard quantitative survey, probably with a complication such as a multi-stage structure. If this could be organized as a set of replicates – miniature surveys each with an identical structure – then an estimate of some key measure could be derived from each one, and that set of estimates treated just as basic statistics treats a simple random sample of data. The replicate-to-replicate standard error would incorporate the whole set of

complexities within the stages of each miniature survey, and we would obtain an easy measure of precision of the final answer.

CHAPTER THREE

1   See Kanbur (2001b) for a parallel debate relating to poverty assessment more generally.
2   All these organizations maintain active websites. A useful single gateway into all of them is the Enterprise Development website: *www.enterweb.org/microcre.htm*
3   For a discussion of these issues in relation to global standards in higher education see Room (2000); for an economic theory perspective, see Hudson and Jones (2002). Skevington (2002), in contrast, explores procedural issues in development of a universal yet cross-cultural protocol for assessing quality of life.
4   This difference arises from the contrasting epistemologies under-pinning the two approaches. Qualitative enquiry addresses the attribution problem by assessing the consistency and coherence of respondents' narratives. Positivist enquiry seeks (often with partial success due to problems of selection bias) to solve the attribution problem through statistical inference.
5   See Copestake (2001) for a discussion of client portfolio classification.
6   Quota sampling starts with a clear definition of subcategories of the population. For example, this might be based on client loyalty. A decision is then made to select an initial quota of respondents from each subcategory. A random mechanism for doing this must then be identified. If the data generated by an initial quota do not reveal a clear pattern, then additional quotas may be sampled. The method is inefficient in enabling statistical inferences to be made about mean values for the whole population. But it is effective in building on prior knowledge of the diversity of the population.
7   See, for example, Copestake (2002), reporting on data collected by visiting a quota sample of 'three-year old' clients on the Zambian Copperbelt who had already been interviewed twice before.
8   As Davidson (1999) has observed, documenting personal histories and struggles can illuminate both an individual's courses of action (or inaction) and the effects of constraints and barriers which evolve over the life course at different times and places.
9   For example, where respondents are asked to score or rank data this may have cultural or symbolic meaning of which the researcher is unaware. Nevertheless, it has been argued that subjective values are amenable to mathematical analysis and quantification (Hanton 2002).

CHAPTER FOUR

1   The work reported on here is only one aspect of the wider bilateral project funded from 2000 to 2003 by the Department for International

Development, on 'Institutional Capacity Building in Monitoring and Evaluation', with the Mexican Environment Ministry and its Regional Sustainable Development Programmes. The work has been undertaken by a wider team of Mexican consultants, ministry staff and ATOS KPMG-led UK-based consultants, and this chapter is only a first sharing (in English) of reflections and analysis on the work at this stage (for published outputs of Phase 1 see Toledo and Bartra 2000). Our comments and conclusions are our own responsibility. Jutta Blauert (at the time of writing based at the Institute of Development Studies, Sussex) has collaborated on the project since March 2001, in those phases and aspects where participatory approaches to M&E are being addressed. Thanks go to Mike Thomson and Julian Laite for their comments on this draft and the collaborative work without which this chapter would not exist. We would also like to thank the staff of the PRODERS offices in Mexico, and community members who helped us learn about the challenges of national PM&E work.

2 The innovative nature of the programme can be seen in its vision of integrating social and environmental benefits and damages into the decision-making process from the beginning (in contrast to the conventional policy approach, which merely adds environmental concerns to those of economic development).

3 This evaluation work was supported from March 2000 onwards by DFID through a bilateral grant for 'Strengthening of Institutional Capacity in Monitoring and Evaluation', with PRODERS as the pilot.

4 This work was coordinated by the social anthropologist Armando Bartra and his research team from the research NGO *Instituto Maya*.

5 For example, standard Likert scales, running from interventions having a negative impact (1) through to those with a very significant positive impact (5).

CHAPTER FIVE

1 There are two underlying dimensions for reliability: repeatability and internal consistency (Zikmund 1994). The Delphi technique is an iterative, interactive cognition process, with the final outcome based on internal consistency, as the outcome represents the consensual opinion of a group of experts relating to the enquiry. It has been suggested that statements relating to the researcher's assumptions, biases and values, and the method and rationale for selection of participants, should be documented as this would enhance the chance of replicating the study in another setting (Creswell 1994).

INTRODUCTION: PART II

1 Generally, income-based and consumption-based measurements of poverty are used either because they are viewed as legitimate

ends in themselves, or because they are regarded as strong predictors or indicators of other welfare variables (Carvalho and White 1997: 2).

2   During a participatory village survey in Gujarat, for example, Jodha (1988) elicited that households whose wellbeing had declined in terms of per capita income were in fact better off according to 37 out of 38 of their own criteria of wellbeing, which included independence from patrons, mobility, security and self-respect.

3   A study that produced numerical indicators of participation in 121 diverse water projects, for instance, produced strong statistical findings that increasing beneficiary participation directly causes more sustainable project outcomes (Isham et al. 1995).

CHAPTER SIX

1   However, it must be noted that hierarchical data structures are more appropriately computerized using a suitable database, rather than as a series of spreadsheets.

2   It is important to recognize that proceeding beyond straightforward data summaries and graphical presentations to formal statistical procedures and tests of significance has little value in helping research conclusions if sampling issues have not been appropri- ately addressed in the sample selection. One issue is whether the sample size gives an adequate representation of the communities targeted for study. Here sample size refers to the number of inde-pendent assessments obtained, either by interviewing respon-dents individually or by holding separate discussions with a number of respondent groups. How large a sample is needed will depend on the specific objectives of the study.

3   Moringa oil comes from pressing the seed of the tree *Moringa oleifera* to yield a high-quality edible oil.

4   Economists often use regression analysis, a special case of a more general linear modelling procedure, where the response variate is quantitative but the explanatory variables can be quantitative or binary or categorical qualitative variables.

5   If ties occur in the data, an adjustment to Friedman's test statistic is available. However, three associated problems need consideration. First, the test is based on an approximation to the chi-squared distribution. If n is the number of farmers and k is the number of items being ranked, then nk must be reasonably large, say ≥ 30, for the approximation to be reasonable. Second, the test makes no allowance for missing data. If missing data do occur, because (say) the number of items ranked varies from farmer to farmer, then ranks need to be converted to numerical scores in some fashion (Abeyasekera et al. 2000), and then analysed using procedures described in the previous section. Third, the test cannot take into account the full data structure.

6   Typically, the modelling procedure is followed by an analysis of residuals (the residual component associated with each data point

after the variation in the main response variable has been adjusted for all other known factors). Some residuals may emerge as outliers. A return to the narratives is then essential for explaining and discussing these extreme cases. Identifying such cases is greatly facilitated by an initial quantitative treatment of the data gathered.

CHAPTER SEVEN

1   Collaborators are greatly acknowledged for their inputs to the case studies from LZARDI Ukiriguru, Biharmulo District Office, Tanzania and the Food Research Institute, Accra, Ghana. This publication is an output from a research project funded by UK Department for International Development (DFID) for the benefit of developing countries: R7543, R7520, R7498, R7497: Crop Post-Harvest Research Programme. The views expressed are not necessarily those of DFID.

2   The significance of a difference can be tested using standard tables with the forced choice using one-sided tests, and a two-sided test to find out if there is a difference in intensity or preference. If no-difference or no-preference replies have been permitted, the results can be ignored (subtracted from the total number of replies from the panel), or half the no-difference or no-preference replies can be allocated to each of the two categories of reply.

3   In order to analyse and interpret the results, samples are decoded and the rank orders for each sample given by each assessor are tabulated. Where there are tied rankings, the mean rank is recorded. The rank sum for each sample is calculated by summing the ranks for each assessor. By comparing the rank sums for the samples it is possible to obtain an evaluation of the differences between the samples.

4   The results may be summarized as frequencies for each category. The chi-squared test can then be used to compare the distributions of two or more types of a product into the different categories.

5   The results obtained for one sample may be summarized as a median or a mean with some method of variation such as the standard deviation. If only two samples are involved and the distribution of the results is normally distributed, the t-test may be used to compare means and the F-test to compare variances. If more than two samples are involved, the analysis of variance (ANOVA) procedure is recommended.

6   There is no simple way of treating the results statistically. ANOVA has been used to determine consensus among the assessors for each single attribute. Because of the multidimensional character of the data (each descriptor provides a dimension) and the numerous interrelationships between the descriptors, a dimension-reducing analysis technique may be needed to analyse the data set (Krzanowski 1988). Multivariate techniques of analysis may include principal components analysis, canonical variates analysis, and generalized procrustes analysis. The purpose of principal

components analysis is to transform the set of original correlated descriptors into a new set of principal components, which are linear combinations of the original descriptors, and which are not correlated with each other (Digby et al. 1989).

7   Our experience of using line scales at a recent project workshop in Tanzania indicates that if the anchors at each end of the scale are too extreme, the results are skewed. In this case, a happy and sad smiley were placed at opposite ends of the scale. Because the majority of participants were happy with the technology, they scored at the extreme end of the happy smiley, making prioritization difficult. Replacing the sad smiley with a neutral face may have been more appropriate.

8   Because the testing environment may not be controlled, however, careful consideration would need to be given to the applicability of the statistical methods so that the assumptions are not violated.

CHAPTER EIGHT

1   This chapter draws heavily on sections of Appleton and Booth's (2001) background paper for a workshop in Uganda which discussed closer coordination between the household survey programme and the participatory appraisals carried out by the Uganda Participatory Poverty Assessment Process.

2   In addition, there are advantages to having a 'panel' aspect to survey design, where some households and communities are revisited over time. This risks undermining the representativeness of the survey due to what is called non-random attrition (particular households drop out or cannot be found, for one reason or another). For this reason not all the sample should be a panel. However, a panel component is extremely useful for analytical purposes, and also provides a cross-check on whether changes in sampling have unintentionally distorted the results.

3   Allowing access to the data via the Internet is arguably the best way of providing open access. Several comparable data sets (such as the Tanzanian Human Resource Development Survey) are available from the World Bank website, while all the demographic and health surveys can be downloaded from MacroInternational (*www.measuredhs.com*).

4   An example of the sensitivity of results to questionnaire design is the omission of a question about public transport fares in the 1992 Uganda survey. Correcting for this raised estimated mean household consumption by 1.7 per cent.

5   Administrative data also provide such information, but surveys may be better in gathering information on control variables – for example, to see if there was a 'pure gender' effect or a government efficiency advantage.

6   Participatory assessments have often drawn attention to the potential for neglect of intra-household relationships. However, in

their normal form – where there is heavy use of focus groups and very little individual interviewing – PPAs are not a particularly good instrument for remedying the deficiency.

7   This matters because many of the arguments about the uses and abuses of participatory methods actually apply to the whole class of case-study approaches (including, for example, the typical form of anthropological fieldwork). Others apply to all rapid-appraisal work. And some apply specifically to PRA/PPA methods.

8   Participatory poverty assessment processes can make use of survey results, and this should probably happen more often. It is a mistake to think that PPA reports should be based on PPA field information alone. But this cannot be a symmetrical relationship. Household survey operations are processes too, but they are, quite rightly, driven by a narrower range of concerns.

9   The recent Policy and Service Satisfaction Survey that is part of the PRSP monitoring system in Tanzania combines focus groups with a tailor-made sample survey (REPOA, 2003). In the research literature there are excellent models of combining household survey analysis and anthropological fieldwork (Francis and Hoddinot 1993) and of PRA and local surveys (Ellis and Freeman 2004).

10   It should be noted, however, that there was a cost in this revision as it prevented comparison with the welfare indicators in two previous monitoring surveys which had revealed an intriguing worsening at the same time as consumption rose. This is an example of the general trade-off between perfecting survey instruments and maintaining comparability over time. For monitoring and related purposes, there is some virtue in maintaining a consistent but imperfect instrument.

11   A good way to complement data on consumption poverty is to use anthropometric data (stunting, wasting, etc.), which in Uganda are collected both by the National Household Survey and by the Demographic and Health Survey series. Although different dimensions of welfare are usually significantly correlated, the strength of the correlation is often surprisingly low. For example, Appleton and Song (1999) found low correlations between consumption poverty, lack of education and ill health at the household level in six countries. Sahn et al. (1999) find evidence from repeated demographic and health surveys in ten African countries that anthropometric indicators may worsen despite improvements in asset-based indicators of welfare.

12   TIP provides a small pack of free agricultural inputs (10 kg fertilizer, 2 kg maize seed and 1 kg legume seed) to smallholder farmers.

13   They adopted a threefold categorization: food-secure households have enough to eat throughout the year from harvest to harvest; food-insecure households have enough food to last from harvest (April/May) up to Christmas but not between Christmas and the next harvest; and extremely food-insecure households start facing severe food shortages before Christmas (Levy 2003).

14 For Uganda see Bird and Kakande (2001), especially their table on findings and policy responses. A more negative case for a change of focus may also be made. This starts from the experience in second-generation PPAs that repeatedly exploring with poor people the dimensions and proximate causes of deprivation and vulnerability eventually generates diminishing returns.

CHAPTER NINE

1 Examples of current research can be found in the *Journal of Artificial Societies and Social Simulation*: *www.soc.surrey.ac.uk/JASSS* (available without subscription). Issues 2 and 3 of Volume 6 (*http://jasss.soc.surrey.ac.uk/6/2/contents.html*) include several articles on the theme of role-playing games, models and negotiation processes, most of which relate to case studies in developing countries.

CHAPTER TEN

1 Much of the research that informed this paper was funded by the UK Department for International Development (DFID; contract number AG1196), to whom we express our gratitude. We are also grateful to CARE International in Zambia, to the Nepal Safe Motherhood Project, and to Population Services International in Cambodia for their cooperation and support in the field testing of the peer ethnographic method. Most importantly, our thanks go to those individuals – too numerous to name – who acted as peer researchers in the three programmes. The usual disclaimer applies: the opinions expressed in this chapter are ours alone, and we accept full responsibility for any errors or shortcomings.

2 We are not using the term 'peer' to refer exclusively to young people, whose peers are often of the same age, but to refer to members of any significant social network, such as friends, neighbours, workmates and kinsfolk, with whom an individual shares relatively equal status.

3 A *ta-ta* is an older man who takes care of a woman financially in return for sex. In *songsar* ('sweetheart') relationships, condoms are usually used initially but discontinued after around three months, invariably at the behest of the man.

4 At the time of writing, a round of peer ethnography has just been completed with non-literate researchers and interviewees in Myanmar, and appears to been successful.

CHAPTER ELEVEN

1 Research is being conducted under the auspices of Research Permit No. OP46/1 XCVI (87) provided by the Government of the Republic of Botswana. Funding was provided by the Explorer's

Club, Royal Scottish Geographical Society and University of Leeds. We are grateful to the Ministry of Agriculture for their ongoing cooperation and support.

CHAPTER TWELVE

1   To give an idea of the spread of the LFA – a simple Internet search produces an output of more than 500 000 hits. These include the web pages of multilateral agencies working in the field of international cooperation, many international and national NGOs, research centres, institutes and universities researching and teaching in the broad area of development.
2   Through a review of more than 200 international cooperation projects, Oakley et al. (1998) showed that the majority of projects planned and implemented on the basis of LFA very seldom even reached the output stage.
3   It can also be argued that there is a third logic within TML that originates from the semantic and conceptual interaction between the first two.
4   It is important to note here that the LFA matrix was realized only at a later stage, when implementation had already begun.
5   The case-study locations were Medellín (Antioquia), Cartagena, Carmen de Bolívar and San Basilio de Palenque (Bolívar), Quibdó (Chocó), Monteria (Córdoba) and Sincelejo (Sucre).
6   In each workshop, target groups were asked to evaluate the state of a range of assets at various points in time: before displacement occurred; during the three months after displacement when the government provided official assistance rations; during the period (variable for group to group) that separated the end of emergency provision and the arrival of the assistance brought by PRRO; and after the arrival of PRRO assistance.

CHAPTER THIRTEEN

1   This chapter is an output from several research projects funded by the UK Department for International Development (DFID) for the benefit of developing countries (R6913, R7190 and R7925, Forestry Research Programme). The views expressed here are not necessarily those of DFID. The PhD research was sponsored by the German Agency for Technical Cooperation (GTZ) with additional funding from the University of London Central Research Fund and the School of Oriental and African Studies.

CHAPTER FOURTEEN

1   Such problems have been raised by a number of donor agencies, and are expressed most succinctly by the evaluators of the European Commission's PHARE/TACIS Democracy Programme

(European Commission 1997: 15). The challenges listed here build on this source.

2   Posed here as a question, Carothers (1999: 287) originally used this statement as a subheading for his critique of USAID's 'managing for results' system.

3   Crawford and Kearton (2002: 14) state that their research did not find such a recommendation by the Development Assistance Committee, but note, in contrast, that the Committee's report on 'Participatory Development and Good Governance' advocates the adoption of 'truly participatory evaluation techniques' (OECD 1997: 26).

4   Participatory evaluation has a history that can be traced back at least 20 years to the discussion edited by Fernandes and Tandon (1981) of participatory research and evaluation in India.

5   A recent survey of DG evaluation studies found that while eight reports (out of 60) involved a degree of participation, only two loosely fulfilled Rebien's three threshold criteria to be counted as a participatory evaluation (Crawford and Kearton, 2002: 66). This finding is supported by Estrella and Gaventa's (1998) review of participatory monitoring and evaluation, in which 20 examples of projects and programmes using participatory monitoring and evaluation methods did not include a single one from the political aid sector. It also confirms unusually blunt statements from the Development Assistance Committee in its synthesis report on Participatory Development and Good Governance that 'While donors' rhetoric favors using more participatory evaluation, actual practice is still limited if not rare' (OECD 1997: 26). Although donor agencies may be prepared to 'listen to stakeholders', they 'typically stop short of bringing them fully into the evaluation process', partly due to an unwillingness to cede control over evaluations (OECD 1997: 26).

6   On completion of this chapter, I came across a speech by Michael Patton (2002) that similarly focuses on the links between evaluation and democracy, highlighting the ways in which a particular form of evaluation is congruent with and can contribute to a strengthening of democracy. While it is beyond the bounds of this chapter to examine Patton's arguments, and those of authors he discusses, they reinforce the perspective advocated here regarding the potential synergy between evaluation and democratization.

7   In this context, indirect stakeholders are those groups and individuals who are not recipients of the assistance, that is with no direct stake as such, but who do have a critical engagement with democratic processes in their country and thus are affected by the political interventions of external actors. Such indirect stakeholders can be subdivided into 'non-beneficiaries' and 'non-recipients', where the former are less involved in the democracy promotion 'business', while the latter are excluded from receipt of such funds. Non-beneficiaries could be representatives of legal bodies (bar

associations, for example), academic institutions, independent think tanks, and so on. Non-recipients are categorized as those denied DG assistance, or excluded from applying by domestic legislation, or self-excluded by their opposition to democracy assistance as external manipulation (Brouwer 2000: 10–11).

CHAPTER FIFTEEN

1   The experience with the Oregon Progress Board and the 'Oregon Shines' programme in the USA is documented in various reports on a regularly updated website: *http://egov.oregon.gov/DAS/OPB/os.shtml*
2   The JASPEV task force is exploring the possibility of using the Internet as a forum for comparison and discussion between local networks.
3   We adopt here Hentschel's (1999) matrix distinguishing methods as more-or-less contextual, and data as quantitative or qualitative.

CHAPTER SIXTEEN

1   The Centre for Development Studies, University of Wales Swansea, managed the project in partnership with the Department of Development Studies, School of Oriental and African Studies, University of London.
2   This project aimed at strengthening and intensifying the design and implementation processes of social integration policies in Bolivia, as well as promoting the immediate implementation of social integration actions that will improve the capacity of institutions to answer new democratic demands. Between January and March 2001, ten consultation workshops were conducted, which came up with '148 ideas to face the crises' with 700 copies distributed in policy, NGO, public, media and academic circles. A copy of the booklet was also personally presented by the Director of the SDRC project in Bolivia to the President of the Republic, and further copies were subsequently sent to every Cabinet Minister. This demonstrated that it is possible to carry out purposeful interventions in response to the urgent needs of the political system.
3   Here we should bear in mind the wider context of neoliberalism and the opening up of Tanzania's development economy to both private sector and donors during the 1980s. By implication, it was only really in the 1990s that that circumstances enabled private research institutes and research NGOs to become established and flourish.
4   This was acknowledged at a lesson-learning workshop after the project's completion, when many individuals who had participated in the project firmly agreed that DFID should not fund capacity-building programmes of fewer than seven years.
5   For more detailed case studies on research capacity-building in development, see Ryan 1999a,b; Molas-Gallart et al. 2000; Puchner 2001; Weber and Mujica 2001.

References

Abbot, J. and Guijt, I. (1998) *Changing Views on Change: Participatory Approaches to Monitoring the Environment*, Sustainable Agriculture and Rural Livelihoods (SARL) Discussion Paper No. 2, International Institute for Environment and Development, London.

Abel, N.O.J. and Blaikie, P.M. (1989) Land degradation, stocking rates and conservation policies in the communal rangelands of Botswana and Zimbabwe, *Land Degradation and Rehabilitation*, 1: 101–23.

Abeyasekera, S., Lawson-McDowall, J. and Wilson, I.M. (2000) *Converting Ranks to Scores for an ad-hoc Procedure to Identify Methods of Communication Available to Farmers*, case study for DFID project on 'Integrating qualitative and quantitative approaches in socio-economic survey work', Statistical Services Centre, University of Reading. *www.reading.ac.uk/ssc*

Agresti, A. (1996) *An Introduction to Categorical Data Analysis*, Wiley, New York.

Anderson, R.L. (1959) Use of contingency tables in the analysis of consumer preference studies, *Biometrics*, 15: 582–90.

Andranovich, G. (1995) *Developing Community Participation and Consensus: The Delphi Technique*, Community Ventures: A Western Regional Extension Publication.

Appleton, S. (2001) *Poverty in Uganda 1999/2000: Preliminary Estimates from the UNHS*, University of Nottingham, UK.

Appleton, S. and Booth, D. (2001) *Combining Participatory and Survey-based Approaches to Poverty Monitoring and Analysis*, Background Paper for Workshop held in Entebbe, Uganda 30 May–1 June 2001, Overseas Development Institute, London.

Appleton, S. and Song, L. (1999) Income and human development at the household level, background paper for *World Development Report 2000/2001*, processed, Department of Economics, University of Nottingham.

Arnstein, S. (1971) A ladder of citizen participation in the USA, *Journal of the Royal Town Planning Institute*, 57: 176–182 (originally in *Journal of American Institute of Planners*, 35 (1969): 216–24).

Ashley, C. (2000) *Applying Livelihood Approaches to Natural Resource Management Initiatives: Experiences in Namibia and Kenya*, ODI Working Paper No. 134, Overseas Development Institute, London.

Atkinson, R. (1998) *The Life Story Interview*, Sage, London.

Axelrod, R. (1995) A model of the emergence of new political actors, in: Gilbert, N. and Conte, R. (eds), *Artificial Societies: The Computer Simulation of Social Life*, UCL Press, London.

Axelrod, R. (1997) Advancing the art of simulation in the social sciences, in: Conte, R., Hegselmann, R. and Terna, P. (eds), *Simulating Social Phenomena, Lecture Notes in Economics and Mathematical Systems*, pp. 21–40.

Banco Interamericano de Desarrollo (BID) (1997) *Evaluación: una herramienta de gestión para mejorar el desempeño de los proyectos*, (EVO), Siglo del Hombre Editores, Santa Fe de Bogotá.

Barahona, C. and Levy, S. (2002) *How to Generate Statistics and Influence Policy Using Participatory Methods in Research*, Working Paper, Statistical Services Centre, University of Reading.

Barreteau, O., Bousquet, F. and Attonaty, J.-M. (2001) Role-playing games for opening the black box of multi-agent systems: method and lessons of its application to Senegal River Valley irrigated systems, *Journal of Artificial Societies and Social Simulation*, 4(2). *www.soc.surrey.ac.uk/JASSS/4/2/5.html*

Bartra, A. (2000) Conciertos y desconciertos del desarrollo sustentable. Participación social y gestión en los programas regionales, in: Toledo, C. and Bartra, A. (eds), *Del Círculo Vicioso al Círculo Virtuoso. Cinco Miradas al Desarrollo Sustentable de las Regiones Marginadas*, Plaza y Valdés/SEMARNAP, Mexico City.

Baum, F. (1995) Researching public health: behind the qualitative–quantitative methodological debate, *Social Science and Medicine*, 40(4): 459–68.

Beetham, D. (1999) *Democracy and Human Rights*, Polity Press, Cambridge.

Beetham, D., Bracking, S., Kearton, I. and Weir, S. (2002) *International IDEA Handbook on Democracy Assessment*, Kluwer Law International, The Hague.

Behnke, R.H., Scoones, I. and Kerven, C. (eds) (1993) *Range Ecology at Disequilibrium: New Models of Natural Variability and Pastoral Adaptation in African Savannas*, Overseas Development Institute, London.

Bellows, B.C. (1995) *Principles and Practices for Implementing Participatory and Intersectoral Assessments of Indicators of Sustainability: Outputs from the Workshop Sessions*, SANREM CRSP Conference on Indicators of Sustainability, Sustainable Agriculture and Natural Resource Management Collaborative Research Support Programme, Research Report 1/95, pp. 243–68.

Berger, P.L. and Luckman, T. (1971) *The Social Construction of Reality: A Treatise in the Sociology of Knowledge*, Penguin, Harmondsworth.

Bernard, H. (1994) *Research Methods in Anthropology: Qualitative and Quantitative Approaches*, Sage, London.

Biggs, S. and Smith, G. (1998) Beyond methodologies: coalition-building for participatory technology development, *World Development*, 26(2): 239–48.

Bird, B. and Kakande, M. (2001) The Uganda participatory poverty assessment process, in: Norton, A. with Bird, B., Brock, K., Kakande, M. and Turk, C. (eds), *A Rough Guide to PPAs: Participatory Poverty Assessment – An Introduction to Theory and Practice*, Overseas Development Institute, London, 43–56.

Blackburn, J. and Holland, J. (1998) *Who changes? Institutionalising participation in development*, Intermediate Technology Publications, London.

Booth, D. and Lucas, H. (2002) *Good Practice in the Development of PRSP Indicators and Monitoring Systems*, Working Paper No. 172, Overseas Development Institute, London.

Booth, D., Holland, J., Hentschel, J., Lanjouw, P. and Herbert, A. (1998) *Participation and Combined Methods in African Poverty Assessment: Renewing the Agenda*, Issues Series (February), Social Development Department, Department for International Development, London.

Booth, D., Leach, M. and Tierney, A. (1999) *Experiencing Poverty in Africa: Perspectives from Anthropology*, Background Paper No. 1(b) for the World Bank Poverty Status Report, 1999.

Born, G. (1997) Computer software as a medium: textuality, orality and sociality in artificial intelligence research culture, in: Banks, M. and Morphy, H. (eds), *Rethinking Visual Anthropology*, Yale University Press, New Haven, CT, USA, pp. 139–67.

Bourguignon, F. (2003) Qualitative and quantitative approaches to poverty analysis: two pictures of the same mountain? in: Kanbur, R. (ed.), *Q-Squared: Qualitative and Quantitative Methods of Poverty Appraisal*, Permanent Black, Delhi, pp. 68–72.

Breckenridge, R.P., Kepner, W.G. and Mouat, D.A. (1995) A process for selecting indicators for monitoring conditions of rangeland health, *Environmental Monitoring and Assessment*, 36: 45–60.

Brinkerhoff, D.W. and Crosby, B.L. (2002) *Managing Policy Reform: Concepts and Tools for Decision-Makers in Developing and Transitioning Countries*, Kumarian Press, Bloomfield, CT, USA.

Brock, K. and McGee, R. (2002) *Knowing Poverty: Critical Reflections on Participatory Research and Policy*, Earthscan, London.

Brokensha, D. (1966) *Applied Anthropology in English-Speaking Africa*, Monograph Series No. 8, Society for Applied Anthropology, Lexington, KY, USA.

Brouwer, I. (2000) *Bringing Democracy Assistance Recipients In*, Discussion Paper No. 3/2000, research project 'Democracy promotion and protection in Central and Eastern Europe and the Middle East and North Africa', European University Institute/Humboldt-Universitat zu Berlin, Florence/Berlin.

Brown, D., Howes, M., Hussein, K., Longley, C. and Swindell, K. (2002) *Participation in Practice: Case Studies from The Gambia*, Overseas Development Institute, London.

Bryman, A. (2001) *Social Research Methods*, Oxford University Press, New York.

Burnside, C. and Dollar, D. (2000) *Aid, policies and growth*, America Economic Review, 90(4): 847-68.

Butler, R.G. (1993) Tourism: an evolutionary perspective, in: Nelson, J.G., Butler, R. and Wall, G. (eds), *Tourism and Sustainable Development: Monitoring, Planning, Managing*, Heritage Resources Centre Joint Publication No. 1, Department of Geography, University of Waterloo, Waterloo, Canada, pp. 27-43.

Calhoun, C. (1995) *Critical Social Theory*. Blackwell, Oxford.

Campbell, B.M., Dore, D., Luckert, M., Mukamuri, B. and Gambiza, J. (2000) Economic comparisons of livestock production in communal grazing lands in Zimbabwe, *Ecological Economics*, 33: 413-38.

Campbell, J. (2002) 'Theory and method in the study of poverty in East Africa', paper presented to the conference on Combined Methods in Development Research, University of Wales, Swansea, July 2002.

Campbell, J. with Holland, J. (eds) (2005) 'Convergent or divergent understandings of Poverty?', *FOCAAL (European Journal of Social Anthropology)*, special issue, volume no. F45, Utrecht, The Netherlands.

Caravias, J., Provencio, E. and Toledo, C. (1994) *Manejo de recursos naturales y pobreza rural*, Fondo de Cultura Económica/UNAM, Mexico City.

Carothers, T. (1999) *Aiding Democracy Abroad: The Learning Curve*, Carnegie Endowment for International Peace, Washington, DC.

Carvalho, S. and White, H. (1997) *Combining the Quantitative and Qualitative Approaches to Poverty Measurement and Analysis: The Practice and the Potential*, Technical Paper No. 366, World Bank, Washington, DC.

CDS (2002) *Resource Book of Processes and Results for Social Development Research Capacity Project State Capacity-Building Component (Eastern India)*, Centre for Development Studies, Swansea.

Cernea, M. (1995) 'Social Organization and Development', Malinowski Award Lecture, World Bank, Washington, DC.

Chambers, R. (1983) *Rural Development: Putting the First Last*, Longman, Harlow.

Chambers, R. (1989) Editorial introduction: Vulnerability, coping and policy, *IDS Bulletin*, 20(2): 1-7.

Chambers, R. (1992) *Rural Appraisal: Rapid, Relaxed and Participatory*, Discussion Paper No. 311, Institute of Development Studies, Brighton, UK.

Chambers, R. (1994a) The origins and practice of participatory rural appraisal, in *World Development* 22(7): 953-69.

Chambers, R. (1994b) Participatory rural appraisal (PRA): analysis of experience, *World Development*, 22(9): 1253-68.

Chambers, R. (1995) Poverty and livelihoods: whose reality counts?, *Environment and Urbanisation*, 7(1): 173-204.

Chambers, R. (1997) *Whose Reality Counts? Putting the First Last*, ITDG Publishing, London.

Chambers, R. (2003) The best of both worlds, in: Kanbur, R. (ed.), *Q-Squared: Qualitative and Quantitative Methods of Poverty Appraisal*, Permanent Black, Delhi, pp. 35-45.

Chambers, R. and Longhurst, R. (1986) Trees, seasons and the poor, *IDS Bulletin*, 17(3): 44–50.

Chen, M.A. (1997) *A Guide for Assessing the Impact of Microenterprise Services at the Individual Level*, AIMS Project, USAID Office of Microenterprise Development, Washington, DC.

Chinsinga, B., Dzimadzi, C., Magalasi, M. and Mpekansambo, L. (2002) TIP Messages: Beneficiary Selection and Community Targeting, Agricultural Extension and Health (TB and HIV/AIDS), Module 2 of the 2001–02 TIP Evaluation, July 2002. *www.reading.ac.uk/ssc*

Chirban, T. (1996) *Interviewing in Depth: The Interactive–Relational Approach*. Sage, London.

Chung, K. (1997) *Identifying Good Practice for the Integration of Qualitative and Quantitative Methods for Poverty Research*, Brown University, Providence, RI, draft.

CIDA (2000a) *CIDA Evaluation Guide*, Canadian International Development Agency, Ottawa.

CIDA (2000b) *Democracy and Governance Programming Lessons for CIDA: Ethiopia Case Study*, Canadian International Development Agency, Ottawa.

Clark, W.C. (1999) *Designing Effective Assessments of Global Environmental Issues: Towards a Conceptual Framework for Learning from Experience*, GEA Project No. 18, Harvard University, Cambridge, MA.

Cline, A. (2000) White Paper: Prioritisation Process Using Delphi Technique, Carolla Development. *www.carolla.com/wp-delph.htm*

Cohen, M. (1999) *Microfinance Impact Evaluation: Going Down Market*, paper presented to Conference on Evaluation and Poverty Reduction, World Bank, USAID, Washington, DC.

Conover, W.J. (1999) *Practical Non-Parametric Statistics*, 3rd edn, Wiley, New York.

Copestake, J. (2001) *Towards a General Framework for Client Monitoring within Microfinance Organisation*, Learning Note No. 5, Imp-Act (Improving the Impact of Microfinance on Poverty), Brighton, UK. *www.imp-act.org*

Copestake, J. (2002) Poverty, inequality and the polarising impact of microcredit: evidence from Zambia's Copperbelt, *Journal of International Development*, 14(6): 743–55.

Copestake, J. et al. (2001a) *Impact Monitoring and Assessment of Microfinance Services Provided by CETZAM on the Zambian Copperbelt: 1991–2001*, Final Report, Centre for Development Studies, University of Bath. *www/bath.ac.uk/cds*

Copestake, J. et al. (2001b) Assessing the impact of micro-credit on poverty: a Zambian case study, *Journal of Development Studies*, 37(4).

Copestake, J.G. (2000) Integrating impact monitoring and assessment of microfinance, *Journal of Development Practice*, 10(4).

Copestake, J.G. and Mlotshwa, W.M. (2000) *Impact Monitoring and Assessment of the Christian Enterprise Trust of Zambia: Report on the First Round of Repeat Client Interviews* (No. 3), Centre For Development Studies, University of Bath.

Cornwall, A. (2002) *Making Spaces, Changing Places: Situating Participation in Development*, Working Paper No. 170, Institute of Development Studies, Brighton, UK.

Cornwall, A. and Gaventa, J. (2001) *From Users and Choosers to Makers and Shapers: Repositioning Participation in Social Policy*, Working Paper No. 127, Institute of Development Studies, Brighton, UK.

Cracknell, B.E. (2000) *Evaluating Development Aid: Issues, Problems and Solutions*, Sage, London.

Craig, D. and Porter, D. (2002) Poverty reduction strategy papers: a new convergence, *World Development*, 31(1): 53–69.

Crawford, G. with Kearton, I. (2002) *Evaluating Democracy and Governance Assistance*, Centre for Development Studies, University of Leeds.

Creswell, J.W. (1994) *Research Design: Qualitative and Quantitative Approaches*, Sage, London.

Crewe, E. and Young, J. (2002) *Bridging Research and Policy: Context, Evidence and Links*, ODI Working Paper No. 173, Overseas Development Institute, London.

Croll, E. (2000) *Endangered Daughters: Discrimination and Development in Asia*, Routledge, London.

Cromwell, E., Kambewa, P., Mwanza, R.l. and Chirwa, R. with KWERA Development Centre (2001) *Impact Assessment using Participatory Approaches: Starter Pack and Sustainable Agriculture in Malawi*, AGREN Network Paper No. 112, ODI Agricultural Research and Extension Network.

Curnan, S., LaCava, L., Langenburg, D., Lelle, M. and Reece, M. (eds) (1998) *Evaluation Handbook*, W. K. Kellogg Foundation, Battle Creek, MI, USA.

Danida (2000) *Danish Support of Human Rights and Democratisation* (vols 1–9), Danish Ministry of Foreign Affairs, Danish International Development Assistance, Copenhagen.

Davidson, G. (1999) *Poverty amidst Plenty: A Study of Disadvantage, Vulnerability and Social Exclusion in Singapore*, University of Liverpool.

de Haan, A. (2000) *Holistic Approaches to Monitoring Changes in Well-Being and Policies*, Workshop Report, Department for International Development, London.

de Vibe, M., Hovland, I. and Young, J. (2002) *Bridging Research and Policy: An Annotated Bibliography*, ODI Working Paper No. 174, Overseas Development Institute, London.

Deininger, K. and Okidi, J. (2003) Growth and poverty reduction in Uganda 1992–2000: panel data evidence, *Development Policy Review*, 21(4): 481–509.

Delbecq, A., Van de Ven, A. and Gustafson, D. (1975) *Group Guide to Nominal Group and Delphi Processes*, Scott, Foresman & Co, Glenview, IL.

den Heyer, M. (2001) *The Temporal Logic Model: A Concept Paper*, Evaluation Unit, International Development Research Centre, Ottawa, Canada, *www.idrc.ca/evaluation*

Denzin, N. (1970) *The Research Act in Sociology*, Butterworths, London.

Denzin, N. and Lincoln, Y. (1994) *Handbook of Qualitative Research*, Sage, London.

Devereux, S. and Maxwell, S. (eds) (2001) *Food Security in Sub-Saharan Africa*, ITDG Publishing, London.

DFID (1997) *Economic and Social Research Guidelines*, Department for International Development, London.

DFID (2000) *Realising Human Rights for Poor People*, Department for International Development, London.

Digby, P., Galwey, N. and Lane, P. (1989) *Genstat 5: A Second Course*, Clarendon Press, Oxford.

Dougill, A.J., Thomas, D.S.G. and Heathwaite, A.L. (1999) Environmental change in the Kalahari: integrated land degradation studies for nonequilibrium dryland environments, *Annals of the Association of American Geographers*, 89: 420–42.

Dunham, R.B. (1998) *Organisational Behaviour: The Delphi Technique*, University of Wisconsin School of Business. *www.instruction.bus.wisc.edu/obdemo/readings/delphi.htm*

Earl, S. and Smutylo, T. (1998) *Supporting Development Research: An Assessment of the specifics of IDRC's Approach to Program Delivery*, Evaluation Unit, Corporate Services Branch, International Development Research Centre, Ottawa, Canada.

Echtner, C.M. and Jamal, T.B. (1997) The disciplinary dilemma of tourism studies, *Annals of Tourism Research*, 24(4): 868–83.

Ellis, F. (2000) *Rural Livelihoods and Diversity in Developing Countries*, Oxford University Press, Oxford, UK.

Ellis, F. and Freeman, H.A. (2004) Rural livelihoods and poverty reduction strategies in four African countries, *Journal of Development Studies*, 40(4): 1–30.

Emery, F.E. (1974) *La Teoria dei Sistemi*, Franco Angeli, Milan.

Epstein, A. (1969) Gossip, norms and social networks, in: Mitchell, J. (ed.), *Social Networks in Urban Situations: Analyses of Personal Relationships in Central African Towns*, Manchester University Press, UK, pp. 117–27.

Epstein, J.M. and Axtell, R. (1996) *Growing Artificial Societies: Social Science from the Bottom Up*, MIT Press, Cambridge, MA.

Estrella, M. and Gaventa, J. (1998) *Who Counts Reality? Participatory Monitoring and Evaluation: A Literature Review*, Working Paper No. 70, Institute of Development Studies, Brighton, UK.

Estrella, M. et al. (eds) (2000) *Learning from Change: Issues and experiences in Participatory Monitoring and Evaluation*, Intermediate Technology Publications and International Development Research Centre, London and Ottawa.

European Commission (1995) *Communication to the Council and Parliament on The European Union and the External Dimension of Human Rights Policy: From Rome to Maastricht and Beyond* [COM (95) 567], European Commission, Brussels.

European Commission (1997) *Evaluation of the PHARE and TACIS Democracy Programme 1992–1997*, European Commission, Brussels.

European Commission (1999) *Evaluation of the MEDA Democracy Programme 1996–98*, European Commission, Brussels.

European Commission (2000) *External Evaluation of Community Aid Concerning Positive Actions in the Field of Human Rights and Democracy in the ACP countries*, European Commission, Brussels.

Evans, A., Nicholson, K. and Porter, C. (2003) *Learning the Lessons on PSIA – A Synthesis of Experience from the DFID Pilot Studies*, PRSP Monitoring and Synthesis Project Briefing Note 8, October, Overseas Development Institute, London.

Eyben, R. (2003) The growth of a profession: social development advisors in the British civil service, *Journal of International Development*, 15(7): 879–92.

Eyre, S. (1997) The vernacular term interview: eliciting social knowledge related to sex among adolescents, *Journal of Adolescence*, 20(1): 9–27.

Fals Borda, O. (1988) *Knowledge and People's Power: Lessons with Peasants in Nicaragua, Mexico and Colombia*, International Labour Organization, Geneva.

Felsing, M., Haylor, G.S., Lawrence, A. and Abeyasekera, S. (2000) *Evaluating some Statistical Methods for Preference Testing in Participatory Research*, DFID Aquaculture Research Programme Project, Department for International Development, London.

Fernandes, W. and Tandon, R. (eds) (1981) *Participatory Research and Evaluation: Experiments in Research as a Process of Liberation*, Indian Social Institute, New Delhi.

Fine, B. (1999) The Developmental State is Dead – Long Live Social Capital? *Development and Change*, 30(1).

Flick, U. (1998) *An Introduction to Qualitative Research*, Sage, London.

Foddy, W. (1993) *Constructing Questions for Interviews and Questionnaires: Theory and Practice in Social Science Research*, Cambridge University Press, Cambridge, UK.

Foran, B.D., Tainton, N.M. and Booysen, P. de V. (1978) *The development of a method for assessing veld condition in three grassveld types in Natal*, Proceedings of the Grassland Society of Southern Africa, 15: 37–42.

Foucault, M. (1980) *Power/Knowledge: Selected Interviews and other Writings 1972–1977*, Harvester Press, London.

Foucault, M. (1998) *Bisogna difendere la societá*, Milano, Feltrinelli (Original title: 1997, *Il faut défendre la société*, Suil-Gallimard, Paris).

Francis, P. (1999) 'Community participation and decision making', draft paper unpublished, World Bank, Washington DC.

Francis, E. and Hoddinott, J. (1993) Migration and differentiation in western Kenya: a tale of two sub-locations, *Journal of Development Studies*, 30(2): 115–45.

Frechtling, J. and Sharp, L. (eds) (1997) *User-Friendly Handbook for Mixed Method Evaluations*, Directorate for Education and Human Resources, Division of Research, Evaluation and Communication, National Science Foundation, Washington, DC.

Freire, P. (1970) *Pedagogy of the Oppressed*, Seabury Press, New York.

Freire, P. (1985) *The Politics of Education: Culture, Power and Liberation*, Macmillan, London.

Gamon, J.A. (1991) The Delphi: an evaluation tool, *Journal of Extension*, 29(4).

Gasper, D. (1997) *Logical Frameworks: A Critical Assessment Managerial Theory, Pluralistic Practices*, Working Paper Series 264, Institute of Social Studies, The Netherlands.

Gaventa, J. and Blauert, J. (2000) Learning to change by learning from change: going to scale with participatory monitoring and evaluation, in: Estrella, M. et al. (eds) *Learning from Change: Issues and experiences in Participatory Monitoring and Evaluation*, Intermediate Technology Publications and International Development Research Centre, London and Ottawa, pp. 229–43.

Gaventa, J. and Valderrama, C. (1999) 'Participation, citizenship and local governance', unpublished background note, June, Institute of Development Studies at the University of Sussex.

Germann, D. and Gohl, D. (1996) *Participatory Impact Monitoring*, Deutsches Zentrum für Entwicklungstechnologien – GATE, Deutsche Gesellschaft für Technische Zusammenarbeit (GTZ) GmbH, Eschborn, Friedr. Vieweg and Sohn Verlagsgesellschaft mbH, Braunschweig/Wiesbaden.

Giddens, A. (1974) *Positivism and Sociology*, Heinemann, London.

Gilbert, N. (1999) Computer simulation in the social sciences, special issue, *American Behavioral Scientist*, 42.

Gilbert, N. (ed.) (1993) *Researching Social Life*, Sage, London.

Gilbert, N. and Troitzsch, K.G. (1999) *Simulation for the Social Scientist*, Open University Press, Milton Keynes.

Gilbert, N., Maltby, S. and Asakawa, T. (2002) Participatory simulations for developing scenarios in environmental resource management, in: Urban, C. (ed.), *Third Workshop on Agent-based Simulation*, SCS-Europe, Passau, Germany, pp. 67–72.

Gordon, J., Schreckenberg, K. and Barrance, A. (2003) Are rare species useful species? Obstacles to the conservation of tree diversity in the dry forest zone agro-ecosystems of Mesoamerica, *Global Ecology and Biogeography*, 12(1): 13–19.

Government of Jamaica (2002) *Jamaica 2015: A Framework and Action Plan for Improving Effectiveness, Collaboration and Accountability in the Delivery of Social Policy*, Government of Jamaica, Kingston, Jamaica.

Grandin, B. (1988) *Wealth Ranking in Smallholder Communities: A Field Manual*, Intermediate Technology Publications, London.

Green, H.C., Hunter, C. and Moore, B. (1990) Assessing the environmental impact of tourism development: the use of the Delphi technique, *International Journal of Environmental Studies*, 35: 51–62.

Greenhalgh, S. (1990) Toward a political economy of fertility: anthropological perspectives, *Population and Development Review*, 16(1): 85–106.

Grindle, M.S. and Thomas, J.W. (1991) *Public Choices and Policy Change: Political Economy of Reform in Developing Countries*, The Johns Hopkins University Press, Baltimore, MA.

Grootaert, C. (1998) *Social Capital: The Missing Link?*, Social Capital Initiative Working Paper No. 3, World Bank, Washington, DC.

Guba, E. and Lincoln, Y. (1998) 'Competing paradigms in qualitative research', in: Denzin, N. and Lincoln, Y. (eds), *The Landscape of Qualitative Research*, Sage, London.

Guba, E.G. and Lincoln, Y.S. (1989) *Fourth Generation Evaluation*, Sage, London.

Guevara, A. and Yúnez-Naude, A. (2000) Evaluación socioeconómica de los proyectos comunitarios en el ámbito de los proders: esencia, méétodo y resultados preliminares, in: Toledo, C. and Bartra, A. (eds), *Del Círculo Vicioso al Círculo Virtuoso. Cinco Miradas al Desarrollo Sustentable de las Regiones Marginadas*, Plaza y Valdés/SEMARNAP, Mexico City.

Guijt, I. and Cornwall, A. (1995) *Critical Reflections on the Practice of PRA*, PLA Notes No. 24, International Institute for Environment and Development, London.

Guijt, I. and Gaventa, J. (1998) *Participatory Monitoring and Evaluation: Learning From Change*, Institute of Development Studies, Brighton, UK.

Habermas, J. (1972) *Knowledge and Human Interests*, Heinemann, London.

Habermas, J. (1990) *Moral Consciousness and Communicative Action*, MIT Press, Cambridge, MA.

Hall, C.M. and Jenkins, J.M. (1995) *Tourism and Public Policy*, Routledge, London.

Hammel, E.A. (1990) A theory of culture for demography, *Population and Development Review*, 16(3): 455–85.

Hammersley, M. (1998) *Reading Ethnographic Research: A Critical Guide*, 2nd edn, Longman, London/New York.

Hammersley, M. (ed.) (1992) *Social Research*, Sage, London.

Hanmer, L., Pyatt, G. and White, H. (1997) *Poverty in Sub-Saharan Africa: What Can We Learn from the World Bank's Poverty Assessments?*, Institute of Social Studies, The Hague.

Hanton, D. (2002) 'From words to numbers: A basis for translating ethnographic description', Paper presented at Conference on Combined Methods in Development Research at the University of Wales Swansea, July 2002.

Hare, M., Gilbert, N., Medugno, D., Asakawa, T., Heeb, J. and Pahl-Wostl, C. (2001) The development of an Internet forum for long-term participatory group learning about problems and solutions to sustainable urban water supply management, in: Hilty, L.M. and Gilgen, P.W. (eds), *Sustainability in the Information Society*, Metropolis, Marburg, pp. 743–50.

Harrison, E.F. (1995) *The Managerial Decision-Making Process*, 4th edn, Houghton Mifflin, Boston, MA, USA.

Harriss, J. and de Renzio, P. (1997) Policy arena: 'Missing link' or analytically missing? The concept of social capital. An introductory bibliographic essay, *Journal of International Development*, 9(7): 919–37.

Hauser, P. (1993) The limitations of KAP surveys. In: Bulmer, M. and Warwick, D. (eds), *Social Research in Developing Countries*, UCL Press, London, pp. 65–9.

Häusermann, J. (1998) *A Human Rights Approach to Development, Rights and Humanity*, DFID, London.

Hawkins, K. and Price, N.L. (2000) *A Peer Ethnographic Approach to Social Appraisal and Monitoring of Sexual and Reproductive Health Programmes*, Centre for Development Studies, University of Wales Swansea.

Heilbronner, R. and Milberg, W. (1995) *The Crisis of Vision in Modern Economic Thought*, Cambridge University Press, Cambridge, UK.

Hentschel, J. (1999) Contextuality and data collection methods: a framework and application to health service utilisation, *Journal of Development Studies*, 35, 64–94.

Henwood, K. and Pidgeon, N. (1995) Remaking the link: qualitative research and feminist standpoint theory, *Feminism and Psychology*, 5(1): 17–30.

Herring, R. (2003) Data as social product, in: Kanbur, R. (ed.), *Q-Squared: Qualitative and Quantitative Methods of Poverty Appraisal*, Permanent Black, Delhi, pp. 141–51.

Hudson, J. and Jones, P. (2002) 'International trade in quality goods: signalling problems for developing countries' (unpublished), Department of Economics and International Development, University of Bath.

Hulme, D. (2000) Impact assessment methodologies for microfinance: theory, experience and better practice, *World Development*, 28(1): 79–98.

Hulme, D. and Mosley, P. (1996) *Finance against Poverty*, vol. 1, Routledge, London.

Interact Evaluation Group (IEG) (2001) Evaluating Participative, Deliberative and Co-operative Ways of Working, Working Paper June 2001, London.

Inter-American Development Bank (IBD) (1997) *Evaluación: Una Herramienta de Gestión para Mejorar el Desempeño de los Proyectos*, Siglo del Hombre Editores, Santa Fe de Bogotá, Colombia.

Isham, J., Narayan, D. and Pritchett, L. (1995) Does participation improve performance? Establishing causality with subjective data, *World Bank Economic Review*, 9(2): 175–200.

ITAD/ODI (2000) *Evaluation of Danida's Bilateral Programme for Enhancement of Research Capacity in Developing Countries* (ENRECA), ITAD Ltd, Hove, UK/Overseas Development Institute, London.

Jellinek, G. (1985) *Sensory Evaluation of Food – Theory and Practice*, Ellis Horwood, Chichester, UK.

Jodha, N.S. (1988) Poverty debate in India: A minority view, *Economic and Political Weekly*, Special Number 2421–2428, November.

Johnson, S., Copestake, J. and W.K. Consultants (2002) *FINCA–Malawi Impact Assessment Research: Final Report*, Centre for Development Studies, University of Bath, UK.

Kabeer, N. (2000) *The Power to Choose: Bangladeshi Women and Labour Market Decisions in London and Dhaka*, Verso, London.

Kanbur, R. (2001a) Economic policy, distribution and poverty: the nature of disagreements, *World Development*, 29(6): 1083–94.

Kanbur, R. (ed.) (2001b) *Qual-Quant: Qualitative and Quantitative Poverty Appraisal: Complementarities, Tensions and the Way Forward*, workshop held at Cornell University, Ithaca, NY, 15–16 March 2001. [Revised version published as Kanbur (2003).] *www.arts.cornell.edu/poverty/kanbur/QQZ.pdf*

Kanbur, R. (2001c) Qualitative and quantitative poverty appraisal: the state of play and some questions, in: Kanbur, R. (ed.), *Qualitative and Quantitative Poverty Appraisal: Complementarities, Tensions and the Way Forward*, contributions to a workshop held at Cornell University, Ithaca, NY, 15–16 March 2001, pp. 17–21, *www.arts.cornell.edu/poverty/kanbur/QQZ.pdf*

Kanbur, R. (ed.) (2003a) *Q-Squared: Qualitative and Quantitative Methods of Poverty Appraisal*, Permanent Black, Delhi.

Kanbur, R. (2003b) Q-Squared? A commentary on qualitative and quantitative poverty appraisal, in: Kanbur, R. (ed.), *Q-Squared: Qualitative and Quantitative Methods of Poverty Appraisal*, Permanent Black, Delhi, pp. 1–21.

Kandiyoti, D. (1998) *Post-Soviet Transitions and Challenges for Social Development Research: The Case for the Inclusion of Central Asia*, School for Oriental and African Studies, London.

Kandiyoti, D. (1999) Poverty in transition: an ethnographic critique of household surveys in post-Soviet Central Asia, *Development and Change*, 30(3): 499–524.

Kelly-Gadol, J. (1987) The social relation of the sexes: methodological implications of women's history, in: Harding, S. (ed.), *Feminism and Methodology*, Indiana University Press, Bloomington, IN, pp. 15–28.

Kepe, T. and Scoones, I. (1999) Creating grasslands: social institutions and environmental change in Mkambati Area, South Africa, *Human Ecology*, 27(1): 29–53.

Killick, T. (2001) 'Donor funding of socio-economic research in southern countries', Paper prepared for the DFID Workshop on Building Southern Socio-Economic Research Capacity, 12–13 June, University of Natal South Africa, Overseas Development Institute, London.

Kipuri, N. (1996) Pastoral Maasai grassroots indicators for sustainable resource management, in: Hambly, H. and Angura, T.O. (eds), *Grassroots Indicators for Desertification Experience and Perspectives from Eastern and Southern Africa*, International Development Research Centre, Ottawa, Canada.

Kothari, U. (2000) *Developing Guidelines for Assessing Achievement in the Eight Focal Areas of Social Development Work and for Assessing Outcomes: Assessment Procedures*, Institute for Development Policy and Management, University of Manchester, UK.

Krzanowski, W.J. (1988) *Principles of Multivariate Analysis: A User's Perspective*, Oxford University Press, Oxford, UK.

Kumar, K. (ed.) (1993) *Rapid Appraisal Methods*, World Bank, Washington, DC.

Lane, C.R. (1998) *Custodians of the Commons: Pastoral Land Tenure in East and West Africa*, Earthscan, London.

Lang, T. (1995) An overview of four futures methodologies, *Manoa Journal*, 7: 1–43.

Lanjouw, P. and Stern, N. (1991) Poverty in Palanpur, *World Bank Economic Review*, 5: 23–55.

Leakey, R., Schreckenberg, K. and Tchoundjeu, Z. (2003) The participatory domestication of West African indigenous fruits, *International Forestry Review*, 5(4): 338–47.

Letherby, G. (2003) *Feminist Research in Theory and Practice*, Open University Press, Buckingham, UK.

Levy, S. (2003) Are we targeting the poor? Lessons from Malawi, *PLA Notes* 47 (August), IIED, London.

Lincoln, Y.S. and Guba, E.G. (1985) *Naturalistic Inquiry*, Sage, London.

Lindquist, E.A. (2001) *Discerning Policy Influence: Framework for a Strategic Evaluation of IDRC-Supported Research*, University of Victoria, Canada.

Linstone, H. and Turoff, M. (1975) *The Delphi Method: Techniques and Applications*, Addison-Wesley, Reading, MA, USA.

Lockwood, M. (1995) Structure and behaviour in the social demography of Africa. *Population and Development Review*, 21(1): 1–32.

Long, N. and Long, A. (1992) *Battlefields of Knowledge: The Interlocking of Theory and Practice in Social Research and Development*, Routledge, London.

Longhurst, R., Chambers, R. and Swift, J. (1986) Seasonality and poverty: implications for policy and research, *IDS Bulletin*, 17(3): 67–8.

McClean, K. (1999) 'Disconnect Between Consumption Data and Perceptions of the Poor in Uganda', processed, UPPAP, Kampala.

McCracken, G. (1998) *The Long Interview*, vol. 13, Sage, London.

McGee, R. (2000) *Analysis of Participatory Poverty Assessment (PPA) and Household Survey Findings on Poverty Trends in Uganda*: Mission Report, 10–18 February 2000, processed, Institute of Development Studies, Brighton, UK.

McGee, R. (2001) What is required to reduce tensions and increase complementarity?, in: Kanbur, R. (ed.), *Qual-Quant: Qualitative and Quantitative Poverty Appraisal: Complementarities, Tensions and the Way Forward*, contributions to a workshop held at Cornell University, Ithaca, NY, 15–16 March 2001, pp. 89–90. *www.arts.cornell.edu/poverty/kanbur/QQZ.pdf*

McGee, R. (2002) Conclusion. Participatory poverty research: opening spaces for change, in: Brock, K. and McGee, R. (eds), *Knowing Poverty: Critical Reflections on Participatory Research and Policy*, Earthscan, London, pp. 189–205.

McGee, R. (2003) Qualitative and quantitative poverty appraisal workshop: some reflections and responses, in: Kanbur, R. (ed.), *Q-Squared: Qualitative and Quantitative Methods of Poverty Appraisal*, Permanent Black, Delhi, pp. 132–40.

McGee, R. and Norton, A. (2000) *Participation in poverty reduction strategies: a synthesis of experience with participatory approaches to policy design, implementation and monitoring*, Working Paper No. 109, Institute of Development Studies, Brighton, UK.

Mair, L. (1957) *Studies in Applied Anthropology*, Athlone Press, London.

Manderson, L. and Aaby, P. (1992) An epidemic in the field? Rapid assessment procedures and health research, *Social Science and Medicine*, 37(7): 839–50.

Marr, A. (2002) Studying group dynamics: an alternative analytical framework for the study of microfinance impacts on poverty reduction, *Journal of International Development*, 14(4): 511–34.

Marsden, D. and Oakley, P. (eds) (1990) *Evaluating Social Development Projects*, Oxfam, Oxford, UK.

Marsden, D., Oakley, P. and Pratt, D. (1994) *Measuring the Process: Guidelines for Evaluating Social Development*, INTRAC, Oxford, UK.

Marshall, C. and Rossman, G.B. (1999) *Designing Qualitative Research*, Sage, London/Thousand Oaks/New Delhi.

Marshall, E., Newton, A.C. and Schreckenberg, K. (2003) Commercialisation of non-timber forest products: first steps in analysing factors influencing success, *International Forestry Review*, 5(2): 128–37.

Marsland, N. et al. (1998) *A Methodological Framework for Combining Quantitative and Qualitative Survey Methods*, Social and Economic Development Department, Natural Resources, Institute and Statistical Service Centre, University of Reading, UK.

Martin, A. and Sherington, J. (1997) Participatory research methods – implementation, effectiveness and institutional context, *Agricultural Systems*, 55(2): 195–216.

Mason, J. (2002) *Qualitative Research*, Sage, London/Thousand Oaks/New Delhi.

Maxwell, S. (2003) Heaven or hubris? Reflections on the new 'new poverty agenda', *Development Policy Review*, 21(1): 5–25.

Maxwell, S. and Bart, C. (1995) Beyond ranking: exploring relative preferences in P/PRA, *PRA Notes* 22 (February): 28–34.

Maynard, M. and Purvis, J. (eds) (1994) *Researching Women's Lives from a Feminist Perspective*, Taylor & Francis, London.

Middleton, V.T.C. and Hawkins, R. (1998) *Sustainable Tourism: A Marketing Perspective*, Butterworth-Heinemann, Oxford, UK.

Mikkelsen, B. (1995) *Methods for Development Work and Research: A Guide for Practitioners*, Sage, London/Thousand Oaks/New Delhi.

Miles, M.B. and Huberman, A.M. (1984) *Qualitative Data Analysis*, 2nd edn, Sage, Thousand Oaks, CA, USA.

Milton, S.J, Dean, W.R. and Ellis, R.P. (1998) Rangeland health assessment: a practical guide for ranchers in the arid Karoo shrublands, *Journal of Arid Environments*, 39: 253–65.

Mitchell, J.C. (ed.) (1980) *Numerical Techniques in Social Anthropology*, Institute for the Study of Human Issues, Philadelphia, PA, USA.

Moëller, G.H. and Shafer, E.l. (1994) The Delphi technique: a tool for long range travel and tourism planning, in: Ritchie, J.R. and Goeldner, C.R. (eds), *Travel, Tourism and Hospitality Research*, 2nd edn, John Wiley and Sons, New York, pp. 473–80.

Molas-Gallart, J., Tang, P. and Morrow, S. (2000) Assessing the non-academic impact of grant-funded socio-economic research: results from a pilot study, *Research Evaluation*, 9: 171–82.

Moore, M. (2001) Empowerment at last?, *Journal of International Development*, 13(3): 321–9.

Moore, M. and Putzel, J. (1999) Thinking strategically about politics and poverty. IDS *Working Paper No. 101*, IDS, Brighton.

Moris, J. and Copestake, J. (1993) *Qualitative Enquiry for Rural Development: A Review*, Intermediate Technology Publications, London.

Morse, S., McNamara, N., Acholo, M. and Okwoli, B. (2001) Sustainability indicators: the problem of integration, *Sustainable Development*, 9: 1–15.

Moser, C. (1998) The asset vulnerability framework: reassessing urban poverty reduction strategies, *World Development*, 26(1): 1–19.

Mosse, D. (1994) Authority, gender and knowledge: theoretical reflections on the practice of participatory rural appraisal, *Development and Change*, 25: 497–526.

Mukherjee, N. (1995) *Participatory Rural Appraisal and Questionnaire Survey: Comparative Field Experience and Methodological Innovations*, Concept Publishing Company, New Delhi.

Narayan D. (1997) *Voices of the Poor: Poverty and Social Capital in Tanzania*, World Bank, Washington, DC.

Narayan, D. and Pritchett, L. (1997) *Cents and Sociability: Household Income and Social Capital in Rural Tanzania*, World Bank Policy Research Working Paper, World Bank, Washington, DC.

Narayan, D. et al. (2000) *Voices of the Poor: Can Anyone Hear Us?*, World Bank, Washington, DC.

Nelson, J.G. (1993) An introduction to tourism and sustainable development with special reference to monitoring, in: Nelson, J.G., Butler, R. and Wall, G. (eds), *Tourism and Sustainable Development: Monitoring, Planning, Managing*, Heritage Resources Centre Joint Publication No. 1, Department of Geography, University of Waterloo, Waterloo, Canada, pp. 3–23.

Nelson, N. and Wright, S. (1997) *Power and Participatory Development: Theory and Practice*, Intermediate Technology Publications, London.

Netley, A. (undated) *Policy Transfer and the Developing-Country Experience Gap: Taking a Southern Perspective*, University of York, UK.

Neuman, W. (2002) *Social Research Methods*, Allen & Bacon, Boston, MA, USA.

Newman, D. and de Haan, A. (2001) *Southern Socio-Economic Research Capacity*, Report of the DFID-sponsored workshop hosted by the School of Development Studies, University of Natal, Department for International Development, London.

Nielson, S. (2001) *IDRC-Supported Research and its Influence on Public Policy*, International Development Research Centre, Ottawa, Canada.

NORAD (1990) *The Logical Framework Approach (LFA): Handbook for Objectives-oriented Project Planning*, Norwegian Agency for Development Cooperation, Oslo.

Norton, A. with Bird, B., Brock, K., Kakande M. and Turk, C. (2001) *A Rough Guide to PPAs: Participatory Poverty Assessment – An Introduction to Theory and Practice*, Overseas Development Institute, London.

Nowak, A. and Latané, B. (1993) Simulating the emergence of social order from individual behaviour, in: Gilbert, N. and Doran, J. (eds), *Simulating Societies: The Computer Simulation of Social Phenomena*, UCL Press, London.

NRI/SSC (2001) *Combining Quantitative and Qualitative Survey Work: Methodological Framework, Practical Issues, and Case Studies*, Project R7033, Report for DFID Natural Resources Systems Programme (NRSP), Socio-Economic Methodologies (SEM). Natural Resources Institute/Statistical Services Centre, University of Reading, Chatham/Reading, UK.

Nutley, S., Davies, H. and Walter, I. (2002) *Learning from the Diffusion of Innovations*, Research Unit for Research Utilisation, Department of Management, University of St Andrews, Scotland.

O'Mahony, M. (1995) Sensory measurement in food science: fitting methods to goals, *Food Technology*, 49(4): 72–82.

Oakley, P., Pratt, B. and Clayton, A. (1998) *Outcomes and Impact: Evaluating Change in Social Development*, INTRAC, Oxford.

OECD (1993) *OECD Core Set of Indicators for Environmental Performance Reviews. A Synthesis Report by the Group on the State of the Environment*, Organisation for Economic Cooperation and Development, Paris.

OECD (1997) *Evaluation of Programmes Promoting Participatory Development and*

Good Governance: Synthesis Report, Organisation for Economic Cooperation and Development, Paris.

OECD (2000) *DAC Guidelines on Poverty Reduction*, Organisation for Economic Cooperation and Development, Paris.

Onselen, V. (1993) The reconstruction of rural life from oral testimony: critical notes on the methodology employed in the study of a Black South African sharecropper, *Journal of Peasant Studies*, 20(3): 494–514.

Pannell, D.J. and Glenn, N.A. (2000) A framework for the economic evaluation and selection of sustainability indicators in agriculture, *Ecological Economics*, 33: 135–49.

Parker, R., Herdt, G. and Carballo, M. (1991) Sexual culture, HIV transmission, and AIDS research, *Journal of Sex Research*, 28(1): 77–98.

Parlett, M. and Hamilton, D. (1972) 'Evaluation as illumination: a new approach to the study of innovatory programmes', Conference Paper, Churchill College, Cambridge, UK.

Pasteur, K. (1999) *Thinking about Logical Frameworks and Sustainable Livelihoods: A Short Critique and a Possible Way Forward*, Institute of Development Studies, Brighton, UK. *www.livelihoods.org/post/logframe1-postit.html*

Pasteur, K. (2003) 'Organisational learning: challenges and actions for donor organisations', unpublished paper, Institute of Development Studies at the University of Sussex.

Pasteur, K. and Blauert, J. (2001) *Participatory Monitoring and Evaluation in Latin America: Overview of the Literature with Annotated Bibliography*, Institute of Development Studies, Brighton, UK.

Patton, M.Q. (1997) *Utilisation-focused Evaluation*, 3rd edn, Sage, Thousand Oaks, CA, USA.

Patton, M.Q. (1999) 'Utilisation-focused evaluation in Africa', Evaluation Training Lectures Delivered to the Inaugural Conference of the African Evaluation Association, Nairobi, Kenya, 13–17 September 1999.

Patton, M.Q. (2002) A vision of evaluation that strengthens democracy, *Evaluation*, 8(1): 125–39.

Pawson, R. and Tilley, N. (1997) Realistic Evaluation, Sage, London.

Pearce, D.G. (1992) *Tourist Organisations*, Longman, Harlow.

Peters, T. (1989) *Thriving on Chaos: Handbook for a Management Revolution*, Pan Books, London.

Pill, J. (1971) The Delphi method: substance, context, a critique and an annotated bibliography, *Socio-Economic Planning*, 5(1): 57–71.

PNUD (1997) *Monitoreo y Evaluación Orientados a la Obtención de Resultados: Manual para los Administradores de Programas*, Serie de Guías OEPE, Programa de las Naciones Unidas para el Desarrollo, Venezuela/OESP (UNDP), New York.

Poole, J. (1997) 'Dealing with ranking/rating data in farmer participatory trials', MSc thesis, University of Reading, UK.

Preece, R. (1994) *Starting Research: An Introduction to Academic Research and Dissertation Writing*, Pinter Publishers, London/New York.

Pretty, J. (2001) *Criteria for Trustworthiness: Excerpts From a Paper on Participatory Inquiry*, Note for Joint IED/IDS Meeting on Alternatives to Questionnaires, 26 October 2001. *www.ids.ac.uk*

Price, N.L. and Hawkins, K. (2002) Researching sexual and reproductive behaviour: a peer ethnographic approach, *Social Science and Medicine*, 55(8): 1327–38.

PSI/Cambodia (2002) *Sweetheart Relationships in Cambodia: Love, Sex and Condoms in the Time of HIV*, Population Services International, Phnom Penh.

Puchner, L. (2001) Researching women's literacy in Mali: a case study of dialogue among researchers, practitioners, and policy makers, *Comparative Education Review*, 45: 242–56.

Raine, J.P. (1992) Experience of using the Delphi forecasting process, in: Targett, D. (1996) *Analytical Decision Making*, Pitman, London.

Ravallion, M. (2003) Can qualitative methods help quantitative poverty measurement?, in: Kanbur, R. (ed.), *Q-Squared: Qualitative and Quantitative Methods of Poverty Appraisal*, Permanent Black, Delhi, pp. 50–7.

RAWOO (1997/98) *Building Bridges in Research for Development*, Netherlands Development Assistance Research Council, The Hague.

RAWOO (2001) *Supporting Capacity Building for Research in the South*, Netherlands Development Assistance Council, The Hague.

Rebien, C.C. (1996) *Evaluating Development Assistance in Theory and Practice*, Avebury, Aldershot, UK.

Reed, M.S. and Dougill, A.J. (2001) Participatory selection process for indicators of rangeland condition in the Kalahari, *Geographical Journal*, 168: 224–34.

Rennie, J.K. and Singh, N.C. (1996) *Participatory Research for Sustainable Livelihoods: A Guidebook for Field Projects*, International Institute for Sustainable Development, Ottawa, Canada.

REPOA (2003) *Policy and Service Satisfaction Survey: Main Survey Results*, Research on Poverty Alleviation, Dar es Salaam.

Research International (2000) *Financial Services Project Exploratory Study: Case Study Reports*, Research International (EA) Ltd and Department for International Development, Nairobi.

Rew, A. (1997) The donors' discourse: official social development knowledge in the 1980s, in: Grillo, R.D. and Stirrat, R.L. (eds), *Discourses of Development: Anthropological Perspectives*, Berg, Oxford, UK.

Rigby, D., Howlett, D. and Woodhouse, P. (2000) *Sustainability Indicators for Natural Resource Management and Policy, Working Paper 1. A Review of Indicators of Agricultural and Rural Livelihood Sustainability*, Institute for Development Policy and Management, University of Manchester, UK.

Rist, G. (1997) *The History of Development: From Western Origins to Global Faith*, Zed Books, London.

Ritchey-Vance, M. (1998) Widening the Lens on Impact Assessment: The Inter-American Foundation and its Grassroots Development Framework – The Cone, in: Blauert, J. and Zadek, S. (eds) *Mediating Sustainability: Growing Policy from the Grassroots*, Kumarian Press, West Hartford, CT, USA.

Robb, C.M. (2002) *Can the Poor Influence Policy? Participatory Poverty Assessments in the Developing World*, 2nd edn, IMF and World Bank, Washington, DC.

Roberts, H. (ed.) (1988) *Doing Feminist Research*, Routledge, London.

Robson, C. (2002) *Real World Research: A Resource for Social Scientists and Practitioner–Researchers*, Blackwell, Oxford.

Room, G. (2000) Globalisation, social policy and international standard-setting: the case of higher education credentials, *International Journal of Social Welfare*, 9(2): 103–19.

Rosenthal, E.J. (1976) Delphi technique, in: Anderson, S. (ed.), *Encyclopedia of Educational Evaluation*, Jossey-Bass, San Francisco, CA, USA, pp. 121–2.

Rowlands, J. (1991) How do we know it is working? The evaluation of social development projects, in: Smith, M.K. (2001) *Evaluation: Theory and Practice, The Encyclopedia of Informal Education*.

Rubin, F. (1995) *A Basic Guide to Evaluation for Development Workers*, Oxfam, Oxford, UK.

Ruth, S. (1990) *Issues in Feminism*, Houghton Mifflin, Boston, MA, USA.

Ryan J.G. (1999a) Assessing the Impact of Policy Research and Capacity Building by IFPRI in Malawi, International Food Policy Research Institute, Washington, DC.

Ryan, J.G. (1999b) *Assessing the Impact of Rice Policy Changes in Viet Nam and the Contribution of Research Policy*, International Food Policy Research Institute, Washington, DC.

Ryan, J.G. (2002) *Synthesis Report on Assessing the Impact of Policy-Oriented Social Science Research*, International Food Policy Research Institute, Washington, DC.

Sahn, D., Stiffel, D. and Younger, S. (1999) *Inter-temporal Changes in Welfare: Preliminary Results from Nine African Countries*, processed, Cornell University, Ithaca, NY, USA.

Salanick, J.R., Wenger, W. and Helfer, E. (1971) The construction of Delphi event statements, *Technology Forecasting and Social Change*, 3: 65–73.

Satterthwaite, D. (2001) Aid and urban development: where are the views of the 'recipients'?, *Environment and Urbanisation*, 13(1): 3–9.

Savory, A. (1988) *Biological Monitoring Notes*, Centre for Holistic Resource Management, Albuquerque, NM, USA.

Schreckenberg, K. (1995) The respective merits of RRA and conventional methods for longer-term research, *PLA Notes*, 24: 74–7.

Schreckenberg, K. (1996) 'Forests, fields and markets: a study of indigenous tree products in the woody savannas of the Bassila region, Benin', PhD thesis, University of London.

Scoones, I. (1995a) 'Investigating Difference: Applications of Wealth Ranking and Household Survey Approaches among Farming Households in Southern Zimbabwe', *Development and Change*, vol.36, pp. 6–15.

Scoones, I. (1995b) New directions in pastoral development in Africa, in: Scoones, I. (ed.), *Living with Uncertainty: New Directions in Pastoral Development in Africa*, Intermediate Technology Publications, London, pp. 1–36.

Scoones, I. (1998) *Sustainable Rural Livelihoods: A Framework for Analysis*, Working Paper No. 72, Institute of Development Studies, Brighton, UK.

Scott, J. (1985) *Weapons of the Weak: Everyday Forms of Peasant Resistance*, Yale University Press, New Haven, CT, USA.

Sebstad, J. and Cohen, M. (2001) *Microfinance, Risk Management and Poverty*, World Bank, Washington, DC.

Sechrist, L. and Sidani, S. (1995) Quantitative and qualitative methods: is there an alternative?, *Evaluation and Program Planning*, 18(1): 77–87.

Sen, A. (1981) *Poverty and Famines: An Essay on Entitlements and Deprivation*, Clarendon Press, Oxford, UK.

Sen, A. (1985) *Commodities and Capabilities*, North-Holland, Amsterdam.

Sen, A. (1992) *Inequality Reconsidered*, Harvard University Press, Cambridge, MA, USA.

Sen, A. (1997) Editorial: Human capital and human capability, *World Development*, 25(12): 1959–61.

Sen, A. (1999) *Development as Freedom*, Oxford University Press, Oxford, UK.

Senge, P. (1990) *The Fifth Discipline: The Art and Practice of the Learning Organisation*, Doubleday, New York.

Shaffer, P. (1996) Beneath the poverty debate: some issues, *IDS Bulletin*, 27(1): 23–34.

Shah, P. (1993) *Questionnaires: Participatory, Reliable and Interesting?*, note prepared for the IIED/IDS workshop on Alternatives to Questionnaire Surveys, 26 October 1993, Institute of Development Studies, Brighton, UK.

Sida (2000) *The Evaluability of Democracy and Human Rights Projects*, Sida Studies in Evaluation 00/3, Swedish International Development Cooperation Agency, Stockholm.

Silverman, D. (1985) *Qualitative Method and Sociology*, Gower, Aldershot, UK.

Silverman, D. (1993) Interpreting Qualitative Data, Sage, London.

Silverman, D. (1997) *Qualitative Research: Theory, Method and Practice*, Sage, London.

Silverman, S. (1966) An ethnographic approach to social stratification: prestige in a central Italian community, *American Anthropologist*, 68: 899–921.

Simanowitz, A. (2001) I*mp-Act: Improving the Impact of Microfinance on Poverty: An Action Research Programme*, see *www.Imp-Act.org*

Skevington, S. (2002) Advancing cross-cultural research on quality of life: observations drawn from the WHOQOL development, *Quality of Life Research*, 11: 134–44.

Smith, H. (1993) On the limited utility of KAP-style survey data in the practical epidemiology of AIDS, with reference to the AIDS epidemic in Chile, Health *Transition Review*, 3(1): 1–16.

Smyth, A.J. and Dumanski, G. (1995) A framework for evaluating sustainable land management, *Canadian Journal of Soil Science*, 75: 401–6.

SSC (2001) *Modern Methods of Analysis*, Statistical Guidelines Series supporting DFID Natural Resources Projects, Statistical Services Centre, University of Reading, UK. *www.reading.ac.uk/ssc*

Stocking, M.A. and Murnaghan, N. (2001) *Handbook for the Field Assessment of Land Degradation*, Earthscan, London.

Stone, D. (2000) *Learning Lessons, Policy Transfer and the International Diffusion of Policy Ideas. http://nt1.ids.ac.uk/eldis/fulltext/poltrans.pdf*

Stone, D., Maxwell, S. and Keating, M. (2001) *Bridging Research and Policy*, paper for an international workshop funded by DFID, Radcliff House, Warwick University, 16–17 July 2001, Department for International Development, London.

Stone, H. and Sidel, J.L. (1998) Quantitative descriptive analysis: developments, applications and the future, *Food Technology*, 52(8): 48–52.

Strauss, A. and Corbin, J. (1990) *Basics of Qualitative Research: Grounded Theory Procedures and Techniques*, Sage, London.

Stuter, L. (1998) 'Using the Delphi technique to achieve consensus', *Education Reporter*, November 1988, Eagle Forum Education and Legal Defence Fund, St Louis, MO, USA.

Surr, M.B., Duncan, A., Speight, M., Bradley, D., Rew, A. and Toye, J. (2002) *Research for Poverty Reduction*, DFID Research Policy Paper, Department for International Development, London.

Sutton, R. (1999) *The Policy Process: An Overview*, ODI Working Paper No. 118, Overseas Development Institute, London.

Swift, J. (1989) Why are rural people so vulnerable to famine?, *IDS Bulletin*, 20(2): 8–15.

Taplin, R.H. (1997) The statistical analysis of preference data, *Applied Statistics*, 46(4): 493–512.

Taylor-Powell, E., Steele, S. and Douglah, M. (1996) *Planning a Programme Evaluation*, Cooperative Extension Publications, Madison, WI, USA, pp. 1–21.

Tjonneland, E. et al. (1998) *The World Bank and Poverty in Africa: A Critical Assessment of the Bank's Operational Strategies for Poverty Reduction*, report for the Norwegian Ministry for Foreign Affairs, Christian Michelsen Institute, Bergen.

Toledo, C. and Bartra, A. (eds) (2000) *Del Círculo Vicioso al Círculo Virtuoso. Cinco Miradas al Desarrollo Sustentable de las Regiones Marginadas*, Plaza y Valdés/SEMARNAP, Mexico City.

Tomlins, K.I. (2000) *Methods for the Sensory Evaluation of Food and Drink Products*, Natural Resources Institute, Chatham, UK.

Toye, J. (2002) A note on building research capacity in Africa, in: Surr, M.B. et al. (eds), *Research for Poverty Reduction*, DFID Research Policy Paper, Department for International Development, London.

Trussler, T., Perchal, P. and Barker, A. (2000) Between what is said and what is done: Cultural constructs and young gay men's HIV vulnerability, *Psychology, Health and Medicine* 5(3): 296–305.

Twyman, C., Dougill, A.J., Sporton, D. and Thomas, D.S.G. (2001) Community fencing in open rangelands: a case study of community self-empowerment in Eastern Namibia, *Review of African Political Economy*, 28(87): 9–26.

Uganda, Republic of (1999) 'Uganda poverty participatory assessment: key findings', paper presented at the Conference 'Assessing outcomes for a Comprehensive Development Framework', Kampala, 26–28 October 1999.

Uganda, Republic of (2000) *Uganda Poverty Participatory Assessment Report*, Ministry of Finance, Planning and Economic Development, Kampala.

UNCSD (1996) *Indicators of Sustainable Development Framework and Methodologies*, United Nations Commission on Sustainable Development, New York.

UNDP (1997) *Who Are the Question-makers? A Participatory Evaluation Handbook*, United Nations Development Programme, New York. *www.undp.org/eo/documents/who.htm*

UNDP (1998) *Evaluation of the Governance Programme for Latin America and the Caribbean*, United Nations Development Programme, New York.

UNDP (2000) *Human Rights and Human Development* (Human Development Report 2000), Oxford University Press, Oxford/New York.

UNEP (1997) *World Atlas of Desertification*, 2nd edn, United Nations Environment Programme, Nairobi.

Uphoff, N. (1992) *Learning from Gal Oya: Possibilities for Participatory Development and Post-Newtonian Social Science*, Cornell University Press, Ithaca, NY/London, UK.

Uphoff, N. (2003) Bridging quantitative–qualitative differences in poverty appraisal: self-critical thoughts on qualitative approaches, in: Kanbur, R. (ed.), *Q-Squared: Qualitative and Quantitative Methods of Poverty Appraisal*, Permanent Black, Delhi, pp. 50–7.

Van Oirschot, Q.E.A, White, J.L., Ngendello, T., Kolijn, S. and Westby, A. (2002) Cassava processing technologies for farmers in Tanzania, *PhAction*, 5 (March): 20–2.

Vorster, M. (1982) The development of the ecological index method for assessing veld condition in the Karoo, *Proceedings of the Grassland Society of Southern Africa*, 17: 84–9.

Wade, R. (2001) Making the World Development Report 2000: attacking poverty, *World Development*, 29(8): 1435–41.

Wallerstein, I. (ed.) (1996) *Abrir las Ciencias Sociales*, Siglo XXI Editores, México, DF. [*Open the Social Sciences: Report of the Gulbenkian Commission on the Restructuring of the Social Sciences*, Stanford University Press, Stanford, CT, USA.]

Warburton, H., Villareal, S. and Subramaniam, P. (1998) Farmers' rice tungro management practices in India and Philippines, in: *Proceedings of a workshop on Rice Tungro Management*, IRRI, Philippines, 9–11 November 1998, International Rice Research Institute, Los Baños, The Philippines.

Warwick, D. (1982) *Bitter Pills: Population Policies and their Implementation in Eight Developing Countries*, Cambridge University Press, Cambridge, UK.

Weaver, T.W. (1972) *Delphi: A Critical Review*, School of Education, Policy Research Centre, Syracuse University, Syracuse, NY, USA.

Weber, E.J. and Mujica, M. (2001) *Lessons from Twenty Years of Research Support in the Central Andes*, International Development Research Centre, Ottawa, Canada.

West, M. and Shackleton, L. (1999) *USHEPiA: Building a Research Capacity Network in Africa. A Report of the ADEA Working Group on Higher Education*, World Bank, Washington, DC.

White, H. (2002a) Combining quantitative and qualitative approaches in poverty analysis, *World Development*, 30(3): 511–22.

White, H. (2002b) *Evaluating International Cooperation: The road to nowhere? Results-based Management in International Cooperation*, Institute of Development Studies, Brighton, UK. *www.oneworld.org/thinktank/evaluate/edit3.htm*

Whitehead, A. and Lockwood, M. (1998) Gender in the World Bank's poverty assessments: six cases from sub-Saharan Africa, *Development and Change*, 30(3): 525–55.

Wickens, E. (1999) 'Tourists' Voices: A Sociological Analysis of Tourists' Experiences in Chalkidiki, Northern Greece', PhD thesis, Oxford Brookes University, Oxford, UK.

Wilks, A. (2003) Poverty research: extractive or empowering?, in: Kanbur, R. (ed.), *Q-Squared: Qualitative and Quantitative Methods of Poverty Appraisal*, Permanent Black, Delhi, pp. 158–63.

Woller, G. (2002) From market failure to marketing failure: market orientation as the key to deep outreach in microfinance, *Journal of International Development*, 14(3): 305–24.

Woodhouse, P., Howlett, D. and Rigby, D. (2000) *A Framework for Research on Sustainability Indicators for Agriculture and Rural Livelihoods*, Working Paper No. 2, Sustainability Indicators for Natural Resource Management and Policy, University of Manchester, UK.

World Bank (1996) *Diseño del sistema de seguimiento y evaluación de los proyectos, Serie Lecciones y Prácticas*, Vol. 2, No. 8, Departamento de Evaluación de Operaciones, World Bank, Washington, DC.

World Bank (2001) *World Development Report 2000/2001: Attacking Poverty*, World Bank, Washington, DC.

World Food Programme (1999) *Protracted Relief and Recovery Operation – Colombia 6139.00: Assistance to Persons Displaced by Violence in Colombia*, Agenda Item 7, World Food Programme, Rome, 19–22 October 1999.

Wright, K. (2001) *Women's Participation in Microcredit Schemes: Evidence from Cajamarca and Lima*, Peru, University of Liverpool, UK.

Wright, K. (2003) Problems, what problems? We have none at all: qualitative data collection for impact assessment, *Journal of Microfinance*, 5(1): 115–39.

Yaron, G., Blauert, J. and Guevara, A. (2002) 'What determines successful sustainable development projects? Some evidence from the PRODERS experience in Mexico', paper presented to the conference 'Combining Qualitative and Quantitative Methods in Development Research', 1–2 July 2002, Centre for Development Studies, University of Wales Swansea, UK.

Zadek, S., Pruzan, P. and Evans, R. (1997) *Building Corporate Accountability, Emerging Practices in Social and Ethical Accounting*, Auditing and Reporting, Earthscan, London.

Zikmund, W.G. (1994) *Business Research Methods*, 2nd edn, Dryden, Fort Worth, TX, USA.

Index